C. B.
gave this book to
Clare Blondie

HOW TO BUILD CABINETS
FOR THE MODERN KITCHEN

R.P. Stevenson

How to
Build Cabinets
for the
Modern Kitchen

WORKING DRAWINGS BY RICHARD MEYER

Simmons-Boardman Publishing Corporation · New York

PREFACE

Friends often asked me, while I was working on this book: "How can you do a whole book on kitchen cabinets when there are only two kinds—wall and floor cabinets?"

I must confess that I too once had this idea. As the book progressed, however, my difficulty was not in finding enough different cabinets to fill it, but to decide which ones could best be omitted. It is true that there are only two *types* of cabinets, but these two types have infinite variations.

Among these variations, the job of construction obviously varies too. Some are easy. Some are comparatively more difficult. But in the main I can subscribe to the contention of one builder who remarked that anyone who can hold a hammer should be able to build kitchen cabinets because in effect they are nothing more than boxes with doors hinged to them.

In this Do-It-Yourself age, kitchen modernization offers rich possibilities to the amateur builder. As a rule, no other room in the house equals it in handyman opportunities. It is a rare kitchen, indeed, that fully satisfies the woman who uses it. Even if the room has a complete complement of up-to-date cabinets, arranged in an approved work-saving plan, there still may be knickknacks to build, or perhaps corner whatnots or other what-have-yous. Whatever it is that motivates an individual Do-It-Yourselfer—a desire to economize, an inherent need for a creative outlet, or perhaps just keeping up with the Joneses—a full or partial program of kitchen modernization will give him what he wants.

I am often asked how much a cabinet-building home owner can

save. The answer obviously requires a basis for comparison. Will you compare your handiwork with the most expensive line of handsome commercial cabinets? Or will you stack them up against the unpainted cabinets you can buy with far less outlay? From this, it is evident that what you save will depend first of all on what would satisfy you if you were buying cabinets.

In building your own cabinets, lumber will be your major expense. Buying in small lots, you will pay more than the commercial builder. But, doing your own work, you will have no labor costs. Nor will there be tacked on to the item the mark-up that is part of a retail price. Considering all these points, it seems likely that home-built cabinets should cost you only about half as much as comparable commercial ones.

A book like this obviously can be written only with the help of others. I wish to thank here all of those who have given me a helping hand—and especially that kind lady who, returning part of the manuscript after reviewing it, wrote that she had become so absorbed that she let her dinner burn.

If the book arouses enough interest among other housewives to cause a number of other dinners to burn, and if it brings about a few hammer-bashed thumbs among those stubborn husbands who still clutch frayed membership cards in the old-fashioned DON'T-Do-It-Yourself School, then I shall certainly feel that it was well worth writing.

R. P. Stevenson

Lebanon, New Jersey,
October 1954

CONTENTS

Which Cabinets Do You Need?

The age of specialization has come to kitchen cabinets. In contrast to the old catchall cupboard, a modern cabinet is usually designed for a specific storage function, often in a particular part of the kitchen. Some have features that suit them especially to hold pots and pans, lids, seasonings, and other supplies used at the range. Some are fitted and equipped to ease the chore of baking a pie or cake—and even the electric mixer may have its own special niche. Some are solely for storing potatoes; some are just for keeping cleaning supplies handy to the sink; some are used only for storing and drying towels. Others have shelves just wide enough to store food supplies one-can deep, with none hidden behind and no waste space above.

The physical features of modern cabinets go far beyond the shelves and drawers that grandmother knew. As often as not, shelves now are adjustable up and down. Some shelves revolve; some slide in and out; some swing wide on doors; and some, turned on edge, support the stored equipment on hooks. Drawers may open in two directions, either into the kitchen or dining room. Dish cabinets, too, may have

STEP-SAVING U-KITCHEN

two fronts and no back—with the same double access. Work counters spread away in largely unbroken sweeps. Doors may slide back and forth instead of swinging on hinges.

The man or woman who wants to build a modern kitchen or modernize an old one would do well first of all to devote considerable time and thought to the planning stage.

Which cabinets will you need? What sizes? Where will you put them? How can you be sure of winding up with enough storage and counter space? How should you arrange the cabinets to save steps and work? To find satisfactory answers, you must consider such points as the size and shape of the room, door and window location, where the kitchen is located in relation to other rooms, and to some extent the size of the family.

Begin by deciding where to place the three fixtures common to all kitchens—sink, range, and refrigerator. These are commonly ar-

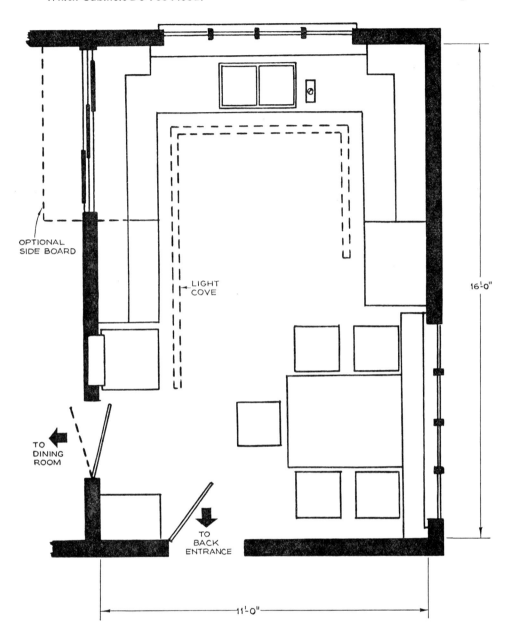

ranged with each at the point of a triangle. The sink, for instance, might go at one end of the room and the range and refrigerator on opposite side walls. But not too far from each other. Some kitchen planners recommend that the sink and refrigerator be four to seven feet apart, the refrigerator and range four to nine, and the range and sink four to six—with the sum of the sides of the triangle being fifteen to twenty feet for greatest working efficiency.

Floor Plans and Work Centers

You can carry out this triangle arrangement in three of the four basic kitchen floor plans—the U-kitchen, the L-shaped, and the corridor or two-wall plan. Where circumstances demand use of the fourth, or one-wall, plan, all three units are located in a line along the single wall. This should be avoided if possible, for the end units are forced too far apart if adequate counter space is provided beside each unit.

Because of its shape, the U-kitchen eliminates through traffic. You can see this layout (and the triangle arrangement) in the accompanying sketches of the step-saving U-kitchen and the modern kitchen-dining area. (The U-kitchen was designed by Lenore Sater Thye of the Bureau of Human Nutrition and Home Economics in the U.S. Department of Agriculture. The other kitchen shown was designed for the M and M Wood Working Company of Portland, Oregon, makers of Malarkey plywoods.) Construction plans are given in succeeding chapters for the cabinets you see in both of these pictures.

The sketch of the combination kitchen and dining area illustrates another feature you may want to consider in your planning—the peninsula arrangement of cabinets. In this case, the peninsula serves two functions—it keeps the kitchen area compact in a U-plan and it separates the kitchen and dining areas. If yours is a large room, or if a partitioning wall can be removed so that your total area embraces an adjoining pantry or other room, a peninsula may enable you to work out a more desirable plan.

Efficient planning calls, too, for dividing your kitchen into work centers. Kitchen authorities usually recognize four distinct areas—the mix or food preparation center, sink center, range or cooking center, and the serve center. Two centers are sometimes combined.

Each center should store equipment and supplies used there, and have enough counter space to handle the activities pertaining to it. The refrigerator is a part of the mix center, the area where different food ingredients are combined. Baking, for instance, begins there. Vegetables, fruits, and other foods that require washing or water are

MODERN KITCHEN — DINING AREA

A peninsula separates the dining area from the work center of this model kitchen. The base cabinet at the left of the range has drawers opening on the side to make table mats, linens, etc., more accessible to the dining area. A corner base cabinet with revolving shelves stands between the range and the sink.

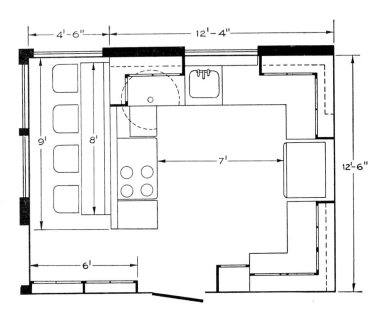

placed at the sink center. Coffee, tea, and other foods that need boiling water go into the range center along with equipment used directly in cooking. In function, the serve center stands between the range and table. It stores cookies, dry cereals, bread, and the like. In the cabinet projects described later, you will find information under the "Uses" heading to suggest where the cabinet might go.

Fitting Cabinets to the Housewife

If you build your own cabinets, or have them built, there is another aspect of planning worth considering—fitting them to the height and reach of the woman who will use them most. This will reduce stretching, stooping, and bending, all of which cause fatigue.

Motion studies show that a woman five feet four inches tall—approximately the average height of American women—usually can work best at a counter 36 inches high. But when she uses long-handled kitchen tools—an egg beater, long mixing spoon, and the like—her elbows tend to rise to an uncomfortable level. To eliminate this, model kitchens may drop the height of the work counter in the mix center to 32 inches—4 inches less than the other work counters where a housewife uses only short-handled tools or none at all.

A woman five feet four inches tall can reach to just above six feet without undue strain. Accordingly, constantly used shelves should be below that level. As suggested in the reach arcs in the accompanying sketch, articles should be stored within the comfortable reach arc as often as possible. This is the circle described by the hand while the elbow is flexed. Maximum reach, of course, is attained by keeping the elbow straight.

You can stick to these dimensions if the housewife is about average height. But if she is only five feet, or if she nudges six, it would be advisable to lower or raise the cabinets to suit her. Adjusting the height of the toe space up or down also can bring the work counter to the proper level.

Kitchen planning has become a science. In this book we only summarize its major principles. A pamphlet well worth the 25 cents it costs is "Planning the Kitchen and Workroom," a Department of Agriculture publication available from the Superintendent of Documents, U.S. Government Printing Office, Washington 25, D. C.

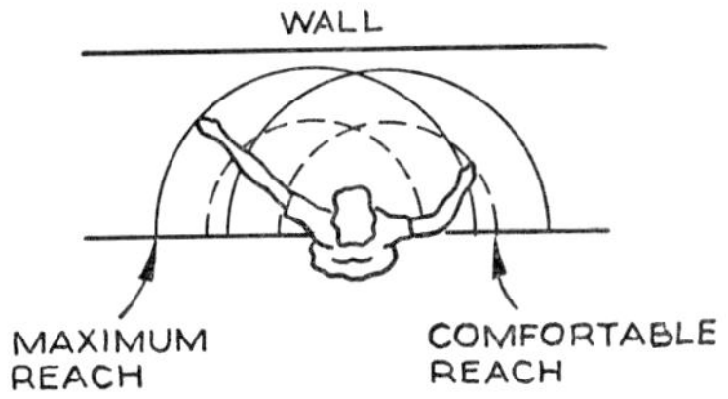

WALL

MAXIMUM
REACH

COMFORTABLE
REACH

MAXIMUM
REACH

COMFORTABLE
REACH

MAXIMUM
REACH

COMFORTABLE
REACH

STRETCHING CAUSES
FATIGUE

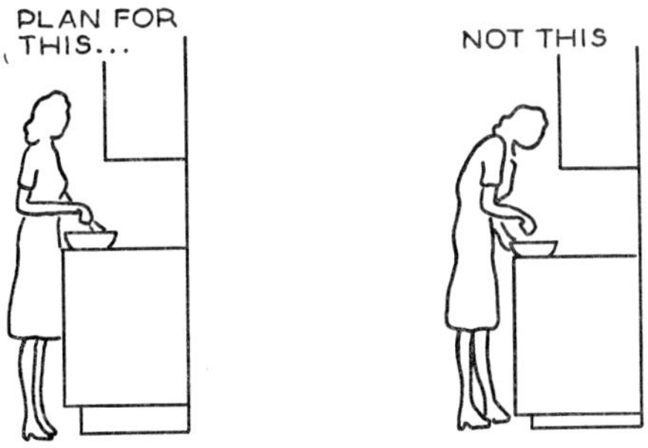

PLAN FOR
THIS...

NOT THIS

STOOPING AND BENDING
CAUSE FATIGUE

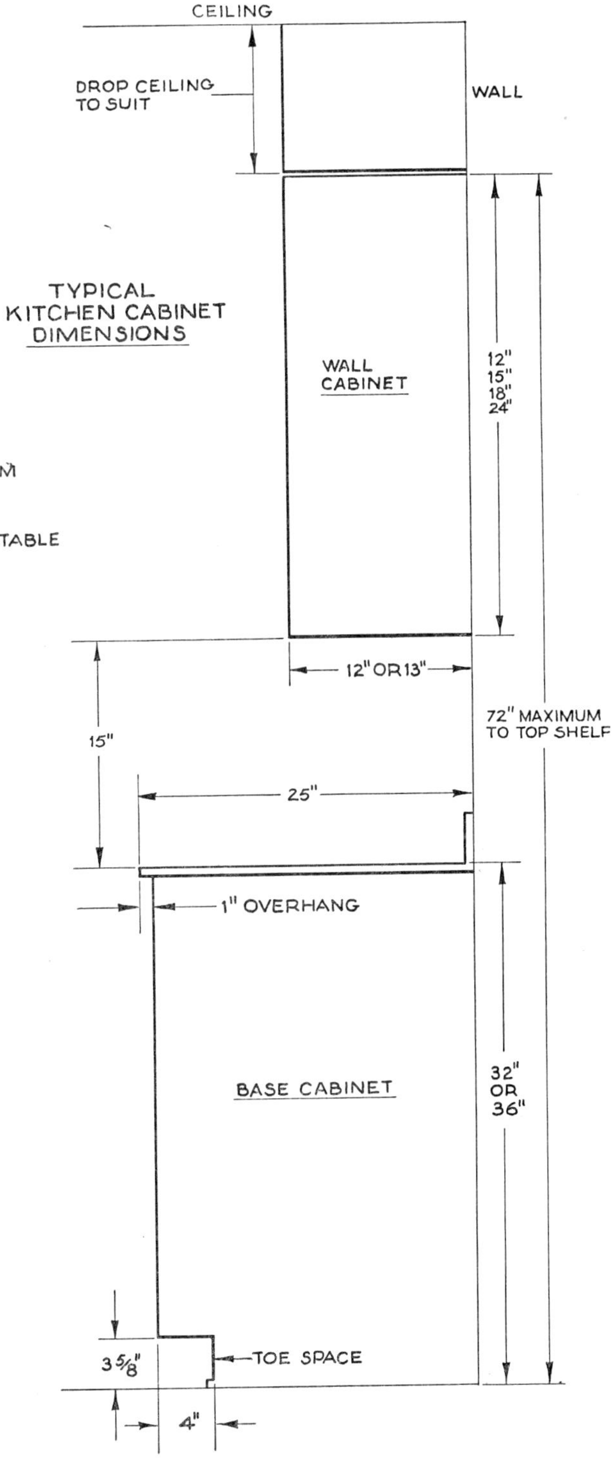

CEILING

DROP CEILING
TO SUIT

WALL

TYPICAL
KITCHEN CABINET
DIMENSIONS

WALL
CABINET

12"
15"
18"
24"

12" OR 13"

15"

72" MAXIMUM
TO TOP SHELF

25"

1" OVERHANG

BASE CABINET

32"
OR
36"

$3\frac{5}{8}$"

TOE SPACE

4"

2

Simplified Approach to Building

Cabinetwork for the living room often has dovetails, mortise-and-tenons, and dovetail dadoes. But kitchen cabinets built with plain butt joints can still look good and do the job for which they were intended. In the long run, what more could you want?

If you already are adept at cutting tenons or dadoes, by all means use them at the points where they should be used in the cabinets you select. If you are a beginning woodworker, you may want to master the advanced techniques for your own satisfaction—if for no other reason. But if you would rather not, you still can build kitchen cabinets that serve their purposes fully and are attractive at the same time.

A butt joint is made by smoothing two surfaces, fitting them together, and holding with glue, dowels, nails, or screws. To strengthen them, the hardware store will supply you with such things as corner irons, mending plates, and corrugated fasteners. Corner irons go inside a corner. Mending plates come in three shapes—straight, right-angle, or T—for use on the edges of the joined members.

A professional cabinetmaker might set shelves in dadoes. You can, too, if you wish. But cleats are a lot simpler, and functionally are just as satisfactory. However, the smart cabinet builder will use neither dadoes nor cleats except in special cases.

Instead, when he visits the hardware store, he will buy a batch of adjustable shelf standards, fasten the standards vertically inside the cabinet ends, and slip in the squared shelves. Some of the finest commercial cabinets have this feature. Not only do standards make cabinet building easier but they keep the cabinet in step with changes in storage needs. They are a logical substitute, too, for the peg-in-hole supports suggested in some of the cabinets in later chapters. If you wish, standards can be fastened directly to the cabinet ends. But setting them into vertical grooves cut in the cabinet ends, if you have the equipment for it, makes a more workmanlike job and reduces the width of the down cracks at the shelf ends.

Some Principles of Cabinet Building

Two of the three pages of drawings accompanying this chapter illustrate some of the simple procedures that can be used in cabinet building. The drawings showing a wall cabinet and a base cabinet were adapted from designs of the Skil Corporation. They provide that the kitchen wall shall serve as the cabinet back. But it is easy enough to add thin plywood, hardboard, or a wallboard-type composition material if you want enclosed units.

The half-lap joint indicated at *A* in the base cabinet requires sawing half the thickness of the stock and chiseling out the waste. End lap joints (made the same way except that one or both joining members are cut on the end) can be used elsewhere on the front facing strips. The simple end rabbet shown on the flush-front drawer is a good one to master. A rabbet is a cut of right-angle section along the edge or end of a piece of wood. This joint usually is glued or nailed. Since glue does not hold well on end wood, it is better to use a rabbet than a butt when you join end wood. A rabbet gives the glue a better chance to do its job because some will be adhering to side wood.

An end rabbet like that shown can be cut by hand. Lay it out by gauging lines on the end, rear surface, and edges of the drawer front, making it half the thickness of the drawer-front stock. Suit the other dimension to the thickness of the stock used for the side of the drawer. Clamp the drawer front in a vise with the end up. Then, using a back saw or rip saw, cut down through the end to the rabbet shoulder line, sawing in the waste area. Begin by nudging the saw into place with the thumb of your left hand. Start the saw in the corner and gradually level off. To cut the shoulder, remove the piece from the vise and clamp a guide block along the line. Again saw in the waste area.

A drawer bottom usually is set into grooves cut in the face and side pieces (and sometimes the back). But it doesn't have to be. It can rest on narrow cleats nailed and glued inside the side and end pieces.

Two types of doors are commonly used—flush and lipped. The flush type is mounted with its face even with the cabinet front. A lipped door has a rabbet around the edges of the rear surface, permitting the door to overlap its frame. A variation is a straight overlapping door without an inset. This usually is made of thin stock. The outer edges of a lipped door should be rounded off. If you want a lipped door, do not be scared away by the need for cutting a rabbet. Build up the door by gluing and bradding together two thin panels, one slightly larger than the other all around.

Cross rails on the back add strength and offer a means of screwing a cabinet to the wall. In standard stud walls, run screws through the rails, spacing them to suit the studs. For a hollow-tile wall, use toggle bolts; for a masonry wall, use bolts and expansion shields.

Important Points About Wood

As a cabinet builder, you have a choice of three major materials— wood, plywood, and hardboard. You can build a complete cabinet of either wood or plywood—or combine plywood or hardboard with a wood frame. For cabinets, specify kiln-dried wood. Poorly seasoned stock will cause the best of joints to open up as it dries.

Some builders may want to limit their use of lumber stock in favor of the working ease provided by the panel materials, plywood and hardboard. But wood usually will still be needed for the framing members. Such parts call for 1 x 2's, 1 x 3's, 1 x 4's, and some 2 x 2's and 2 x 4's. These are nominal (or rough) size designations.

All dressed lumber is less than the rough size by which it usually

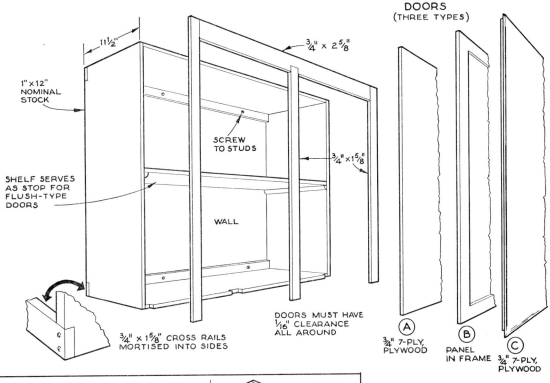

DOORS
(THREE TYPES)

11½"

¾" × 2⅝"

1" × 12"
NOMINAL
STOCK

SCREW
TO STUDS

¾" × 1⅝"

SHELF SERVES
AS STOP FOR
FLUSH-TYPE
DOORS

WALL

Ⓐ
¾" 7-PLY,
PLYWOOD

Ⓑ
PANEL
IN FRAME

Ⓒ
¾" 7-PLY,
PLYWOOD

¾" × 1⅝" CROSS RAILS
MORTISED INTO SIDES

DOORS MUST HAVE
1/16" CLEARANCE
ALL AROUND

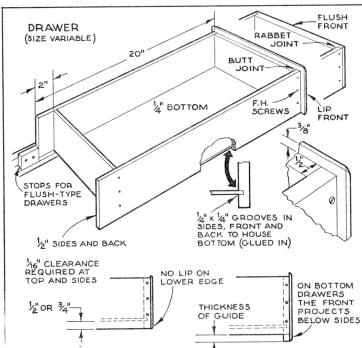

DRAWER
(SIZE VARIABLE)

20"

2"

FLUSH
FRONT

RABBET
JOINT

BUTT
JOINT

¼" BOTTOM

F.H.
SCREWS

LIP
FRONT

⅜"

STOPS FOR
FLUSH-TYPE
DRAWERS

½" SIDES AND BACK

¼" × ¼" GROOVES IN
SIDES, FRONT AND
BACK TO HOUSE
BOTTOM (GLUED IN)

½"

1/16" CLEARANCE
REQUIRED AT
TOP AND SIDES

NO LIP ON
LOWER EDGE

½" OR ¾"

THICKNESS
OF GUIDE

ON BOTTOM
DRAWERS
THE FRONT
PROJECTS
BELOW SIDES

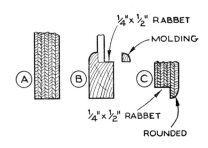

¼" × ½" RABBET

MOLDING

Ⓐ   Ⓑ   Ⓒ

¼" × ½" RABBET

ROUNDED

WALL CABINET
(Size Variable)

is designated, the difference having been planed away in the process of dressing. Because of this, stock 1″ thick in its rough state actually measures nearer ¾″ after being dressed—and is frequently referred to as such. These variations, of course, do not apply to plywood.

Cabinet parts in the project drawings throughout this book usually are indicated in actual dimensions. In the materials lists, however, lumber stock is designated in nominal sizes as an aid to the builder in making lumber-yard purchases.

Board Widths
(Inches)

NOMINAL	DRESSED
2	1⅝
3	2⅝
4	3⅝
5	4⅝
6	5½ or 5⅝
7	6½
8	7½
9	8½
10	9½
11	10½
12	11½
14	13½
16	15½

Board Thicknesses
(Inches)

NOMINAL	DRESSED
1	¾ *
1¼	1⅟₁₆
1½	1⁵⁄₁₆

* According to American Lumber Standards the minimum thickness of nominal 1″ boards is ²⁵⁄₃₂″ dressed. However, for practical measures ¾″ is close enough.

The builder should particularly note the actual dimensions of lumber used, which may vary. Occasionally slight recalculations may have to be made when following drawings, especially when notching or when cutting butted frame or supporting cross-members.

When possible, the cabinets utilize lumber stock in the width received to minimize ripping—or the need for jointing. For most wall cabinets, for example, 1″ x 12″ (nominal) stock will do nicely for sides, top, and bottom. Its actual dressed width of 11½″ gives adequate depth. Shelves, too, can often be made of stock widths.

Although most of the cabinets are presented as separate units, you will usually find it economical of material and time to frame and build adjoining ones as a single assembly. The sub-base on which a line of base cabinets rest should of course be a single unit. This can be made of 2 x 4's, 1 x 4's, or a combination of the two. The 3⅝″ actual dimension of the 4″ (nom.) stock establishes the height of the toe space. Combining several cabinets into one unit also may make it possible to use thin material, or perhaps nothing if partitions are not needed, in place of the ¾″ plywood generally specified for cabinet ends.

When combining two or more of the cabinet projects, it often will be possible to consolidate the separate materials lists into a more economical single one, making use of waste that may result from the individual lists. An hour spent with pencil and paper before buying materials should help you get only what you need. Lumber stock usually is sold in lengths in multiples of 2 feet up to about 16 feet. If your projects require 1″ x 4″ (nom.) stock in a total of, say 24 feet, you may wind up with less waste from one 8-foot length and one 16 than from two 12-foot lengths, or vice versa.

For most economical use of plywood panels, you should have a cutting plan before you pick up the saw. Squared paper will help you work this out. When ¾″ plywood is being used for a counter 25″ wide, the 23″ strip remaining from a 48″-wide panel can be utilized for the base cabinet ends. Make the cut so that the saw kerf falls within the 25″ width. The metal edging that you'll want to apply to the counter will compensate for the saw-kerf loss.

Facts to Remember About Plywood

There are two major types of plywood—lumber core and veneer. Lumber core has a fairly thick middle layer of solid wood with a ¹⁄₁₆″ layer on each side and a ¹⁄₂₈″ face veneer. In all ways except cost, this is the most desirable for cabinet work. On the edge, veneer plywood shows from three to seven layers. In thickness, it ranges from ⅛″ to ¾″. Lumber core usually begins at ½″ and goes up to 1⅜″.

Plywood is divided further into interior and exterior types, made with different kinds of adhesives. More expensive, the exterior type will stand up under permanent exposure without going to pieces. In a kitchen, this type would be a good choice for a sink counter. For other uses, the interior type would do.

Plywood is available in a series of grades with facings of fine hardwoods—birch, butternut, cherry, elm, gum, ash, mahogany, walnut, maple, oak, and many others. But fir plywood is the most common and most economical. The panels—usually 4′ x 8′, although you can get other sizes—are clearly marked as to type (interior or exterior) and grade.

Grade is determined by the quality of both faces. Faces are rated as good, sound, or utility. A good face is a perfect piece of veneer over the entire panel. A sound face may consist of two pieces of veneer per panel, perfectly joined but with small imperfections such as patches, stains, or sapwood. A utility face may have knots, pitch pockets, knot holes, and small splits that impair the strength but not the looks of the panel. Another grading system designates faces as A, B, C, and D. Under this, an A-A panel would have two good faces, an A-C panel a good face and utility back, and so on.

A fir plywood panel may have any combination of faces. The top grade has a good face on each side and may be marked G2S. Kitchen cabinets would rarely require this top grade. Even where both sides will show, as in a cabinet door, a money-saving alternate is G1S, good on one side and sound on the other. If cabinets are to be painted, the sound-two-sides (S2S) or even S1S will reduce the materials cost even more. The wallboard grade (WB), which has a sound face and a utility back, will do nicely for cabinet backs. Sheathing (SH) has two utility faces.

Plywood comes with many different surface treatments. You can also get it with hardboard bonded to the face. This combines the surface smoothness of hardboard with the strength of plywood. Other plywood panels have plastic impregnated or plastic sheet facings, making them especially suitable for counter tops, since grease, alcohol, ammonia, fruit juices, and boiling water will not mar the surface. In some cases, plastic sheets are laminated over hardwood plywood, providing a durable natural finish that needs no further attention. Laminates also come in a variety of colors.

How to Hide Plywood Edges

Because of the plies, exposed edges and corner joints in plywood construction present an appearance problem. You should tackle this first in the design stage, planning the cabinet to minimize the number of visible edges. Edge grain can be hidden in a number of ways. One procedure is to butt a wood strip (half round will do in some

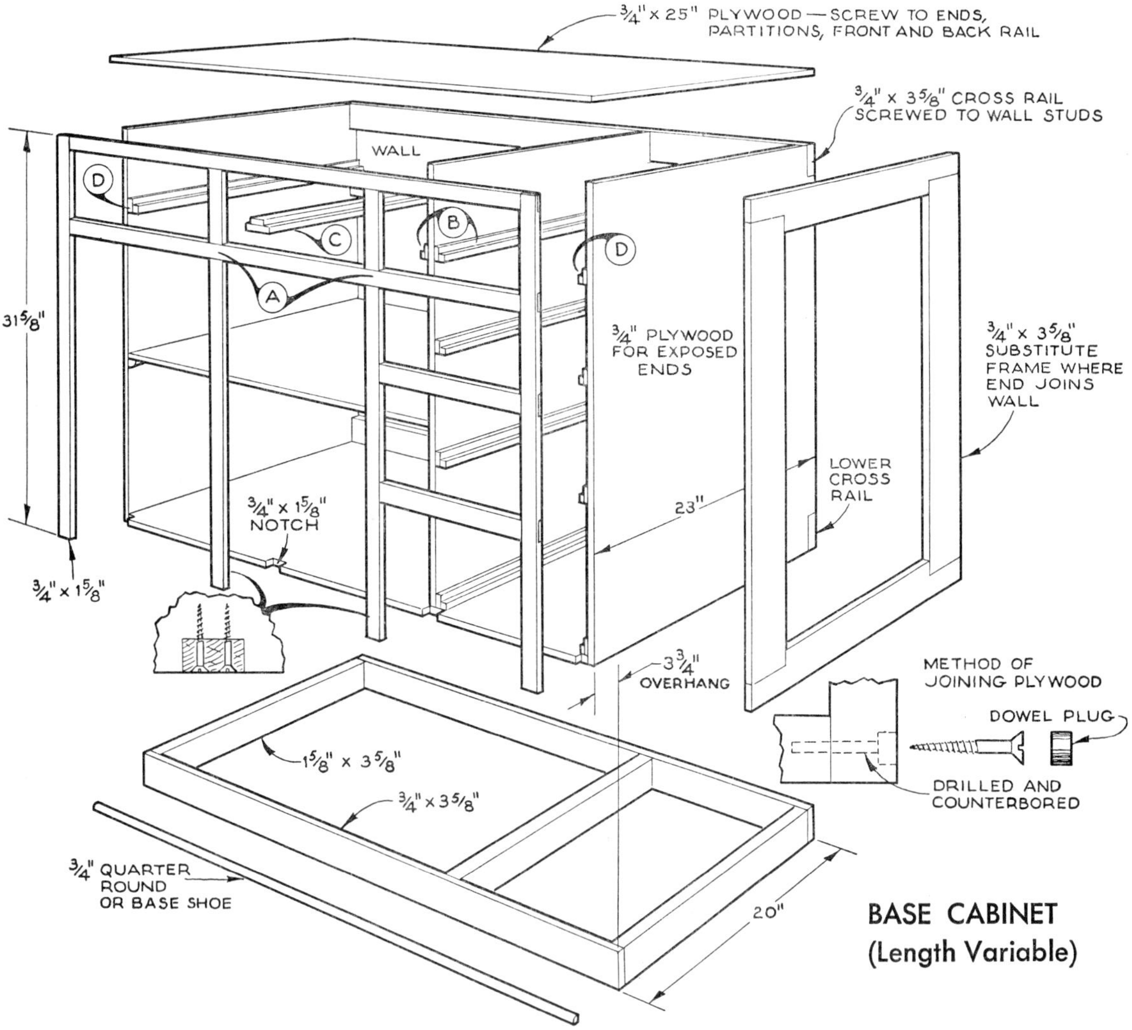
3/4" x 25" PLYWOOD — SCREW TO ENDS, PARTITIONS, FRONT AND BACK RAIL
3/4" x 3 5/8" CROSS RAIL SCREWED TO WALL STUDS
WALL
D
C
B
D
A
31 5/8"
3/4" PLYWOOD FOR EXPOSED ENDS
3/4" x 3 5/8" SUBSTITUTE FRAME WHERE END JOINS WALL
LOWER CROSS RAIL
23"
3/4" x 1 5/8" NOTCH
3/4" x 1 5/8"
3 3/4" OVERHANG
METHOD OF JOINING PLYWOOD
DOWEL PLUG
DRILLED AND COUNTERBORED
1 5/8" x 3 5/8"
3/4" x 3 5/8"
3/4" QUARTER ROUND OR BASE SHOE
20"

BASE CABINET
(Length Variable)

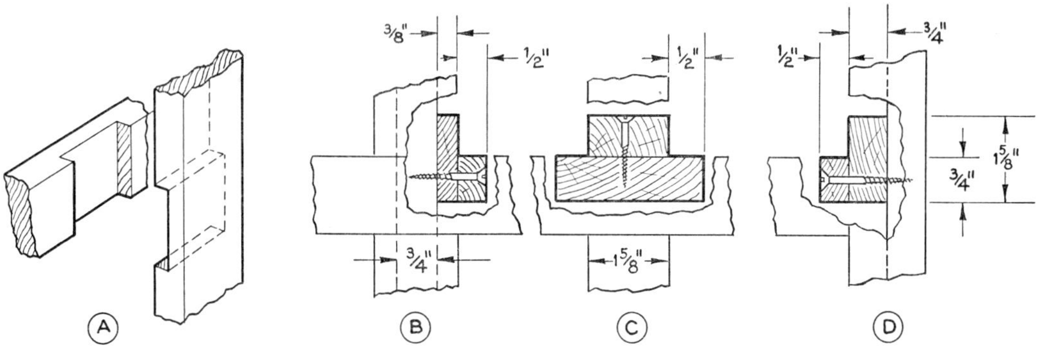
3/8"
1/2"
3/4"
1/2"
1 5/8"
1/2"
3/4"
1 5/8"
3/4"
A
B
C
D

HALF-LAP JOINT

DRAWER GUIDES — SCREW TO PARTITIONS OR ENDS. DOUBLE GUIDE "C" IS SUPPORTED AT REAR ON CROSSRAILS (NOT SHOWN)

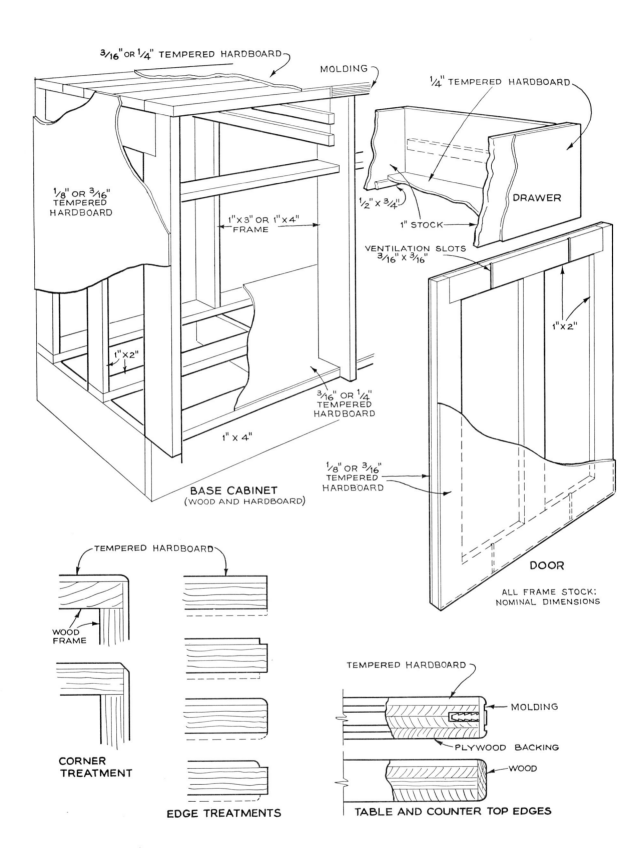

3/16" OR 1/4" TEMPERED HARDBOARD

MOLDING

1/4" TEMPERED HARDBOARD

1/8" OR 3/16" TEMPERED HARDBOARD

1" X 3" OR 1" X 4" FRAME

DRAWER

1/2" X 3/4"

1" STOCK

VENTILATION SLOTS 3/16" X 3/16"

1" X 2"

1"X 2"

3/16" OR 1/4" TEMPERED HARDBOARD

1" X 4"

1/8" OR 3/16" TEMPERED HARDBOARD

BASE CABINET
(WOOD AND HARDBOARD)

DOOR

ALL FRAME STOCK:
NOMINAL DIMENSIONS

TEMPERED HARDBOARD

WOOD FRAME

CORNER TREATMENT

EDGE TREATMENTS

TEMPERED HARDBOARD

MOLDING

PLYWOOD BACKING

WOOD

TABLE AND COUNTER TOP EDGES

cases) to the edge with brads and glue. Or, if you have power equipment, lock the strip on with a tongue and groove. In addition, a strip
of veneer can be glued in place. A triangular strip ripped off the
edge at 45 degrees, with the cut slanting toward the rear, can be re-
versed and then bradded and glued back on the edge to bring the
bottom surface to the front. A 90-degree V-cut underneath, starting
from the panel edge, will yield a 45-degree strip that can be swung
down from the top against the angled edge. This makes a front edge
that matches the top. The method has some disadvantage, in that
the width of the panel is reduced in an amount equal to its own
thickness. But all such tricks are usually unnecessary if the plywood
is to be painted. Just force plastic composition wood into the edge
grain, let it set, and sand the surface smooth.

At corners, the plies can be hidden by using a miter joint, splined
or reinforced with corner blocks. A rabbet joint with a single-ply
overlap looks good enough for even the finest construction. Quarter-
round can be used to hide two plywood edges at a corner. Assemble
the plywood panels over a frame or support them with inside corner
blocks. Stop the edges of the panels short before they reach the corner. Then fill the corner with the quarter-round, butting one of its
flat faces against each plywood edge. Similarly, the plywood can be
joined to a corner post with tongue and groove.

Types of Hardboard

Hardboard, the other major panel material, comes in various types,
but only two, standard and tempered, are of major interest to the
cabinet builder. The tempered type is recommended for use where
hard wear is expected and where high or changing humidity condi-
tions may prevail. A third type, with a smooth finish on both sides,
would be an excellent choice for a single-panel cabinet door or for
sliding doors. Standard and tempered hardboards come in thicknesses
of $\frac{1}{8}''$, $\frac{3}{16}''$, $\frac{1}{4}''$, and $\frac{5}{16}''$, in panels 48'' wide and in a choice
of lengths. The two-faced type, $\frac{1}{8}''$ and $\frac{3}{16}''$ thick, is commonly
available in panels 60'' wide.

The accompanying page of sketches, adapted from plans drawn
by the Masonite Corporation, shows how extensively tempered hardboard (Presdwood) can be used in cabinets. Supported by a wood

frame, tempered hardboard serves as a counter covering. On a frame of (nom.) 1 x 2 material a sheet of hardboard becomes a shelf surface.

When a door is made by sandwiching a wood frame between two hardboard panels, ventilation slots should be cut in the frame as indicated. This allows air to circulate inside the door, causing the hardboard to react equally on both surfaces to humidity changes. In the plans, drawer construction calls for a box of 1″ (nom.) stock with a hardboard bottom and facing. The drawer rides on wood slides that fit between parallel guides in the cabinet. Corners or exposed edges of hardboard can be beveled or rounded with sandpaper or a plane.

When sawing hardboard, turn up the surface that will be exposed. This will avoid scratches if the panel should slide on the supports. A sharper edge is also obtained on the upturned face. If you use a hand saw, the crosscut type with 8 to 12 points per inch and a No. 6 set is usually the most suitable for straight cutting. For most drilling operations, a twist drill is preferred to an auger bit.

A basement filled with power tools might help you turn out better cabinets, and do it more easily, but expensive equipment will never substitute for the application of common sense, a bit of ingenuity, and proper use of hand tools.

3

Special-Purpose Wall Cabinets

Wall cabinets are the device by which real economy of floor space is achieved and the kitchen is drawn together into a unit small enough to cut down the housewife's steps. The list of supplies and equipment needed in the ordinary kitchen is so extensive that only by stacking up part of them in cupboards or shelves, at or above chest height, can the working area be kept compact. Important too is the fact that wall cabinets can offer storage at a height where the housewife needs only to reach forward and up. The more she can store in wall cabinets the less bending she will have to do in pulling what she needs from a base cabinet. The easy reach arc of a housewife standing at work normally embraces only the first row of drawers under the work counter. Storage below that level therefore may require extra effort. Bear these points in mind as you do your planning, and try to arrange for the most convenient and work-saving storage areas.

Include all the wall cabinets you can in your kitchen. The following pages offer various types, each designed for a specialized job.

OVER-REFRIGERATOR CABINET

Uses

This cabinet is a convenient place to store canned juices that eventually will go into the refrigerator for chilling. Large economy-size cans fit nicely at the rear of the bottom shelf, smaller sizes go above and on the two door shelves. Jellies and jams can be kept here too. Since the cans are aligned only one deep, everything in the cabinet comes into view when the doors swing open. Even though the refrigerator top is high, the cabinet door shelves bring their contents within reach.

Materials

1″ x 12″ (nom.) stock (12 linear feet) to make—

    2 pc. 14½″ long — ends.

    2 pc. 26″ long — top and bottom.

    1 pc. 5½″ x 24½″ — shelf.

    4 pc. 5¼″ x 9½″ — door-shelf bottoms.

¼″ plywood or hardboard to make—

    8 pc. 1½″ x 5¼″ ⎫

                   ⎬ door-shelf sides.

    4 pc. 1½″ x 10″ ⎭

1″ x 2″ (nom.) stock (10 linear feet) to make—

    2 pc. 16″ long — facing strips.

    4 pc. 10″ long — door battens.

    2 pc. 6″ long — shelf cleats.

    1 pc. 26″ long — cross rail.

1″ x 4″ (nom.) pine tongue-and-groove (12 linear feet) to make—

    8 pc. 16″ long — doors.

2 pr. H-hinges.

2 door knobs.

2 pr. cabinet spring catches.

4 corner braces 2″ x 2″.

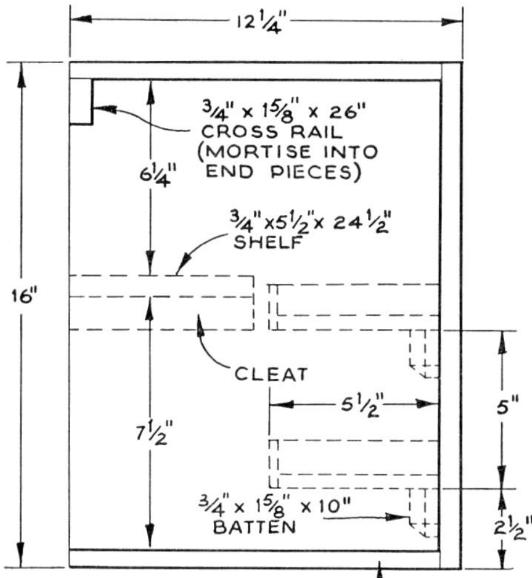

END DETAIL

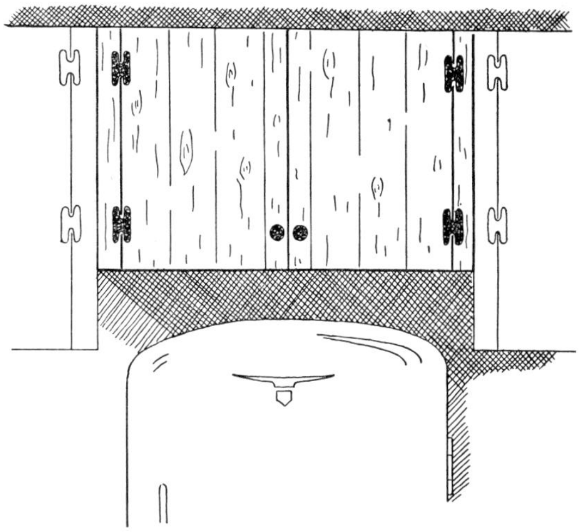

3/4" x 15/8" x 26"
CROSS RAIL
(MORTISE INTO
END PIECES)

3/4" x 5 1/2" x 24 1/2"
SHELF

CLEAT

3/4" x 15/8" x 10"
BATTEN

12 1/4"

6 1/4"

16"

7 1/2"

5 1/2"

5"

2 1/2"

OVER-REFRIGERATOR CABINET

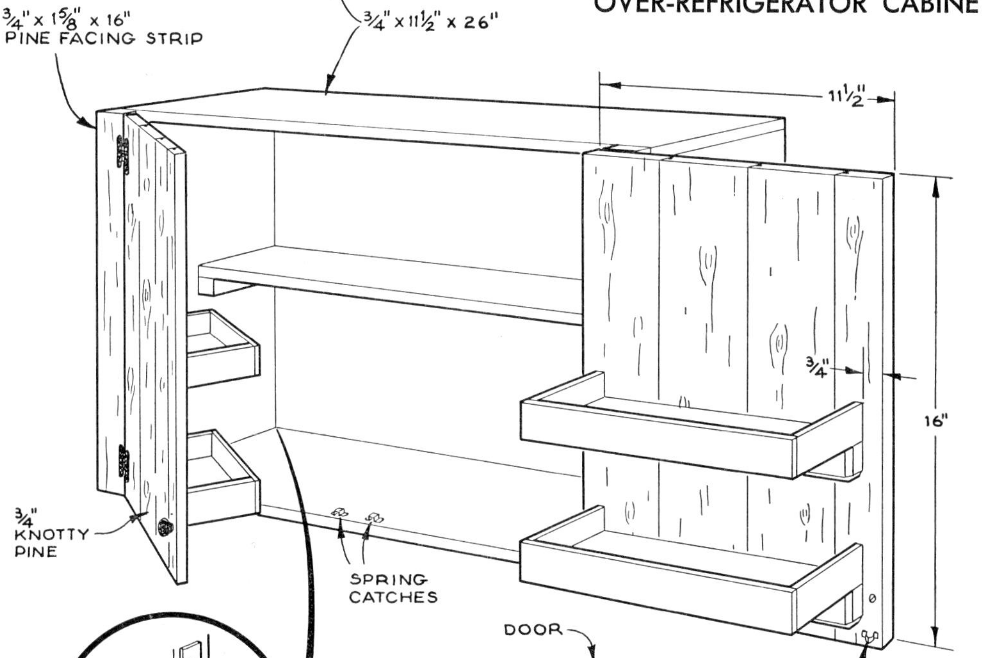

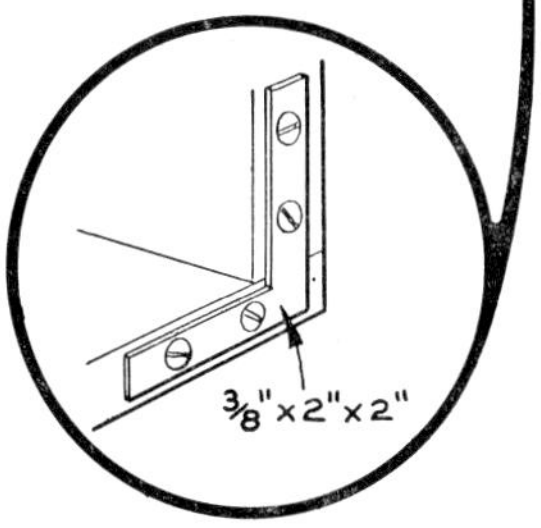

3/4" x 15/8" x 16"
PINE FACING STRIP

3/4" x 11 1/2" x 26"

11 1/2"

3/4"

16"

3/4"
KNOTTY
PINE

SPRING
CATCHES

DOOR

CABINET
CATCH

SCREW BATTEN
TO DOOR

SCREW SHELF
TO BATTEN

3/4" x 5 1/4" x 9 1/2"

1/4" x 1 1/2" x 5 1/4"

1/4" x 1 1/2" x 10"

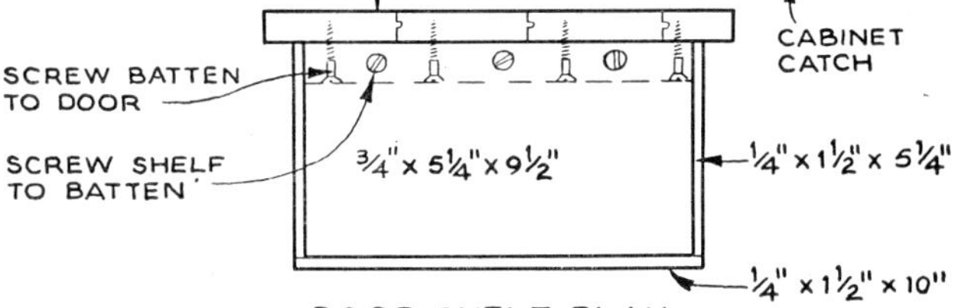

DOOR SHELF PLAN

3/8" x 2" x 2"

REAR CORNER DETAIL
(SCREW BRACES TO ALL REAR CORNERS)

Pointers for Building

A cabinet as simple as this can be built with a hammer, saw, square, screwdriver, and twist drill. In sawing the pieces, be careful to make square cuts. Mortise the ends for the cross rail by marking with the squared end of the rail and sawing inside the lines. All assembly can be with wood screws, countersunk and filled, although glue can be used if desired. Position and attach the two cleats for the middle shelf before assembling the cabinet proper. Screw the bottom to the ends, the middle shelf to the cleats, and the top to the ends, in that order. After making sure the assembly is square, screw a metal brace to each rear corner for extra strength if you wish. These will not be needed if you nail on a back of thin plywood or hardboard. The back can be set into rabbets cut in the rear edges of the cabinet top, bottom, and sides. But it actually is not necessary for you to go to the trouble of cutting rabbets. Just nail the back on, making its edges flush with the cabinet sides.

If you plan to give the doors a natural finish, use dowel plugs to hide the heads of the screws with which you attach the two pine facing strips. Two of the door strips will have to be ripped to make the desired 11½″ width. Battens serve the double function of holding the door sections together and providing a base for the shelves. Beveling the edges of the battens will give the job a more professional look. Because the door shelves must support considerable weight, it would be advisable to use both glue and screws to attach them to the battens.

Alternate Construction

As you might expect, any cabinet can be built in different ways. The second page of drawings shows variations you may prefer in this case. All parts can be cut from a 4′ x 4′ panel of plywood. The wide shelf will probably turn the rear area into dead storage space, but some housewives may prefer this.

Polished and lacquered, the brass sash rod suggested for the door shelf would add an attractive touch to natural pine doors. Use a hacksaw to cut it to the desired lengths. Screw the dowel posts to the shelf after the rods have been forced into holes drilled for them.

The sketch of the rabbet joint illustrates a principle often used to

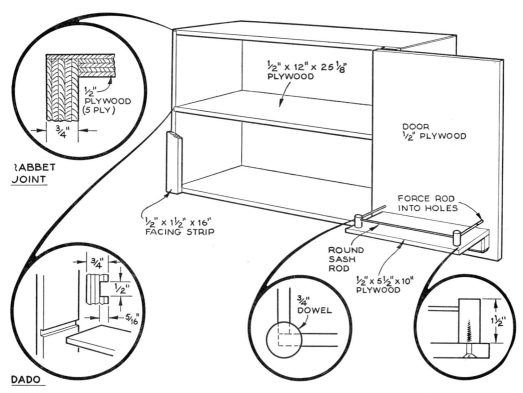

RABBET JOINT

½"
PLYWOOD
(5 PLY)

¾"

½" x 12" x 25⅛"
PLYWOOD

DOOR
½" PLYWOOD

FORCE ROD
INTO HOLES

½" x 1½" x 16"
FACING STRIP

ROUND
SASH
ROD

½" x 5½" x 10"
PLYWOOD

¾"

½"

5⁄16"

DADO

¾"
DOWEL

1½"

OVER-REFRIGERATOR CABINET
(Alternate Construction)

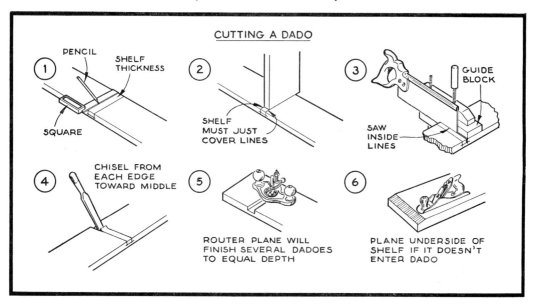

CUTTING A DADO

1 PENCIL SHELF THICKNESS

SQUARE

2 SHELF MUST JUST COVER LINES

3 GUIDE BLOCK

SAW INSIDE LINES

4 CHISEL FROM EACH EDGE TOWARD MIDDLE

5 ROUTER PLANE WILL FINISH SEVERAL DADOES TO EQUAL DEPTH

6 PLANE UNDERSIDE OF SHELF IF IT DOESN'T ENTER DADO

disguise a plywood edge. Only one ply is left when the rabbet is cut. When the joint is fitted, this results in just a thin line showing along the edge. The joint can be glued and nailed after being carefully fitted together.

Cutting a dado to support a shelf is a more difficult bit of construction than tacking on a cleat, but a dado eliminates the down cracks left at the shelf ends when cleats are used. Food particles collect in such cracks and attract insects. (A dado runs across the wood grain, a groove runs with it.) With care, a dado in solid stock can be completed with a chisel after being sawed to depth, but a router plane will give a surer fit. In plywood, the chisel must be used cautiously or it may chip out a ply to an unwanted depth. Everything considered, a dado cutter on a circular saw is a worthwhile investment for the man who expects to do any extensive dado cutting. A dado should be a tight fit. Join the two members with glue, holding them with clamps until the glue has set.

In the sequence of dado-cutting operations shown in the sketches on the preceding page, you can finish the job with the use of a chisel as shown in step 4. A router plane is a useful tool, but you can get by without it. If the end of the shelf doesn't quite enter the dado, plane or sand off the under edge until it does.

LID AND PAN RACK

Uses

Since this cabinet could go either near the range or in the mixing center, you may want one for each location. Lids and flat pans such as pie tins or small cooky sheets are stored upright. Storage bins of two different widths offer a choice for pans and lids of different thickness. The shelves slant downward to the rear to keep round tins from falling out. The spice rack and storage area on the bottom shelf can be used for other items frequently needed at the range or mixing center. This cabinet was adapted from a design of the makers of Malarkey plywoods.

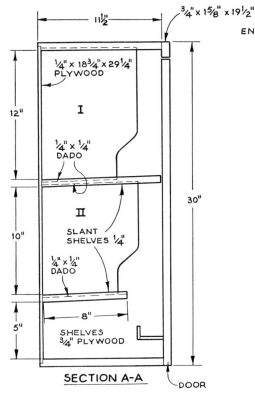

11½"

¾" x 1⅝" x 19½"

¼" x 18¾" x 29¼"
PLYWOOD

I

12"

¼" x ¼"
DADO

30"

II

10"

SLANT
SHELVES ¼"

¼" x ¼"
DADO

8"

5"

SHELVES
¾" PLYWOOD

SECTION A-A

DOOR

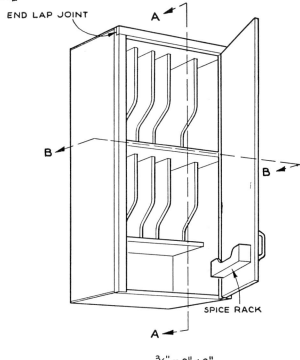

END LAP JOINT

A

B

B

B

SPICE RACK

A

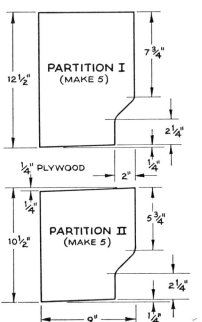

PARTITION I
(MAKE 5)

12½"

7¾"

2¼"

¼"

¼" PLYWOOD

2"

¼"

PARTITION II
(MAKE 5)

10½"

5¾"

2¼"

9"

1¼"

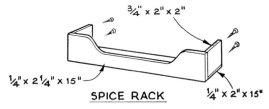

¾" x 2" x 2"

¼" x 2¼" x 15"

SPICE RACK

¼" x 2" x 15"

LID AND PAN RACK

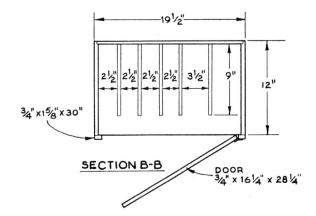

19½"

2½" 2½" 2½" 2½" 3½"

9"

12"

¾" x 1⅝" x 30"

SECTION B-B

DOOR
¾" x 16¼" x 28¼"

Materials

¾″ plywood (4′ x 4′ panel) to make—

    2 pc. 12″ x 30″ — sides.

    2 pc. 12″ x 19½″ — top and bottom.

    1 pc. 12″ x 18½″ — top shelf.

    1 pc.   8″ x 18½″ — bottom shelf.

    1 pc. 16¼″ x 28¼″ — door.

    2 pc.   2″ x 2″ — rack ends.

¼″ plywood (4′ x 4′ panel) to make—

    1 pc. 18¾″ x 29¼″ — back.

    5 pc.   9″ x 10½″ — lower partitions.

    5 pc.   9″ x 12½″ — upper partitions.

    1 pc.   2¼″ x 15″ — rack front.

    1 pc.   2″ x 15″ — rack bottom.

2 pc. ¾″ x 1⅝″ x 30″ pine — front facing strips.

1 pc. ¾″ x 1⅝″ x 19½″ pine — top facing strip.

Pointers for Building

Cut ⅜″ x ¾″ rabbets in the ends of the top and bottom pieces to take the side pieces. Rabbet all four of these pieces ¼″ x ⅜″ for the ¼″ plywood back. Cut ¾″ dadoes ¼″ deep in the sides for the two shelves, slanting them as shown. Stopped dadoes are indicated in both the top and bottom surface of the upper shelf for the partitions, but these can be full dadoes if you want the partitions to be adjustable. Corresponding dadoes also are needed in the 8″ bottom shelf and the under side of the cabinet top. Cut the partitions ¼″ off square as indicated in the drawing. To get exactly the same angle on all the partitions, clamp them together and cut them all at once. After fitting the partitions into the dadoes, position the shelves between the sides of the cabinet and you will find that they slant downward toward the rear as desired.

The spice rack can be attached with flathead screws sunk in the face of the door. Hide the screw heads with putty or other filler.

OVER-THE-RANGE CABINET 1

Uses

A cupboard above the range saves many steps. This one is designed for that spot, although it could be used to advantage on either side if a ventilating hood or other above-range object should interfere. The open shelf holds seasonings and other supplies that the cook needs frequently. Door storage brings pan lids within reach. Breakfast cereals that require cooking can be kept on the cabinet shelves. The narrow vertical and horizontal compartments take large platters or frying pans.

Materials

1″ x 12″ (nom.) stock (24 linear feet) to make—

    2 pc. 35¼″ long — ends.

    1 pc. 40″ long — top.

    1 pc. 39″ long — shelf.

    1 pc. 22⅝″ long — shelf.

    1 pc. 22½″ long — partition.

    1 pc. 18¾″ long — partition.

    1 pc. 8″ x 16⅝″ — shelf.

    2 pc. 7″ x 16⅝″ — shelves.

1″ x 2″ (nom.) stock (14 linear feet) to make—

    2 pc. 25¼″ long — facing strips.

    2 pc. 39″ long — braces.

    1 pc. 11″ long — spoon holder.

¾″ plywood to make—

    2 pc. 18½″ x 25¼″ — doors.

¼″ plywood to make—

    2 pc. 2″ x 20″ — rack.

⅛″ asbestos.

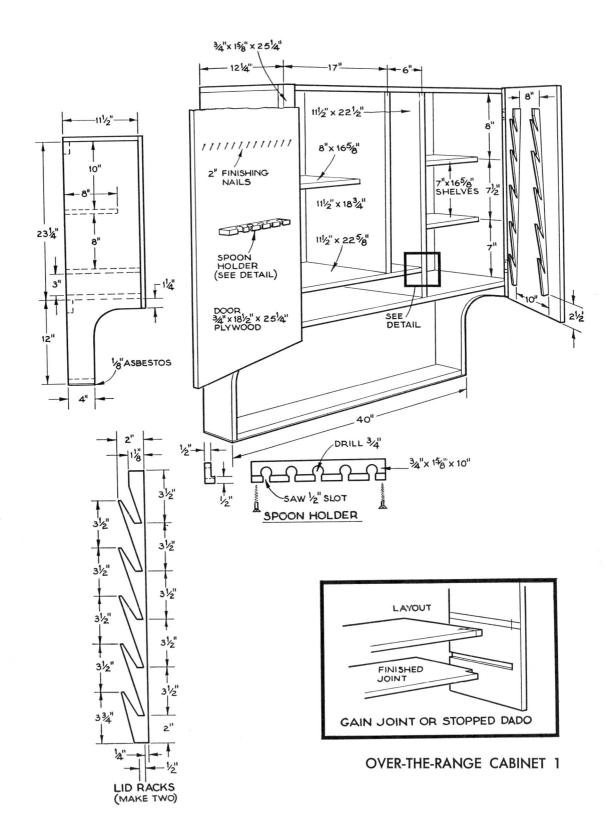

¾" x 1⅝" x 25¼"

12¼"   17"   6"

11½" x 22½"

2" FINISHING
NAILS

8" x 16⅝"

11½" x 18¾"

7" x 16⅝"
SHELVES

8"

7½"

11½"

10"

SPOON
HOLDER
(SEE DETAIL)

11½" x 22⅝"

8"

7"

10"

2½"

DOOR
¾" x 18½" x 25¼"
PLYWOOD

SEE
DETAIL

40"

10"

8"

8"

3"

23¼"

1¼"

12"

⅛" ASBESTOS

4"

2"

1⅛"

3½"

3½"

3½"

3½"

3½"

3½"

3½"

3½"

3½"

3½"

3½"

3¾"

2"

¼"

½"

LID RACKS
(MAKE TWO)

½"

½"

DRILL ¾"

¾" x 1⅝" x 10"

SAW ½" SLOT

SPOON HOLDER

LAYOUT

FINISHED
JOINT

GAIN JOINT OR STOPPED DADO

OVER-THE-RANGE CABINET 1

Pointers for Building

The boxed inset shows a type of joint that the beginning cabinet-maker would do well to master. The gain, or stopped, dado provides the rigidity and strength of the straight dado but, unlike the latter, does not make its presence known by a visible notch in the vertical member. A professional also would probably dado the other shelves into the uprights. But if these seem difficult, well-fitted butt joints will serve as well. In either case, mortise two cross braces into the back edges of the ends at the points indicated and screw them into place.

Lay out one side of the lid rack on ¼″ plywood, tack it to another piece of the same stock, and saw both sides simultaneously. The rack can be screwed or nailed in place, but gluing it would make a firmer construction.

OVER-THE-RANGE CABINET 2

Uses

Salt, pepper, tea, cocoa, sugar, flour, and other supplies used frequently at the range can be kept on the lower of the two open shelves; such staples as rice, corn meal, and breakfast cereal that require cooking can go on the upper shelf. Kept narrow, these open shelves do not extend far enough to interfere with range operations. Asbestos installed under them guards against fire.

The wall cabinet itself, set 24″ above the range, has double-fold doors. These are hinged to fold back flat, lessening the chances of head bumping. Large meat platters slide into the lower shelf. On the shelf above, a vertical file stores pot lids and vegetable dishes. There also is space for additional staples needed at the range. The top shelf can be used for reserve supplies.

Materials

1″ x 12″ (nom.) stock (28 linear feet) to make—

  2 pc. 42½″ long — ends.
  4 pc. 38½″ long — shelves and top.
  1 pc. 5″ x 38½″ — shelf.
  1 pc. 4″ x 38½″ — shelf.
  4 pc. 9⅛″ x 28″ — doors.

1″ x 2″ (nom.) stock (6 linear feet) to make--

  2 pc. 28″ long — facing strips.

¼″ plywood (4′ x 5′ panel) to make—

  1 pc. 39½″ x 42″ — back.
  1 pc. 9″ x 23¼″ — backing for dividers.
  10 pc. 7⅝″ x 9″ — dividers.

⅛″ asbestos.

8 pr. hinges.

Pointers for Building

Since the rabbetted plywood back provides rigidity, the shelves can be installed with butt joints if desired. The adjustable shelf of course should be cut to fit easily between the ends in either case. Dowel plugs support it. You could also use short pieces of adjustable shelf standards here. The easy curves on the end pieces can be cut with a compass saw. In installing the doors, mount the middle hinges with the pins toward the inside of the cabinet, the end ones out in the usual way.

The front edge of the shelf on which the dividers rest is cut out as in plan A-A. The end dividers are nailed permanently to the shelf and the divider backing piece. The loose dividers are set in any desired position by means of three headless nails that press into holes punched in the shelf and backing strip. You can also set the dividers in grooves or between wood strips, as shown elsewhere.

The two open shelves below the doors can be simply nailed or screwed between the end pieces of the cabinet.

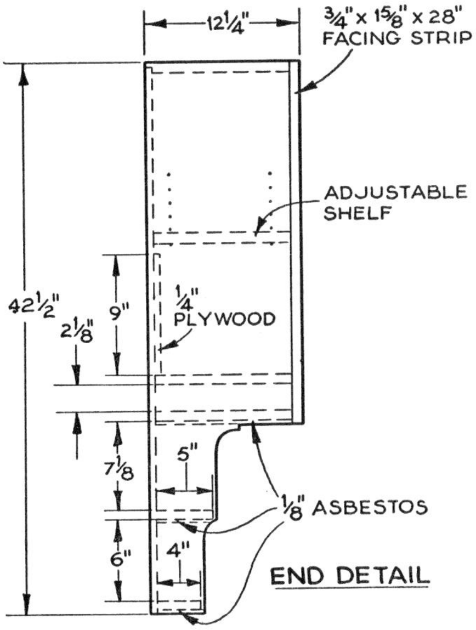
12¼"
¾" x 1⅝" x 28" FACING STRIP
ADJUSTABLE SHELF
42½"
9"
2⅛"
¼" PLYWOOD
7⅛
5"
⅛" ASBESTOS
6"
4"

END DETAIL

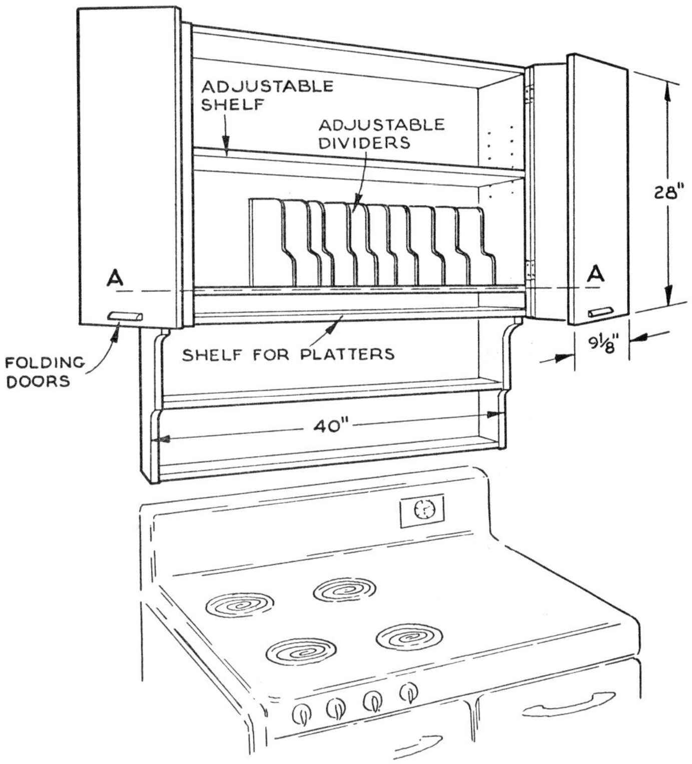
ADJUSTABLE SHELF
ADJUSTABLE DIVIDERS
28"
A
A
9⅛"
FOLDING DOORS
SHELF FOR PLATTERS
40"

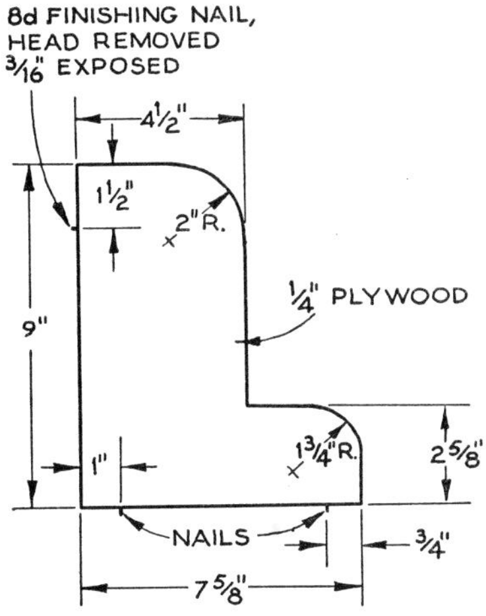
8d FINISHING NAIL, HEAD REMOVED 3/16" EXPOSED
4½"
1½"
2" R.
9"
¼" PLYWOOD
1¾" R.
2⅝"
1"
NAILS
¾"
7⅝"

SHELF DIVIDER

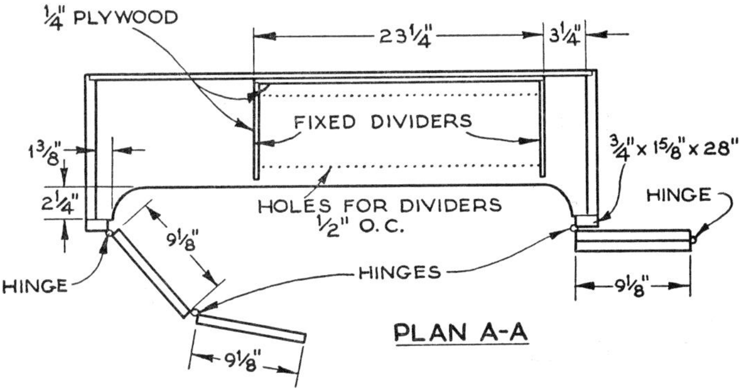
¼" PLYWOOD
23¼"
3¼"
FIXED DIVIDERS
1⅜"
¾" x 1⅝" x 28"
2¼"
HOLES FOR DIVIDERS ½" O.C.
HINGE
9⅛"
HINGE
HINGES
9⅛"
9⅛"

PLAN A-A

OVER-THE-RANGE CABINET 2

SLIDING DOOR CABINET

Uses

Because swinging doors on wall cabinets frequently present a head-bumping hazard, cabinets with sliding doors are preferred by many home owners. In some cases, too, sliding doors offer a solution to a space problem where conventional doors would not open fully. The cabinet shown could be used for general utility anywhere in the kitchen. If desired, sliding doors could be adapted to many other cabinets in this book. This one is presented only as an example of what it is possible to do. The same principles can be used on base cabinets too where that may be desirable.

Materials

1″ x 12″ (nom.) stock (16 linear feet) to make—

    2 pc. 36″ long — top and bottom.

    2 pc. 30″ long — ends.

    2 pc. 10″ x 35″ — shelves.

¼″ plywood or hardboard (4′ x 4′ panel) to make—

    2 pc. 18″ x 29″ — doors.

    1 pc. 30″ x 36″ — back (if desired).

11′ ¾″ x ⅞″ cove.

1 pc. ¼″ x ½″ x 28″ pine — door strip.

2 door pulls.

Pointers for Building

The cabinet itself can be built by any conventional construction method. Rabbet or butt joints can be used at the corners, with cleats, dadoes, metal standards or movable pegs supporting the shelves. Corner irons on inside corners will strengthen the structure.

    The door tracks are the big job. If power equipment is available, cut a ¼″ x 5/16″ rabbet on the front edge of the bottom, and ¼″ behind this cut a ¼″ x 5/16″ groove. Cove mold or a ¼″ x ⅞″

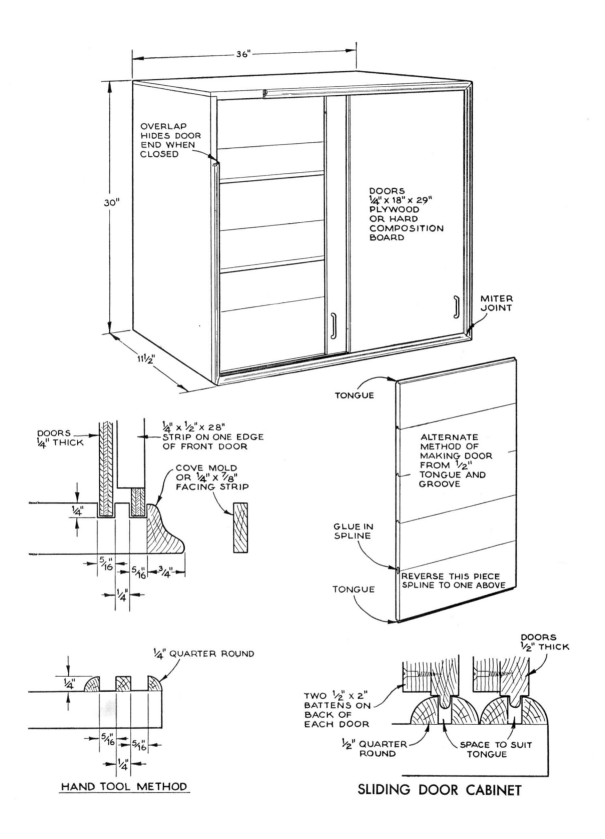

36"

30"

11½"

OVERLAP HIDES DOOR END WHEN CLOSED

DOORS ¼" x 18" x 29" PLYWOOD OR HARD COMPOSITION BOARD

MITER JOINT

DOORS ¼" THICK

¼" x ½" x 28" STRIP ON ONE EDGE OF FRONT DOOR

COVE MOLD OR ¼" x ⅞" FACING STRIP

¼"

5/16"   5/16"   ¾"

¼"

TONGUE

ALTERNATE METHOD OF MAKING DOOR FROM ½" TONGUE AND GROOVE

GLUE IN SPLINE

REVERSE THIS PIECE SPLINE TO ONE ABOVE

TONGUE

¼" QUARTER ROUND

¼"

5/16"   5/16"

¼"

HAND TOOL METHOD

DOORS ½" THICK

TWO ½" x 2" BATTENS ON BACK OF EACH DOOR

½" QUARTER ROUND

SPACE TO SUIT TONGUE

SLIDING DOOR CABINET

pine facing strip nailed and glued to the edge closes up the rabbet as a track for the front door. Some may choose to dispense with the cove or face strips and cut two grooves as the door tracks. On the under side of the cabinet top, cut corresponding tracks—but make these $\frac{1}{16}''$ deeper. Thus, when the doors at rest are just high enough to rise $\frac{1}{32}''$ into the upper tracks, it will be possible to lift up and pull them out of the cabinet to clean dust or food particles from the tracks. Cut enough off the 29" indicated length of the doors to make this possible.

The hand-tool method of making the tracks is equally satisfactory. In this case, cut the doors first, making them $\frac{1}{16}''$ shorter than the inside vertical dimension of the cabinet. Then use the doors as a guide in positioning the track strips, putting a thin piece of cardboard between door and strip to assure good clearance for sliding. Using a sanding block, reduce the height of the lower track members sufficiently to allow the doors to be pressed into place—or pulled out for cleaning of the grooves. The chance of dirt collecting in the grooves is a disadvantage of sliding doors.

Make the sliding doors $1\frac{1}{2}''$ wider than half the inside width of the cabinet. This allows adequate overlap when they are closed, and provides space for mounting the pull on the inside door. For smooth operation, sand the door edges with progressively finer paper. Finish with two coats of shellac, each well rubbed with the finest steel wool. Then rub a light coating of candle wax on them. Smooth and wax the tracks in the same way.

Making the doors from tongue-and-groove lumber results in a heavier construction, and the method is best suited to large cabinets. But some people may pick it for the sake of appearance. Vertical battens, screwed in place, join the door parts together. Tracks might be made of $\frac{1}{4}''$ quarter-round instead of $\frac{1}{2}''$.

Many builders may prefer to use $\frac{1}{8}''$ hardboard for the doors instead of the $\frac{1}{4}''$ shown. In a cabinet this size, the $\frac{1}{8}''$ material will have sufficient rigidity for easy use. The smooth surface of hardboard makes it ideal for sliding-door use.

Rather than build his own sliding doors from scratch, the builder may find it an advantage to shop around and see if he can make use of one of the commercial sliding-door assemblies, especially the hardware.

ADJUSTABLE SHELF CABINET

Uses

Shelves that adjust up and down permit a housewife to make more efficient use of available cabinet space. If items of equal height are grouped, dead space above can be eliminated and devoted to an upper or lower shelf. In the cabinet shown, you could have two or even three movable shelves supported on pegs, instead of only one. Kitchen planners would be smart to settle on adjustable shelves for every cabinet in the room. In this case, the shelf dividers also are adjustable.

The cabinet's place in the kitchen would depend on what is to be stored in it, but the dividers make it a good candidate for the lids and flat pans required at the range or mix center. Without the dividers and open shelf below, and with shelf pegs or metal standards running the full height, the cabinet could be used as the design for all the general-purpose units in the kitchen.

Materials

1″ x 12″ (nom.) stock (22 linear feet) to make—

    2 pc. 36″ long — sides.

    3 pc. 22½″ long — shelves and bottom.

    2 pc. 10½″ x 35¼″ — doors.

    1 pc. 12¼″ x 22½″ — top (nail or glue ¾″ x ¾″ strip to rear edge).

    1 pc. 5½″ x 22½″ — open shelf.

    2 pc. 5½″ x 8¾″ — shelf ends.

2 pc. 1″ x 2″ (nom.) stock 36″ long — face strips.

¼″ plywood (4′ x 4′ panel) to make—

    1 pc. 24″ x 36″ — back.

    7 pc. 11″ x 16″ — dividers.

2 pc. 2″ x 4″ stock 5″ long — shelf supports.

¼″ dowel 5″ long.

2 pr. hinges.   2 door pulls.   2 cabinet catches.

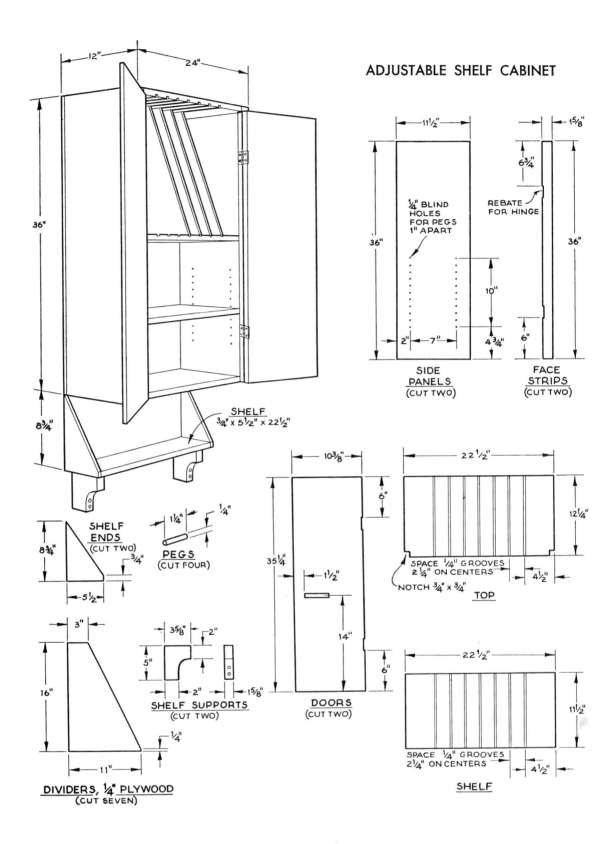

ADJUSTABLE SHELF CABINET

SIDE PANELS (CUT TWO)

¼" BLIND HOLES FOR PEGS 1" APART

FACE STRIPS (CUT TWO)

REBATE FOR HINGE

SHELF ¾" x 5½" x 22½"

SHELF ENDS (CUT TWO)

PEGS (CUT FOUR)

SHELF SUPPORTS (CUT TWO)

DOORS (CUT TWO)

SPACE ¼" GROOVES 2¼" ON CENTERS

NOTCH ¾" x ¾"

TOP

DIVIDERS, ¼" PLYWOOD (CUT SEVEN)

SPACE ¼" GROOVES 2¼" ON CENTERS

SHELF

Pointers for Building

The top, notched 3/4" x 3/4" at the front corners for the face strips, is butted between the sides, extending 3/4" in front of them. The shelves can be cut to identical 22½" lengths and the fixed one butted between the sides or supported on cleats. The fixed shelf could also be cut 23" long and dadoed in place. Grooves for the dividers under the cabinet top and on the upper surface of the fixed shelf must match exactly as to spacing. Locate the top edge of the fixed shelf 16½" from the upper end of the side pieces. Locate the holes for the adjustable shelf pegs with a sharp pencil and center-punch them for exact drilling. Drill the holes ½" deep. Screwed in place, or simply nailed, the ¼" plywood back gives rigidity to the entire cabinet. But here, as in many other cabinets in the book, you may find it possible to omit a back to conserve material and cut costs, letting the kitchen wall serve as the back.

The open shelf below the main cabinet is built as a separate unit. After cutting the parts, nail them together. Four screws about 3" long will attach the shelf to the wall. If you wish, this shelf can be used elsewhere in the kitchen.

COMBINATION WALL CABINET

Uses

This wide wall cabinet combines storage facilities sometimes found in two separate units. Its adjustable vertical dividers keep pie and cake pans and pot lids handy and tidy. Its lower shelves, adjustable for height, serve as a cupboard for packaged baking and cooking supplies and a variety of staples. Set between the sink and refrigerator, the wall cabinet and a companion base cabinet form an efficient baking and mixing center.

For a picture of how the cabinet would appear in such an assembly, see page 99 in the chapter on base cabinets.

Materials

1″ x 12″ (nom.) stock (36 linear feet) to make—

    2 pc. 36″ long — sides.

    1 pc. 38½″ long (with ¾″ x ¾″ strip glued to rear).

    4 pc. 38½″ long — shelves.

    4 pc. 35¼″ long — doors.

    1 pc.   8¾″ long — support for dividers.

1″ x 2″ (nom.) stock (12 linear feet) to make—

    3 pc. 36″ long — hinging strips.

    2 pc. ¾″ x ⅞″ x 11″ — shelf cleats.

¼″ plywood (4′ x 4′ panel) to make—

    1 pc. 36″ x 40″ — cabinet back.

    5 pc. 8¼″ x 9¾″ — shelf dividers.

10 dowels ¼″ x 1¼″ — shelf pegs.

3 pr. 1½″ x 1½″ cabinet hinges.

Pointers for Building

To save work, this cabinet uses the shelving full width for the sides, the bottom and the shelves. The width of the top board can be increased by 3/4″ to bring its front edge out flush with the upright hinging strips by tacking or gluing a fill strip on the rear edge.

When the sides are in place, the notches form a recess for the top ends of the far left and far right hinging strips. Setting the strips back this way provides an overhang for the doors. Front edges of the shelves below serve as door stops.

Cleats support the one fixed shelf. In boring the peg holes for the other shelves, be careful about horizontal alignment of each pair or the shelves will not rest level.

If available, a dado plane will make quick work of the grooves in which the dividers rest in the fixed shelf and the upright piece set into the rear edge. For an easier job, and as satisfactory one, use the alternative method of forming grooves by tacking down parallel strips.

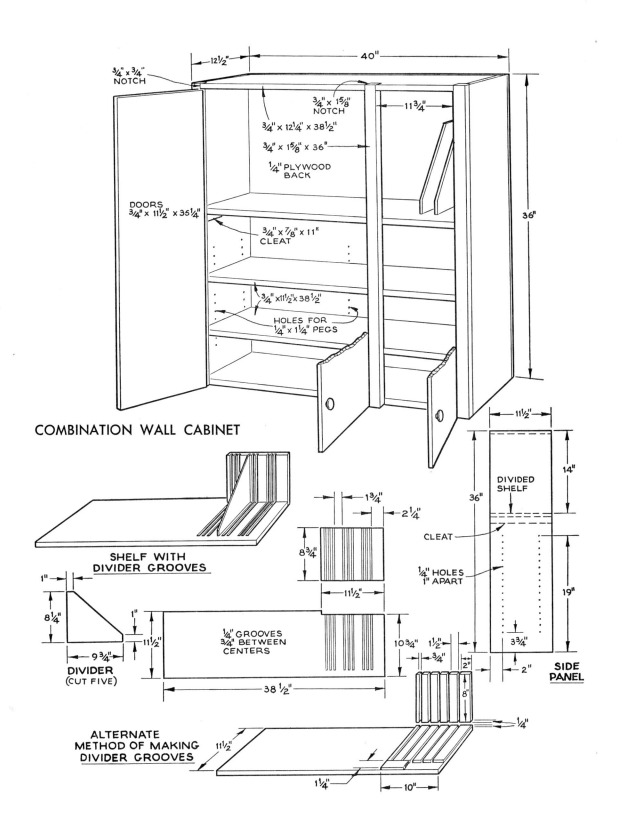

COMBINATION WALL CABINET

3/4" x 3/4" NOTCH

12 1/2"

40"

3/4" x 1 5/8" NOTCH

11 3/4"

3/4" x 12 1/4" x 38 1/2"

3/4" x 1 5/8" x 36"

1/4" PLYWOOD BACK

36"

DOORS 3/4" x 11 1/2" x 35 1/4"

3/4" x 7/8" x 11" CLEAT

3/4" x 11 1/2" x 38 1/2"

HOLES FOR 1/4" x 1 1/4" PEGS

SHELF WITH DIVIDER GROOVES

1"

8 1/4"

1"

11 1/2"

9 3/4"

DIVIDER (CUT FIVE)

1/4" GROOVES 3/4" BETWEEN CENTERS

38 1/2"

1 3/4"

2 1/4"

8 3/4"

11 1/2"

10 3/4"

1 1/2"

3/4"

2"

8"

1/4"

ALTERNATE METHOD OF MAKING DIVIDER GROOVES

11 1/2"

1 1/4"

10"

11 1/2"

36"

14"

DIVIDED SHELF

CLEAT

1/4" HOLES 1" APART

19"

3 3/4"

2"

SIDE PANEL

MIX CENTER WALL CABINET

Uses

Supplies for making cookies, cakes, pies, and other baked goods sometimes present a storage problem. But not so if your kitchen has this
cabinet. Its bins not only store good amounts of flour, sugar, meal,
etc., but the housewife can get what she wants without fuss and
bother. The large storage bin holds about 40 pounds of flour, and a
metal shutter feeds it into a small bin below. This and other small
bins, all removable for cleaning, take the place of the conventional
row of canisters.

Shelves provide space for several mixing bowls, measuring spoons
and cups, casseroles, and custard cups. Pie, cake, muffin, and bread
pans can be filed between the dividers on the top shelf. Another
vertical file (not adjustable in height) can be placed above the flour
bin for such articles as a pudding pan, tube cake pan, and salad mold.

Materials

1″ x 12″ (nom.) stock (40 linear feet) to make—

    2 pc. 52″ long — cabinet ends.

    2 pc. 48″ long — top and bottom.

    1 pc. 35½″ long — partition.

    3 pc. 30¾″ long — adjustable shelves.

    1 pc. 14″ long — fixed shelf.

    1 pc. 5¾″ x 45½″ — bin framing (back).

    4 pc. 6¾″ x 8″ — bin partitions.

    1 pc. 5½″ x 45½″ — bin framing (bottom).

1″ x 2″ (nom.) stock (12 linear feet) to make—

    1 pc. 48″ long — top facing strip.

    3 pc. 36″ long — facing strips.

    1 pc. 45½″ long — bin framing.

1 strip ½″ x ¾″ x 45½″ — bin molding.

¾″ plywood (4′ x 4′ panel) to make—

    2 pc. 14¾″ x 35¼″ — doors.

    1 pc. 14″ x 20½″ — flour bin facing.

    1 pc. 14″ x 14¾″ — upper door.

¼″ plywood (4′ x 6′ panel) to make—

    1 pc. 44¾″ x 47¼″ — cabinet back.

   10 pc. 7⅝″ x 9″ — shelf dividers.

    1 pc. 9″ x 30½″ — divider backing.

About 18 square feet 24- or 26-gauge galvanized iron — small bins.

About 7 square feet 16-oz. copper — flour bin.

1 pc. 1/16″ strap iron 1″ x 25″ (approx.) — flour bin arm.

4 pr. hinges.

8 door or drawer pulls.

Pointers for Building

The ends of the cabinet may be extended down to the work counter or may be stopped flush with the lower edge of the bins. This decision will mostly depend on what the cabinet adjoins. In the original layout, which you can see in the picture of the step-saving U-kitchen shown in the first chapter, a merry-go-round corner cupboard is located on the left, and the full-length side of the wall cabinet is common to the corner unit.

All shelves are adjustable except the 14″ one above the flour bin. After cutting the ends and vertical partition, drill holes for the shelf pegs. Rabbet the ¼″ plywood back to the rear edges of the top and ends to help give rigidity to the cabinet. Corner irons or blocks also are desirable. The shelf dividers are similar to those used in the range wall cabinet (No. 2) previously described. Dividers may be placed above the flour bin or the space may be left clear, depending on the needs of your particular kitchen.

To make the flour bin, first lay out a full-size pattern on wrapping paper or cardboard, taking your dimensions from Section C-C and the front elevation. You will need a sheet of metal approximately 20″ x 50″, the greater dimension being used for bending the metal at three of the vertical corners and making the seam at the fourth.

The funnel bottom can be shaped in one of two ways: either by extending the bin sides down, cutting the extensions to the indicated triangles, and soldering the corners; or by making the funnel separately and attaching it to the body of the bin. You will note that the mouth of the funnel fits into a flared chute that carries flour through the wood bottom of the compartment and into the smaller bin below. The collar into which the shutter slides consists of two rectangular pieces of metal (with openings to match the funnel mouth), joined at the edges so as to allow enough clearance for the shutter to slide in and out between them at the fourth edge. The shutter passes through a thin slot cut in the bin door. Two pieces of strap iron, joined with a pin to give an elbow action, limit the opening of the bin when it is to be filled. The bin itself is attached to the wood facing, which is hinged at the bottom.

The framing for the small bins is simple but requires careful work to assure a smooth bin fit and operation. First attach the strengthening (nom.) 1″ x 2″ member that runs under the rear corner of the main cabinet. Then cut the four wood partitions. Detail B shows the curving rabbets against which the bin lips fit when the bins are closed. Detail A is a section of the 1/2″ x 3/4″ molding that faces the front top edge. The 1/16″ saw kerf in this is designed to receive one end of the metal that lines the compartment. After the framing is in place, one sheet of metal can be run from this slot across the top (curving as indicated), down the back, and out the floor to the metal edging that finishes off the front of the compartment. Other pieces of sheet metal can be placed over the wood partitions at the ends of each compartment.

As the half pattern shows, each bin can be shaped from two pieces of metal. A slightly flaring V formed by the 1/4″ edges of the bottom and back supports the bin on the metal shelf edging and allows the necessary pivoting action. A metal stop, aligned with a projecting dowel pin, keeps each bin from falling out.

Instead of using the galvanized iron and sheet copper specified in the materials list for the bins, the builder might, with a little ingenuity, substitute sheet aluminum in whole or in part. This is now available as a "do-it-yourself" item in most hardware stores.

Aluminum could be substituted with ease as the lining of the small-

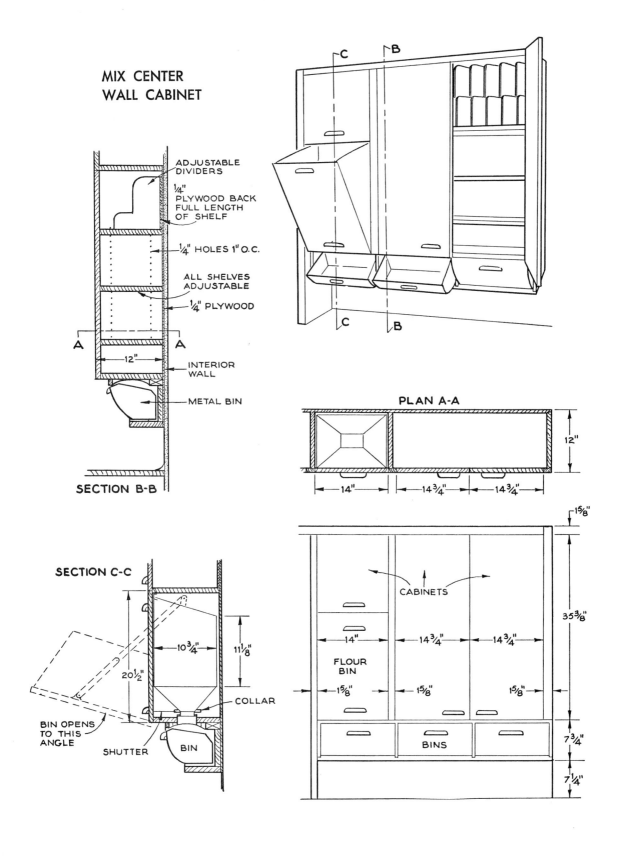

MIX CENTER
WALL CABINET

ADJUSTABLE
DIVIDERS

¼"
PLYWOOD BACK
FULL LENGTH
OF SHELF

¼" HOLES 1" O.C.

ALL SHELVES
ADJUSTABLE

¼" PLYWOOD

A   A

12"

INTERIOR
WALL

METAL BIN

SECTION B-B

SECTION C-C

10¾"   11⅛"

20½"

COLLAR

BIN OPENS
TO THIS
ANGLE

SHUTTER   BIN

PLAN A-A

12"

14"   14¾"   14¾"

1⅝"

CABINETS

14"   14¾"   14¾"

FLOUR
BIN

1⅝"   1⅝"   1⅝"

35⅜"

BINS

7¾"

7¼"

bin compartments. Just cut it, shape it, and tack it in place as you would the specified metal.

If aluminum were used for the bins, its edges might be crimped together instead of soldered. In the case of the small bins, the builder could shape the ends from wood—and then line them inside with metal. Aluminum could be curved around the front and tacked in place on the bottom and back. The wood ends would also ease the bin-construction job if other metals were used.

A wood frame might be used to provide rigidity if aluminum were used for the larger expanses of the flour bin.

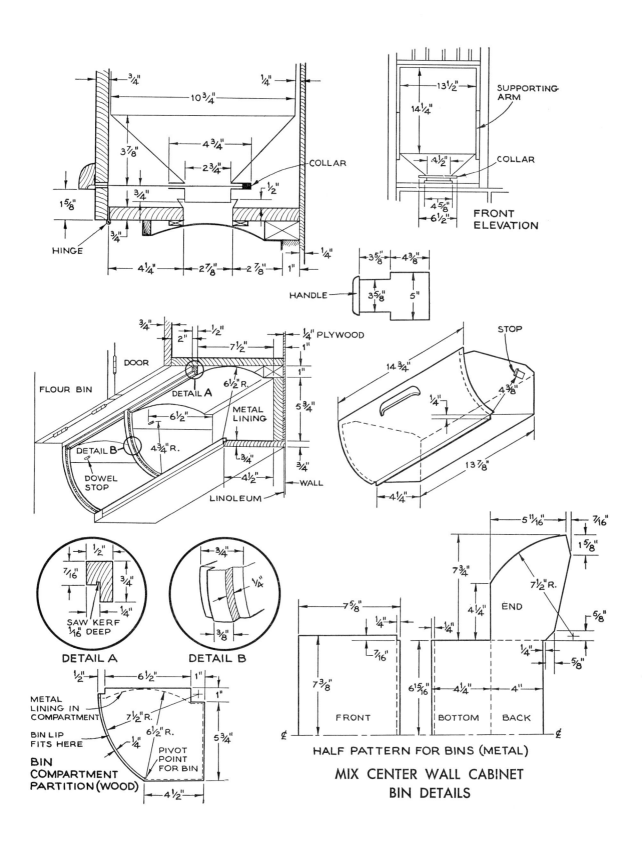

FRONT
ELEVATION

COLLAR

SUPPORTING
ARM

HINGE

HANDLE

DOOR

FLOUR BIN

DETAIL A

METAL
LINING

DETAIL B

DOWEL
STOP

LINOLEUM

WALL

¼" PLYWOOD

STOP

SAW KERF
1/16" DEEP

DETAIL A

DETAIL B

METAL
LINING IN
COMPARTMENT

BIN LIP
FITS HERE

PIVOT
POINT
FOR BIN

BIN
COMPARTMENT
PARTITION (WOOD)

FRONT

BOTTOM

BACK

END

HALF PATTERN FOR BINS (METAL)

MIX CENTER WALL CABINET
BIN DETAILS

OVER-THE-SINK CABINET

Uses

Where a sink faces a blank wall, this quickly built cabinet will provide storage space for bar soap, powdered soap, and other cleaning supplies and equipment used at the sink. The open shelf in the center, if not needed for utilitarian purposes, might be reserved for a couple of small potted plants or knicknacks. Hooks can be placed under the bottom shelf to hang brushes and utensils. Alternatively, a flourescent lamp could be mounted there to put more light on the dishwashing chore. This cabinet was adapted from a design of the Douglas Fir Plywood Association.

In addition to use at the sink, the cabinet might go at other spots in the kitchen. Placed on an otherwise blank wall, it could be devoted exclusively to potted plants and knickknacks. Or it could be used for storage of cookbooks, housekeeping records, and perhaps a box containing recipes on file cards.

Materials

1 panel ⅜″ plywood, 4′ x 4′.
2 pr. hinges.
2 cabinet catches.

Pointers for Building

Lay out the parts as shown and you will wind up with little waste. All parts go together with butt joints. If clamps are available, assemble the parts with glue and nails. If not, flathead wood screws will do a good job alone. Counterbore and fill the screw heads on visible faces of the cabinet. A couple of door knobs can be fashioned from the scrap material as shown.

The layout of parts on the opposite page, incidentally, shows a planning step you should always take for other cabinets throughout the book, before starting work, in order to reduce waste.

OVER-THE-SINK CABINET

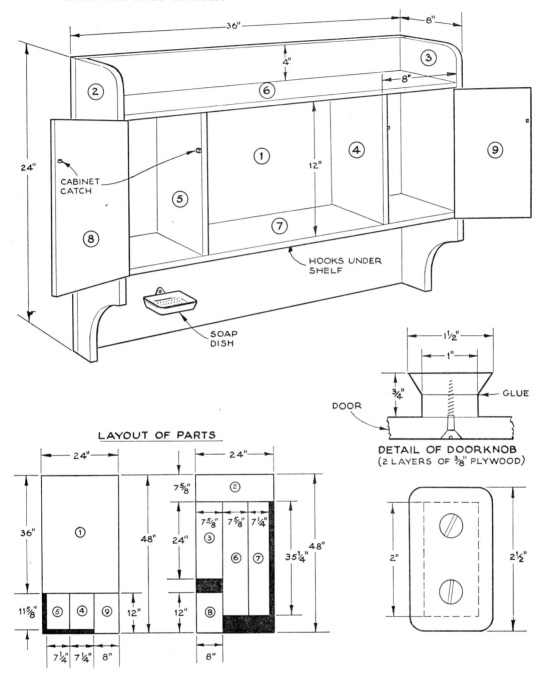

CABINET CATCH

36"

8"

8"

4"

24"

12"

HOOKS UNDER SHELF

SOAP DISH

DETAIL OF DOORKNOB
(2 LAYERS OF ⅜" PLYWOOD)

DOOR

GLUE

1½"

1"

¾"

2"

2½"

LAYOUT OF PARTS

24"

24"

36"

48"

48"

24"

11⅝"

12"

12"

35¼"

7⅝"

7⅝" 7⅝" 7¼"

7¼" 7¼" 8"

8"

WALL VEGETABLE BIN

Uses

Set into the wall back of the sink area, this bin stores vegetables and
fruits within reach of the sink where they will be cleaned for cooking.
A row of the bins, located under a wide casement window, is a feature of a functional U-shaped kitchen designed by Lenore Sater
Thye of the U.S. Bureau of Human Nutrition and Home Economics.
Behind the bin compartments, a sheet of rigid insulation is substituted for the sheathing normally placed under house siding. This
keeps winter temperatures from nipping the stored vegetables—and
prevents house heat from escaping. Each bin lifts out so both it and
the wall compartment can be easily cleaned. A stool (window base)
10″ wide above the bins can be used for house plants. Although the
drawings show the bin located under a window, a row of them could
also be placed below a line of wall cabinets at the back edge of a wide
working counter, either set into the wall or built against it.

Materials

FOR ONE BIN:

⅝″ plywood (2′ x 4′ panel) to make—

    1 pc. 10¼″ x 17¾″ — front.

    3 pc. 1½″ x 17⅜″ — back.

    1 pc. 7¼″ x 17⅜″ — bottom ⎫
                                  ⎬ for all wood construction.
    2 pc. 6⅝″ x 9⅝″ — ends   ⎭

24-gauge galvanized iron to make—

    1 pc. 9¾″ x 40″ — bin sides and bottom.

    1 pc. 18″ x 28″   ⎫
                      ⎬ compartment lining.
    2 pc. 8⅛″ x 10″ ⎭

(Note: Instead of using galvanized iron for the bin and compartment lining, the builder could substitute sheet aluminum, available
at most hardware stores. For this, however, it probably would be
necessary to build a wood framework for the bin.)

FRAMING FOR COMPARTMENT:

1 pc. 2″ x 4″ (nom.), length optional — window plate.

1 pc. 1″ x 10″ (nom.) length optional — window stool.

1 pc. ¾″ x 8⅛″ stock, length optional — compartment base.

1 sheet 1″ insulation board.

2 pc. 2″ x 4″ (nom.) stock, 10″ long — studs in each compartment.

2 pc. 2″ x 2″ (nom.), 11½″ long — front compartment uprights.

2 pc. ¾″ x 1⅞″ x 11½″ — vertical facing strips.

1 pc. ¾″ x 1¼″, length optional — window apron.

Pointers for Building

As shown, the framing for this bin ties in with the framing for the window and would be easiest if done by the contractor as part of the original house construction. In any case, you will have to adapt the framing to suit your circumstances, especially the length of the space available. In the model U-kitchen designed by Lenore Sater Thye, four bins—two 17¾″ wide and two 10½″ wide—and a 16″-wide soap compartment with sliding doors are installed under the window. The soap compartment was centered behind the sink with two bins on either side.

If you prescribe the bins in a house not yet built, you can have the builder put the insulation in place before the siding. A strip 12″ wide will be sufficient. If you install the insulation as part of a remodeling job, you probably will have to remove some of the siding temporarily.

The plate, or double 2 x 4's, customarily located under a window is dropped below the compartment base in this case, and a single 2 x 4 goes under the sill. A stool wider than usual is required since this serves as the top of the compartment.

Ten-inch lengths of 2 x 4 can be spaced vertically as desired against the insulation to frame and separate the compartments. Butt them between the compartment base, which rests on the plate, and the horizontal 2 x 4 that supports the window. Lengths of 2 x 2 stock go in front of the 2 x 4's. Vertical facing strips 1⅞″ wide are nailed to the 2 x 2's. Butt them against the 1¼″-wide apron that goes under the stool.

WALL
VEGETABLE BIN

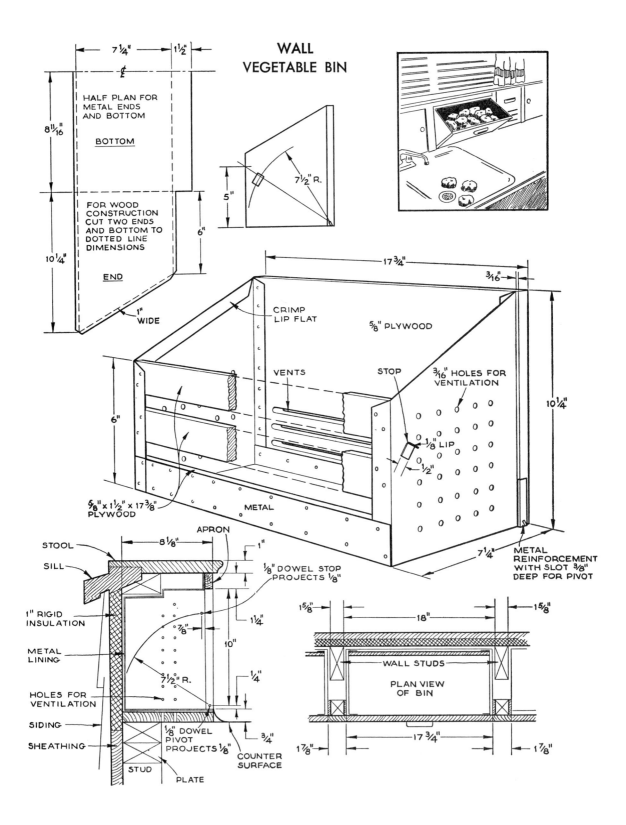

7 1/4"   1 1/2"

¢

HALF PLAN FOR
METAL ENDS
AND BOTTOM

BOTTOM

8 11/16"

FOR WOOD
CONSTRUCTION
CUT TWO ENDS
AND BOTTOM TO
DOTTED LINE
DIMENSIONS

10 1/4"

6"

END

1" WIDE

7 1/2" R.

5"

17 3/4"   3/16"

CRIMP
LIP FLAT

5/8" PLYWOOD

VENTS   STOP   3/16" HOLES FOR
VENTILATION

6"

10 1/4"

1/8" LIP

1/2"

5/8" x 1 1/2" x 17 3/8"
PLYWOOD

METAL

7 1/4"

METAL
REINFORCEMENT
WITH SLOT 3/8"
DEEP FOR PIVOT

STOOL

SILL

APRON

8 1/8"

1"

1/8" DOWEL STOP
PROJECTS 1/8"

1 1/4"

1" RIGID
INSULATION

7/8"

10"

METAL
LINING

7 1/2" R.

1/4"

HOLES FOR
VENTILATION

SIDING

SHEATHING

STUD

PLATE

1/8" DOWEL
PIVOT
PROJECTS 1/8"

3/4"

COUNTER
SURFACE

15/8"   18"   15/8"

WALL STUDS

PLAN VIEW
OF BIN

1 7/8"   17 3/4"   1 7/8"

The metal lining for the compartment can best be made as a unit and then slipped in before the facing strips are in place. Bottom, back, and top can be bent from a single sheet of metal and the ends then soldered on. Sheet metal thinner than the gauge specified might be used here. Punch vent holes in the ends and bottom, drilling matching holes through the wood base of the compartment. If this metal work stumps you, take it to a tinsmith.

The bin itself offers no difficulties. All-wood construction is easiest, but in such a unit wood absorbs odors. Metal is a better long-range bet for sanitary reasons. Here again, if cutting and bending the metal is beyond your capabilities and equipment, a tinsmith will make quick work of the job. Punch holes in the edges for tacking the metal to the wood front and back. A keyhole saw, started by drilling a $\frac{1}{2}$" hole, can be used to cut the vents in the face of the bin. Slant the vents upward toward the inside about 45 degrees.

Careful location of the pivot and pivoting slot are essential to smooth operation of the bin. Drill $\frac{1}{8}$" holes in the edges of the $1\frac{7}{8}$" facing strips for the $\frac{1}{8}$" dowels that serve as pivots. Center the holes in the edge $\frac{1}{4}$" above the compartment base. Cut slots in the lower corners of the bin face and reinforce them with metal. You then can set the bin down over the pivots and swing it back into the compartment. Bend the metal stops on the bin temporarily so they will pass the $\frac{1}{8}$" dowel stops that are set into the framing 2 x 2's, on a $7\frac{1}{2}$" radius.

SOAP COMPARTMENT

Uses

Designed as a companion piece to the fruit and vegetable bin just described, this soap compartment goes directly behind the sink to provide handy storage space for the washing materials used there. Like the bin, it utilizes the space within the wall. Sliding doors give access to the materials stored in it.

Materials

1 pc. 2″ x 4″ (nom.), length optional — window plate.

1 pc. 1″ x 10″ (nom.) , length optional — window stool.

1 pc. 1″ stock, 8⅛″ wide, length optional — compartment base.

1 sheet 1″ insulation board.

2 pc. 2″ x 4″ (nom.), 10″ long — studs in each compartment.

2 pc. 2″ x 2″ (nom.), 11½″ long — front compartment uprights.

2 pc. ¾″ x 1⅞″ x 11½″ — vertical facing strips.

1 pc. ¾″ x 1¼″, length optional — window apron.

1 pc. ¾″ x 1¼″ x 15½″ — inside top door guide.

2 pc. ⅝″ x 8½″ x 10¼″ hardwood — doors.

2 pc. ⅛″ metal rod 16″ long — door tracks.

24-gauge galvanized iron to make—

    1 pc. 15½″ x 28″ ⎫
    2 pc. 8⅛″ x 10″ ⎭ compartment lining.

NOTE: End framing members and some other parts in this cabinet are also common to the wall vegetable bin.

Pointers for Building

Build this compartment by the same procedure outlined for the wall vegetable bin. In installing the metal lining, note that the 2 x 2's at the front corners are shimmed out to give a 1⅞″ dimension. A second strip, 15½″ long, behind the apron strip is grooved to mate the tongue cut in the upper edge of the rear door. Butt this strip between the 2 x 2's. In cutting the doors, keep the grain horizontal. The ⅛″ metal rods, cut just a trifle longer than the width of the compartment, can be sprung into the holes bored in the bottom edges of the vertical facing strips (for the front door) and the 2 x 2's for the rear one. Rout grooves in the bottom board for the metal-rod door track as shown in the inset.

The doors are captive within the structure after final assembly. So make a trial assembly first to be sure they slide easily. Then put all the various parts into place.

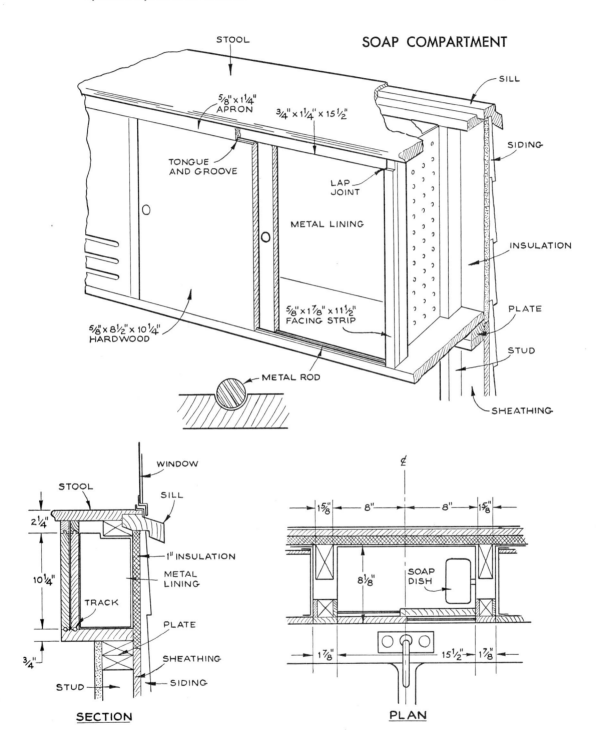

SOAP COMPARTMENT

STOOL

SILL

$\frac{5}{8}" \times 1\frac{1}{4}"$ APRON

$\frac{3}{4}" \times 1\frac{1}{4}" \times 15\frac{1}{2}"$

TONGUE AND GROOVE

LAP JOINT

METAL LINING

SIDING

INSULATION

$\frac{5}{8}" \times 1\frac{7}{8}" \times 11\frac{1}{2}"$ FACING STRIP

PLATE

STUD

$\frac{5}{8}" \times 8\frac{1}{2}" \times 10\frac{1}{4}"$ HARDWOOD

METAL ROD

SHEATHING

SECTION

WINDOW

STOOL

SILL

$2\frac{1}{4}"$

1" INSULATION

METAL LINING

$10\frac{1}{4}"$

TRACK

PLATE

$\frac{3}{4}"$

SHEATHING

STUD

SIDING

PLAN

$\mathcal{C}$

$1\frac{5}{8}"$ 8"   8" $1\frac{5}{8}"$

$8\frac{1}{8}"$

SOAP DISH

$1\frac{7}{8}"$ $15\frac{1}{2}"$ $1\frac{7}{8}"$

WALL CABINET IDEAS

Crisping Cabinet

As any housewife knows, crackers, cereals, and some cookies will absorb moisture and become soggy after the container is opened. These usually can be made crisp again by heating in the oven. But why not utilize some of the available heat in the kitchen to keep such foods crisp? Sources of heat that might be utilized include the range, the room-warming outlet or fixture, and the vent of a gas refrigerator.

Any of the wall cabinets for installation over range or refrigerator already described might be adapted for crisping uses. Simply storing cereals and crackers above the range may be sufficient. The crisping procedure would be more certain, however, if an opening is provided in the bottom of the cabinet so warm air can sweep up through the stored foods and out vents in the top or upper part of the cabinet front. In the case of gas appliances, you might install a metal duct to channel heat to the cabinet from the appliance heat-exhaust vent.

End Cabinet

When a line of wall cabinets comes to an end, for instance at a door or window, you have the chance of creating a cabinet that will solve special storage problems. Install a door on the side of the final cabinet, instead of on the front, and you have a compartment suitable for storage of trays, cooky tins, and similar flat equipment. The door can be omitted if you wish and the flat articles simply shoved between vertical partitions in the cabinet. You could vary the amount of this storage space to suit the amount of equipment to be stored, and still use the front part of the cabinet for shelves accessible through a standard door on the front. The shelves might be made just wide enough (from front to back) to take a row of canned foods. Or some persons might prefer to omit the door and install open shelves to vary the appearance of the cabinets.

You could also install two banks of vertical partitions in such an end cabinet, one bank above the other, and use the compartments for storage of pan lids, pie pans, and similar equipment of this size. Adapting the cabinet to this type of storage would be most appropriate if it is located near the range or baking center.

Tool-Hanging Cabinet

Even when a drawer is compartmented, kitchen tools such as can openers, measuring spoons, and potato mashers often wind up in a jumble from which it is difficult to extract the needed item. A shallow wall cabinet with a large backboard where each tool has its own hanger—the way many home workshop enthusiasts store their tools— will keep each utensil free from the others and in plain sight for quick use. Items suitable for hanging on hooks, nails, or other supports in such a cabinet include egg beaters, large serving spoons, ladles, scissors, strainers, long-handled forks, graters, spatulas, pastry cutters, rolling pins, and cooking thermometers.

A board to accommodate the usual number of such tools found in the ordinary kitchen should have a surface area of not less than 576 square inches—a square board measuring 24″ by 24″ or a rectangular one that is longer than 24″ and less than that wide. The shape can be suited to the space available. A piece of Masonite peg board could be used as the backboard. A variety of hooks and hangers are available for insertion in the holes punched in this hardboard. An inside depth of 4″ (front to back) is enough for such a cabinet. Making it any deeper would just waste space. In some cases it might be possible to install the cabinet on a wall apart from a line of wall cabinets of conventional depth. But for greatest utility, it probably should go in the line of regular cabinets. If the kitchen-planning goal is an unbroken line of cabinets all of the same depth, you face a problem of how to do it. One way is to make the tool cabinet the front part of the end wall cabinet described elsewhere in this chapter. Here, the distance needed for storage of trays and large flat items parallel to the wall (with access from the side of the cabinet) would not be too much less than the size the tool-supporting backboard should be.

Above the range is a logical location for a tool cabinet, for it is here that many of these tools will be used most frequently. A shallow cabinet here, flanked by others of standard depth on either side, would look good and present less of a head-bumping hazard than a deeper one might.

Instead of building this cabinet, you could accomplish the same result by simply nailing a sheet of peg board to the wall. But then of course the tools would not be hidden from sight. Frame the sheet with a decorative molding. When peg board is applied to an existing wall, spacers should be placed behind the board to permit insertion of the hooks.

Waxed-Paper Slot

Practically all kitchens boast a boxed roll of waxed paper—and perhaps one of aluminum foil. Here's one way of keeping this wrapping material handy. Saw a narrow slot in the bottom of a wall cabinet above the area where the paper or foil is most frequently used. Cut the slot as long as the paper is wide. Screw an old hacksaw blade flat against the underside of the cabinet with its teeth projecting into the slot area but leaving space to pull the paper or foil through from above. Inside the cabinet, tack small strips of wood in a rectangle shape just large enough to keep the paper or foil box from moving around on the cabinet floor. Thread the paper down through the slot. When a piece is needed, pull it down and tear quickly against the saw teeth.

Swing-Shelf Cabinet

A useful wall cabinet can be built like the upper part of the swing-storage cabinet shown in the chapter on floor-to-ceiling cabinets. Vary the width and height as desired to suit the available space. One swing-shelf section might be preferred rather than the two shown. Or two might be used, with each hinged at the outer edge, in the manner of swing-apart doors. Above or near the range would be one useful location for such a cabinet.

4

Open Shelves

Some authorities believe open shelves are the most practical storage device for any kitchen. And even though fashion decrees closed cabinets, it is obvious that open shelves do have advantages. First, they keep most of the stored supplies and equipment in full view and quickly accessible. Second, the housewife doesn't waste time and energy opening and closing doors. And finally, they cost less than cabinets.

You probably will want some open shelves even though you use closed storage units through most of your kitchen. These are easily provided. In some cases, they can be just pieces of shelving supported by metal brackets. Open shelves can be provided too as an integral part of wall cabinets. In your planning, you may find spots where you will have space for a few narrow shelves, but not for a cabinet of full depth.

On the pages that immediately follow, you'll find several examples of how shelving can be applied. But these are only a start. The ingenious builder will find many more chances to use them.

WALL SHELVES

Uses

Placed on two walls, the open shelves would supply most of the storage needs of a kitchen. Located at the end of a line of cabinets, or mounted in duplicate by a window that breaks a line of cabinets, the end shelves would provide a place for cookbooks and decorative knickknacks, if nothing else. This drawing was adopted from a design of the makers of Malarkey plywoods. The recessed shelves are located under a line of wall cabinets. Frequently used dishes, a radio, and many other items can be placed there within easy reach without robbing the work counter of the space needed for normal kitchen operations. In the drawing, you will notice that there still is a counter 20″ wide. The reach arc of the average woman indicates that this width will help reduce the fatigue-causing reaching that may occur with counters of conventional width.

Materials

Open shelves — 1″ stock in 12″, 10″, 8″, 6″, and 4″ (nom.) widths.
Recessed shelves — ¾″ x 6″ plywood, length to suit; 3″ cove.
End shelves — 1″ x 12″ (nom.) stock (12 linear feet) to make—

   4 pc. 24″ long — shelves.

   1 pc. 24″ long — end.

1″ x 3″ (nom.) stock (8 linear feet) to make—

   4 pc. 24″ — back pieces.

1⅝″ x 24″ dowel post.

Pointers for Building

OPEN SHELVES.   Space these shelves so the top one will be no more than 72″ above the floor, or it will be useful only for dead storage. Good workmanship will determine whether such shelves give satisfaction from an appearance standpoint. Keep them neat by using

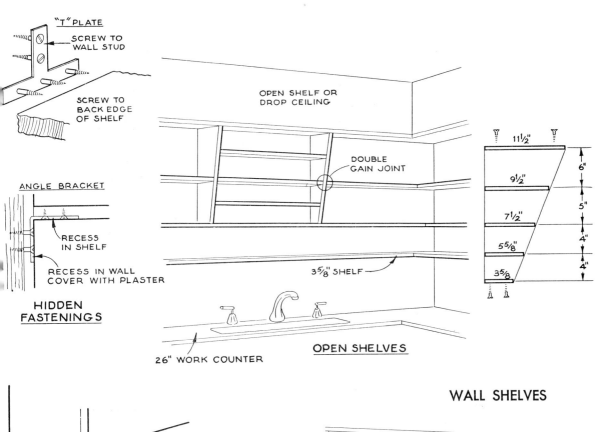

"T" PLATE
— SCREW TO WALL STUD
— SCREW TO BACK EDGE OF SHELF

HIDDEN FASTENINGS

ANGLE BRACKET
— RECESS IN SHELF
— RECESS IN WALL COVER WITH PLASTER

OPEN SHELF OR DROP CEILING

DOUBLE GAIN JOINT

$3\frac{5}{8}$" SHELF

26" WORK COUNTER

OPEN SHELVES

$11\frac{1}{2}$"
$9\frac{1}{2}$"
$7\frac{1}{2}$"
$5\frac{5}{8}$"
$3\frac{5}{8}$

6"
5"
4"
4"

WALL SHELVES

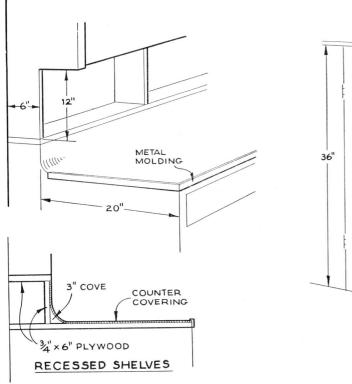

6"
12"

METAL MOLDING

20"

3" COVE
COUNTER COVERING

$\frac{3}{4}$" × 6" PLYWOOD

RECESSED SHELVES

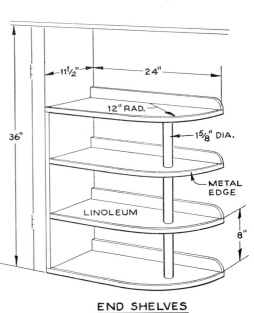

$11\frac{1}{2}$"
24"
12" RAD.
$1\frac{5}{8}$" DIA.
36"
METAL EDGE
LINOLEUM
8"

END SHELVES

stopped dado (gain) joints when possible. However, where the end of a vertical member meets the face of a shelf, butt joints secured by screws will be best. Assemble and glue up the three middle shelves of the five-shelf sink (or range) unit to the triangular side pieces. Mount the top ($11\frac{1}{2}''$) and bottom ($3\frac{5}{8}''$) shelves on the wall. Then place the three-shelf unit between. Snug gain joints, cut and fitted earlier, can be used to support the outside $7\frac{1}{2}''$ shelves on a line with the similar inside shelf. Conventional metal shelf brackets can be used to support the ends of the main shelves. But use only as many as absolutely needed, for they steal useful space from the shelves. The sketches suggest two ways you can hide fastenings. If a drop ceiling is used above the top shelf, it will help support the five-shelf sink or range unit.

RECESSED SHELVES.   As shown, these tie in as part of the original construction of wall cabinets above and the counter surface below. Whatever type wall cabinets you build, you can plan for the recessed shelves by extending the outer sides of the two end cabinets down far enough to serve as supports for the shelves. But vertical members 6″ x 12″ cut from $\frac{3}{4}''$ plywood also could be bracketed at intervals under the bottoms of a line of wall cabinets already in place. Attach the shelf to the verticals with screws driven from underneath. Nail the shelf to the $\frac{3}{4}''$ x 6″ strip that backs up the cove. Cement down the cove as part of the job of applying the counter covering. A set of shelves of this type might easily be installed in an existing modern kitchen. If desired, the shelf could be just a ledge, the vertical members up to the wall cabinets being omitted.

END SHELVES.   Cut gains in the $11\frac{1}{2}''$ x 24″ vertical end piece for the two middle shelves. Butt the top and bottom shelves against the ends of the vertical pieces, joining them with countersunk flathead screws. Screw the back strips to the top surfaces of the shelves (from underneath), mortising the ends of the bottom three into the vertical member. Bore blind holes in the top and bottom shelves for the ends of the $1\frac{5}{8}''$ post, with through holes in the middle two. Glue the post in place, also placing screws into the ends through the top and bottom shelves. Toenail the middle pair of shelves to the post (from underneath) after applying glue.

OPEN MIXING CENTER

Uses

This mix center would be very appropriate for the kitchen where open shelves are the rule. With space for bowls and pans, and perhaps a pull-out cutting board in a base cabinet below, it brings into one handy working area all the equipment and supplies for typical mixing and baking tasks. Two sets of adjustable racks for pie plates and cake tins are within easy reach of the woman of average height. Two gravity feed bins (obtainable from several manufacturers of kitchen equipment) let sugar and flour run directly into the measuring cup. Small equipment can be placed on the rear wall between the bins. A recessed light in the soffit board of the drop ceiling gives the center its own illumination. Drop ceilings are commonly used above a line of wall cabinets these days to give the room a better appearance and keep the cabinet tops from being a work-making dust collector.

Materials

MIX CENTER:

1" x 12" (nom.) stock (32 linear feet) to make—

    2 pc. 50" long — sides.

    2 pc. 47½" long — shelves.

    2 pc. 14" long   ⎫
                   ⎬ pan rack.
    2 pc. 12½" long ⎭

¼" plywood (4' x 8' panel) to make—

    8 pc. 11½" x 11½" — rack dividers.

    1 pc. 48" x 50" — back.

DROP CEILING:

1" x 2" (nom.) stock.

2" x 2" (nom.) stock.

Plaster board.

Pointers for Building

MIXING CENTER.   A 50″ length of a 4′-wide panel of ¼″ plywood
will provide the back. Attach this to the wall first, spacing the screws
or nails to hit the wall studs. Countersink and fill the heads. Center
notches 7½″ deep in the two shelves, adjusting their length to suit
the dimensions of the two bins. The pan racks above can also be
made to match by lengthening or shortening the four dadoed rack
pieces. Match the spacing of the ¼″ x ¼″ dadoes in each pair, top
and bottom, very carefully so the dividers will stand straight. For
greatest strength join the two shelves to the uprights with dado or
gain joints. The bottom ends of the uprights can probably be fastened
by running screws through the counter from underneath. The spacing and location of hooks on the backboard will depend on individual needs and equipment.

DROP CEILING.   When used above wall cabinets, construction will
probably be easiest before the cabinets are in place. With this mix
center or open shelves, the drop ceiling can come last. Above cabinets,
a bottom covering, or soffit board, can be omitted. The finished front
of the drop ceiling should of course come flush with the front of wall
cabinets. Some kitchen cabinet manufacturers use an L-section trim
between the drop-ceiling front and cabinets. One leg of the L points
up, the other goes between the drop ceiling and cabinet. Screws
driven through the top of the cabinet from below hold the trim to
the drop-ceiling frame.

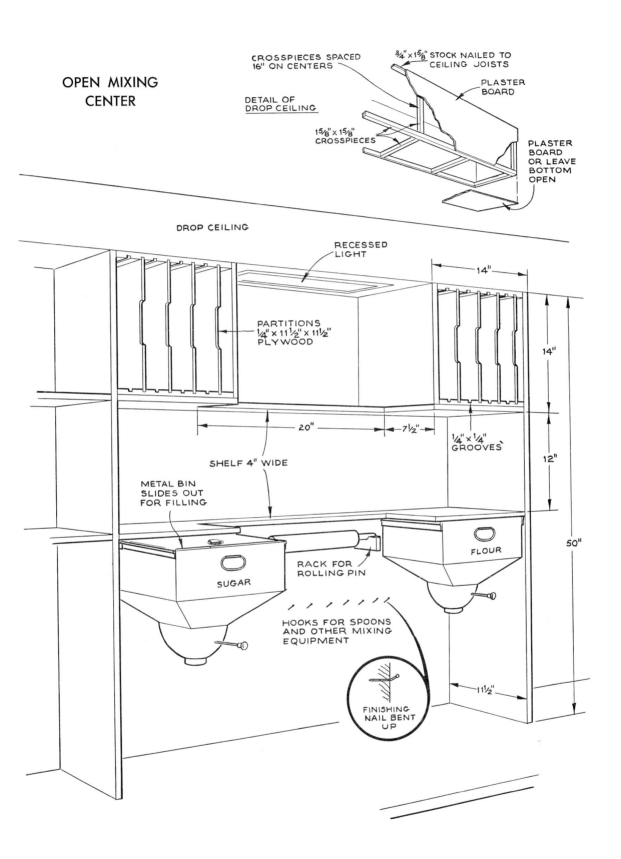

OPEN MIXING CENTER

DETAIL OF DROP CEILING

CROSSPIECES SPACED 16" ON CENTERS

$\frac{3}{4}$" × $1\frac{5}{8}$" STOCK NAILED TO CEILING JOISTS

PLASTER BOARD

$1\frac{5}{8}$" × $1\frac{5}{8}$" CROSSPIECES

PLASTER BOARD OR LEAVE BOTTOM OPEN

DROP CEILING

RECESSED LIGHT

PARTITIONS $\frac{1}{4}$" × $11\frac{1}{2}$" × $11\frac{1}{2}$" PLYWOOD

14"

14"

20"

$7\frac{1}{2}$"

$\frac{1}{4}$" × $\frac{1}{4}$" GROOVES

12"

SHELF 4" WIDE

METAL BIN SLIDES OUT FOR FILLING

FLOUR

50"

SUGAR

RACK FOR ROLLING PIN

HOOKS FOR SPOONS AND OTHER MIXING EQUIPMENT

$11\frac{1}{2}$"

FINISHING NAIL BENT UP

5

Sink Cabinets

More activity revolves around the sink than any other piece of kitchen equipment. When vegetables must be cleaned, meal preparation begins there. Its faucets supply water for cooking. And every meal time has an aftermath at the sink in the drudgery of dishwashing. In laying out a kitchen, it is wise therefore to consider this first equipment first and plan well for it.

Sinks come in two general types, roll-rim and flat-rim. Roll-rim sinks may or may not have an apron around the edge. Newer ones usually do not, for an apron makes it difficult to add the base cabinet that a modern housewife wants. In the past, roll-rim sinks were practically always leg- or wall-supported. Now, most manufacturers supply roll-rim as well as flat-rim types especially designed for custom cabinet building.

Whether to buy a sink with one or two bowls hinges on personal preference and the space available for the installation. If your choice is a two-bowl type, you would do well to consider whether one should be deeper than the other or not. A deep bowl may serve two func-

TYPES OF SINKS AND THEIR DIMENSIONS

Flat-Rim Sinks (for setting into counter)

Type of sink	OUTSIDE (INCHES)		INSIDE (INCHES)		Depth
	Length (side to side)	Width (front to back)	Length (side to side)	Width (front to back)	
SINGLE BOWL	18	18	16	16	8
	18	24	16	22	7
	20, 21	16, 18, 20	17, 19	13–15	6–7
	24	16, 18, 20, 21	20–22	13–19	6–8
	30	18, 20, 21	27–28	15–18	6–8
SINGLE BOWL ONE DRAINBOARD	42	20, 21, 25	20	16–17	8
SINGLE BOWL TWO DRAINBOARDS	54	25	20	16–18	8
	60	21, 25	20	17–18	8
DOUBLE BOWL	32, 36	18, 20, 21	13–17	14–18	7–8
	38, 42	20, 21	17–19	14–18	8

Roll-Rim Sinks (with or without apron)

Type of sink	OUTSIDE (INCHES)		INSIDE (INCHES)		Depth
SINGLE BOWL	20–21	15, 18			6–8
	24	18–21			6–8
	30	18, 20			6, 8
	36	20			6, 8
SINGLE BOWL ONE DRAINBOARD	42	20–25	19–20	15–17	6, 7, 8
SINGLE BOARD TWO DRAINBOARDS	54	25	20	15–17	6, 7, 8
	60	25	20	18	8
DOUBLE BOWL	38, 48	22, 25	18	15–18	8
DOUBLE BOWL TWO DRAINBOARDS	60	21	13	15–18	8
	72	25	16–18	15–18	7–8

tions—provide a place for small amounts of laundry and offer a more comfortable dishwashing level for the woman of short stature. Some double-bowl sinks of this type have a drainboard that slides from side to side—over the bowl not in use.

Typical flat-rim sinks give a smooth, continuous work counter to the edge of the bowl or bowls. Drainboards, found on most roll-rim sinks, take away this general work space to a large extent because of their grooved construction. Liquids may tend to stand on the counter around a flat-rim sink, but this can be avoided by giving the counters on either side a slight downward tilt toward the bowl.

Whether to pick a flat-rim sink or one with a drainboard, right or left, or even a sink with double drainboards, is also a matter of choice. Motion studies have shown that the right-handed person normally works best from dishes stacked on the counter at the right of the sink to a drainboard at the left. A point to remember about roll-rim types is that they usually have a rear splashboard as an integral part of the surface. Newer ones also have a convenient ledge just behind the bowl.

When you build a sink cabinet, whether the sink is cast iron or steel will be a factor to consider. Cast-iron sinks as a rule weigh more than twice as much as steel types. A typical flat-rim single basin made of steel weighs 24 pounds; the same size in cast iron weighs 50 pounds. A cast-iron double bowl can weigh as much as 116 pounds. A double-drainboard, single-bowl cast-iron roll-rim type may go as high as 205 pounds. Consequently, a sturdier supporting framework may be needed for the cast-iron types.

RECESSED SINK FRONT

Uses

Most manufacturers of kitchen equipment offer sink fronts in several widths. Some are just what their name implies, fronts to hide the plumbing below the sink. Others have a floor. The front goes be-

Sink Cabinets

RECESSED SINK FRONT

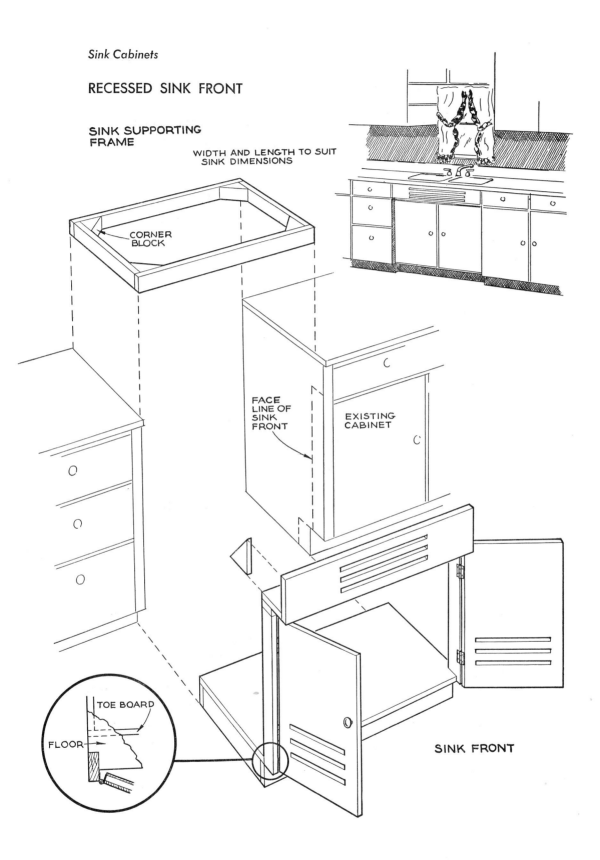

SINK SUPPORTING
FRAME

WIDTH AND LENGTH TO SUIT
SINK DIMENSIONS

CORNER
BLOCK

FACE
LINE OF
SINK
FRONT

EXISTING
CABINET

TOE BOARD

FLOOR

SINK FRONT

tween two standard base cabinets, one end of each doing double duty as a wall for the sink enclosure.

If you build your own cabinets, you would do well to consider this procedure. It saves material. It simplifies the job of putting in a sink. Given two base cabinets that can be spotted on either side of where you intend to place the sink, your job is already well along. A front can be used to enclose either a roll-rim or flat-rim sink.

The lower part of the front shown is recessed. The toe board is set back a little farther than those under the cabinets on either side. The cupboard doors are farther back too. This allows the housewife an easier stance (more knee room) closer to her work. A sink front of course can also be installed flush with the adjoining cabinets if you wish.

Materials

¾″ plywood to make—

   2 doors, floor, vent board (about 5″ wide).

1″ x 2″ (nom.) stock — sink frame, door frame.

1″ x 4″ (nom.) stock — base and recess board.

NOTE: Amount of materials needed will depend on the size of the sink and how far the existing cabinets are placed apart.

Pointers for Building

After buying your sink and positioning the adjoining cabinets, measure and cut the 1″ x 2″ stock to fit around the sink, using corner blocks to strengthen the frame. Screw the frame to the ends of the adjoining cabinets at the proper height to bring the sink at the correct level for installing a counter.

The sink front can be built as a complete unit and then shoved into place. Cut the floor to size and notch the two front corners to allow the vertical framing members to project ¾″, the thickness of the doors. Support the floor on a base made of 1″ x 4″ nominal stock. Set back the toe board a distance equal to that used under the adjacent cabinets.

Cap the two vertical framing members with another piece of 1″ x 2″ stock placed edgewise. On top of this align a piece of 1″ x 4″ stock to bring the vent board flush with the fronts of the adjoining cabinets. Support the vent board with corner blocks or corner irons. The ventilating louvers in the doors and vent board can be started by drilling a hole at each end and then sawing out the slot. The front edge of the sink-front floor acts as a stop for the doors. Push the sink front between its companion cabinets and fasten it with screws driven through the vertical framing members.

COMBINATION SINK CABINET

Uses

Most of the conveniences needed at or near the sink are embraced within this one unit. It might well be the starting point for the handyman who wants to build a full complement of kitchen cabinets over a period of time; for, until the others are completed, this one alone will give the housewife a generous sample of how a modern kitchen can lighten her chores.

The unit was adapted from the model U-shaped kitchen designed by the U.S. Bureau of Human Nutrition and Home Economics. In the original, a series of built-in compartments line the wall behind the sink and work counter. Plans for building these are given in the wall cabinet chapter.

The garbage-disposal method will appeal to many. Fruit and vegetable peelings or scrapings and refuse from the table can simply be swept or dropped through the counter opening into a container in the metal-lined compartment below. A recessed handle in the lid avoids interference with normal use of this part of the counter as a flat work surface. The garbage is removed through a door opening into the compartment from outside the house; no need to carry it through the kitchen to the back door. A pull-down door opens into the cabinet from inside, providing access for cleaning the walls and empty container, positioning the container, or disposing of waste too bulky to go through the counter opening. Insulation on and around the outer door cuts down heat loss from the house.

Two drawers offer storage facilities below the garbage compartment, the shallow one perhaps for paper bags, the large one for bulky utensils. Four drawers at the left of the sink are topped by a pull-out board which provides a handy cutting surface or a place to clamp a food grinder. One of these drawers is metal lined for storage of cookies and cakes.

Materials

1″ x 2″ (nom.) stock (90 linear feet) — framing.

1″ x 4″ (nom.) stock (22 linear feet) — framing and base.

¾″ plywood (two 4′ x 8′ panels) to make—

    4 pc. 23″ x 31⅝″ — ends, vertical divisions.

    1 pc. 12″ x 28″ — garbage compartment flooring.

    1 pc. 11⅝″ x 12″ — inner door of compartment.

    1 pc. 12″ x 12⅜″ — outer door of compartment.

    2 pc. 14⅜″ x 22⅝″ — doors.

    1 pc. 7½″ x 28¾″ (or 1″ x 8″ (nom.) stock) — vent board.

    1 pc. 25″ x 56″ — counter (for this cabinet alone).

    1 pc. 11½″ x 32″ (or 1″ x 12″ (nom.) stock) — shelf.

    1 pc. 10″ x 10″
    1 pc. 9¾″ x 10″ } rack.
    2 pc. 5½″ x 8″

    1 pc. 6⁹⁄₁₆″ x 12″
    2 pc. 7¼″ x 12″
    1 pc. 8⅛″ x 12″ } drawer fronts.
    1 pc. 6″ x 12″
    1 pc. 10¾″ x 12″

½″ plywood (4′ x 5′ panel) — drawers.

¼″ plywood (4′ x 8′ and 2′ x 4′ panels) to make—

    1 pc. 31⅝″ x 59″ — back.

    1 pc. 23″ x 32″ — flooring.

    6 pc. 11¼″ x 22″ — drawer bottoms.

1 breadboard.

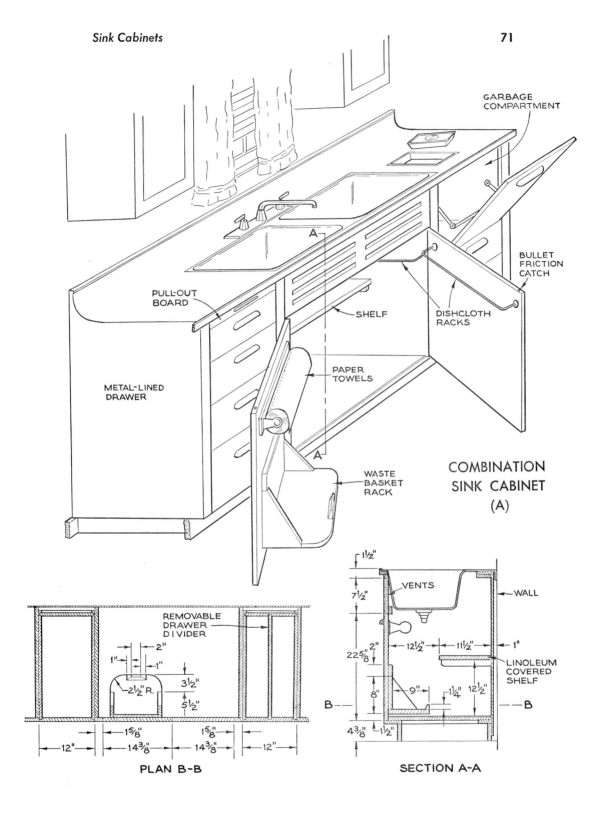

GARBAGE COMPARTMENT

BULLET FRICTION CATCH

PULL-OUT BOARD

SHELF

DISHCLOTH RACKS

METAL-LINED DRAWER

PAPER TOWELS

WASTE BASKET RACK

COMBINATION SINK CABINET (A)

REMOVABLE DRAWER DIVIDER

2"

1" 1"

3½"

2½" R.

5½"

15⅝"

1⅝"

12"

14⅜"

14⅜"

12"

PLAN B-B

1½"

VENTS

WALL

7½"

2"

12½"

11½"

1"

LINOLEUM COVERED SHELF

22⅝"

8"

9"

1¼"

12½"

B

B

4⅜"

1½"

SECTION A-A

Pointers for Building

When you come to a cabinet as extensive as this one, you will get along faster and better if you first resolve the construction job into its component parts. That is, if you can divide the whole into sub-assemblies and do a good job on these first, the final assembly will amount to practically nothing at all.

The basic sub-assemblies here are the frames. These are of four types and they go into the final assembly as indicated by the numerals on the framing drawing. Nominal 1″ x 2″ pine stock (actual measurements ¾″ x 1⅝″) is used without change except for cutting to length in frames 1, 2, and 3. Frames 4 differ only in that they have a piece of 1″ x 4″ stock (¾″ x 3⅝″ actual) across the front to fill in the overhang of the toe space. Frames 2 and 3 are identical except that the five No. 3's are ¾″ shorter to allow for a bottom lip on the face of the drawers they support. The front edges of all other framing units are visible when the full cabinet is complete. Several types of joints might be used for the frames, but an easily cut lap will do as well as any other. Glue corner blocks in all frames.

The front corners of frame 1 and its corresponding frame 4 are notched to take the two vertical facing strips. No such notches are shown in the end frames since it is contemplated that these would be in the framing for any adjoining cabinets at either end of this one. If this cabinet is built as a unit unto itself, the end verticals can be moved inward.

The use of ¾″ plywood partitions and ends makes a vertical framework unnecessary. When the horizontal framing units are complete and the partitions cut to size, carefully mark the positions of the framing units on the partitions. Then drill the latter for flathead wood screws to support the frames. Be careful to assemble all parts square and according to dimensions or you will run into serious trouble when it comes to fitting the drawers. Do not, of course, make any final assembly until all units of the cabinet (including the drawers, etc.) are complete and you have put the whole cabinet through a dry run to be sure everything fits. This is a good rule to follow in all cabinet making.

The framing around the sink (frame 1) may have to be varied, strengthened, or added to, depending on the sink you use. In the

COMBINATION SINK CABINET (B)

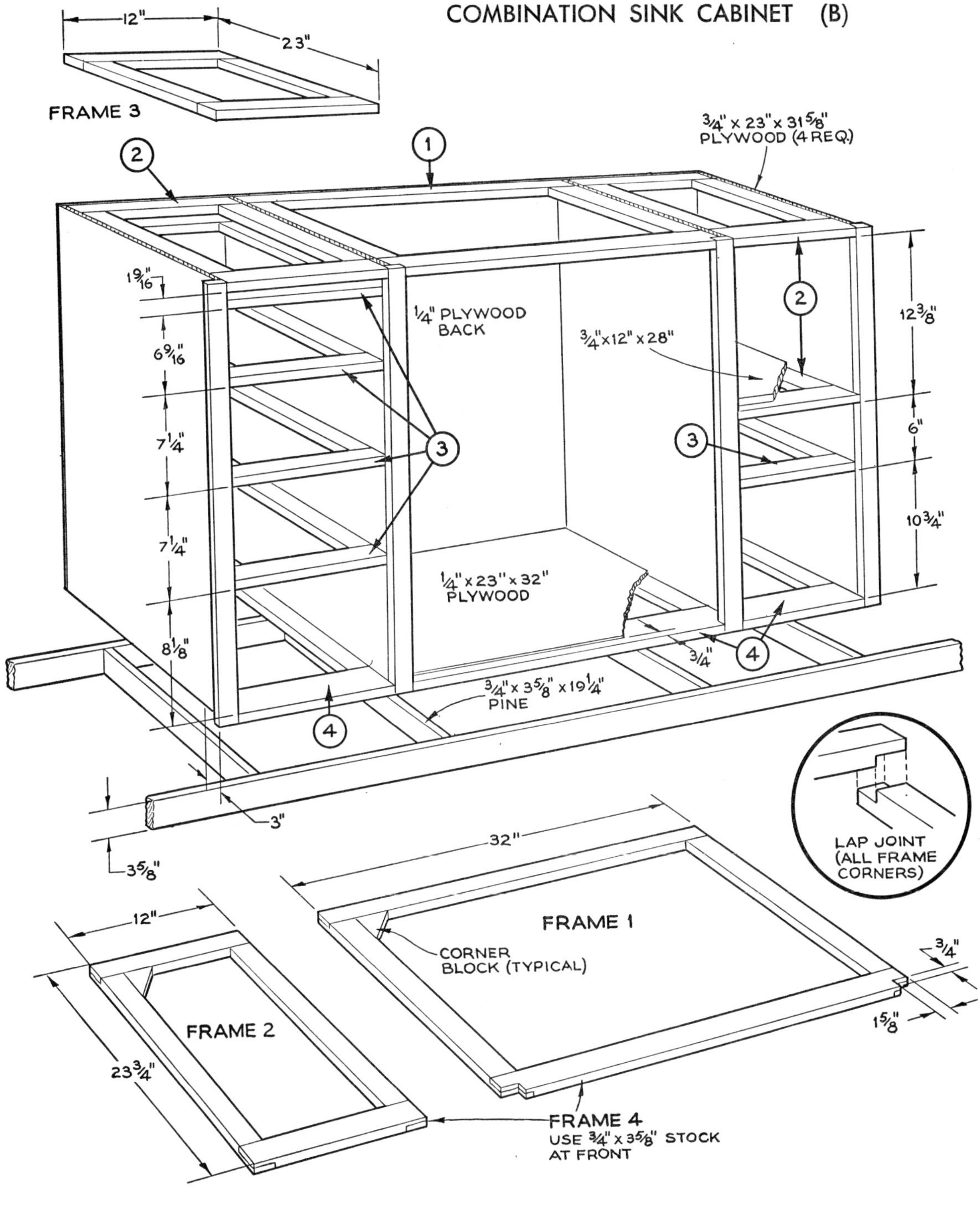
12"
23"
FRAME 3
3/4" x 23" x 31 5/8"
PLYWOOD (4 REQ.)
1
2
1 9/16"
6 9/16"
7 1/4"
7 1/4"
8 1/8"
1/4" PLYWOOD
BACK
3/4"x12"x28"
2
12 3/8"
6"
3
3
10 3/4"
1/4"x23"x32"
PLYWOOD
3/4"
4
3/4"x 3 5/8" x19 1/4"
PINE
4
3"
3 5/8"
LAP JOINT
(ALL FRAME
CORNERS)
32"
FRAME 1
CORNER
BLOCK (TYPICAL)
3/4"
1 5/8"
12"
FRAME 2
23 3/4"
FRAME 4
USE 3/4" x 3 5/8" STOCK
AT FRONT

original, a two-bowl, flat-rim sink of special design was used, one bowl being deeper than the other. An additional piece of 1″ x 2″ stock across the center of the bottom frame (from front to back) will enable you to use the ¼″ plywood bottom as indicated.

Frame 2 at the right of the sink opening needs interior framing to take the garbage-compartment lid. No dimensions are indicated for the lid, but an opening 5″ x 8″ should be large enough. Cut the lid from 1½″ solid stock or from two ¾″ pieces glued together. Mount a recessed metal handle, available from a hardware store, in an opening cut in the lid block. Saw all four edges to an angle of about 15 degrees as indicated in the sketch to match corresponding angles on the edges of the surrounding frame. Cover the top of the lid with a piece of your counter covering, tack or cement a piece of sheet metal on the bottom, and run counter molding around the edges. If you select a flat-surface molding (without fancy decorations) you can also use this to finish off the inner edge of the counter opening.

The sink cabinet must be exactly located in the kitchen before the wall opening can be cut for the garbage compartment. If at all possible, try to locate the opening between two wall studs so as to avoid structural changes in the wall. Frame the opening inside with 2 x 4's.

The 1″ rigid insulation shown in the drawings is specified mostly for use with the line of recessed wall cabinets at the rear of the counter in the original kitchen that uses this sink unit. Unless you also use these wall cabinets, you can forget about the insulation here —except for a piece over the outer door and strips around it. Although they are not shown in the sketch, vertical framing strips should go over the house siding on either side of the opening to finish it off. Galvanized sheet metal of fairly heavy gauge can be used to line the compartment, although lighter stuff will do nicely and will be easier to handle. Sheet copper also might be used.

Allow a spacing of 1³⁄₁₆″ between the two frames where the pull-out board fits. For a board ¾″ thick, this will then give a clearance of ¹⁄₁₆″ for easy action. The stops under the board are spaced so that they overlap the front member of the bottom frame when the board is pulled out. Pushing up the front stop with the fingers allows the board to be shoved back into the cabinet.

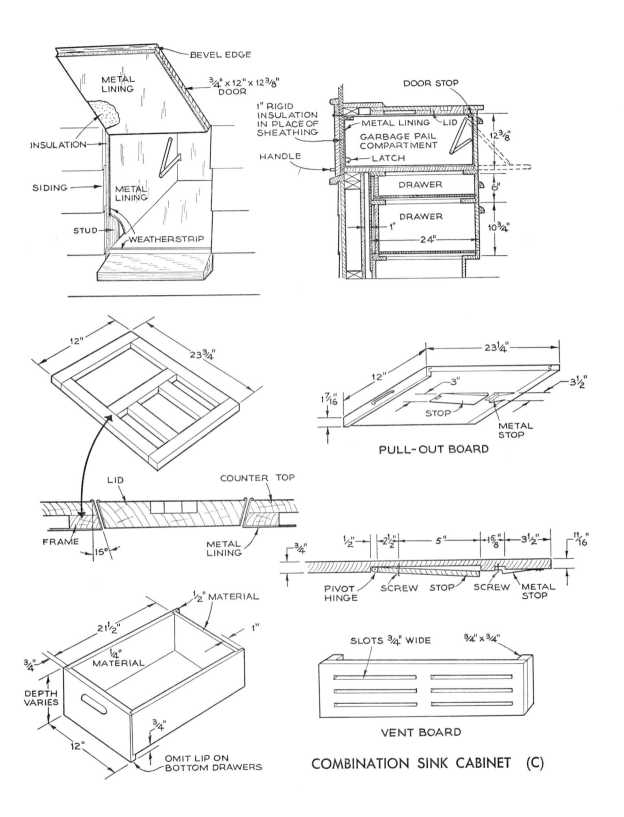

BEVEL EDGE

METAL LINING

3/4" x 12" x 12 3/8" DOOR

DOOR STOP

1" RIGID INSULATION IN PLACE OF SHEATHING

METAL LINING LID

12 3/8"

INSULATION

GARBAGE PAIL COMPARTMENT

LATCH

HANDLE

DRAWER

6"

SIDING

METAL LINING

DRAWER

10 3/4"

STUD

WEATHERSTRIP

1"

24"

12"

23 3/4"

23 1/4"

12"

3 1/2"

1 7/16"

3"

STOP

3 1/2"

METAL STOP

PULL-OUT BOARD

LID

COUNTER TOP

FRAME

15°

METAL LINING

3/4"

1/2"   2 1/2"   5"   1 5/8"   3 1/2"   1 1/16"

PIVOT HINGE   SCREW   STOP   SCREW   METAL STOP

1/2" MATERIAL

21 1/2"

1"

1/4" MATERIAL

3/4"

SLOTS 3/4" WIDE   3/4" x 3/4"

DEPTH VARIES

12"

3/4"

OMIT LIP ON BOTTOM DRAWERS

VENT BOARD

COMBINATION SINK CABINET   (C)

Hardwood should be used for the board, preferably several sections glued up and then finished off smooth. A single piece could be used, however, if available. You might also prefer to adapt a ready-made bread board.

The drawers are varied in height to suit the indicated spaces. The metal lining for the cookie drawer can be any easily worked sheet. Rather than make this a permanent part of the drawer, you would do better to form the metal into a snug-fitting box, with soldered or riveted seams, that can be slipped in and out of the drawer for washing.

SIMPLE SINK CABINET

Uses

Like the sink front previously described, this unit becomes an integral part of two adjoining base cabinets, and it is built as such. Ends of the adjoining cabinets serve as its side walls. The base, including the recessed toe board, is common to all three cabinets.

It is designed for a single-bowl sink, one large enough to hold two dishpans or a dishpan and a drainer. The cabinet is left without shelves or other obstructions, so that two dishpans and a drainer can be stored in it. Additionally there still is room for a bucket or basket of fruit or vegetables for daily use. Soap flakes and scouring powder can be kept in the rack on the left door. A garbage pail placed on the holder mounted on the other door is always easy to reach.

Materials

CABINET:

¾″ plywood (4′ x 4′ panel) to make—

    1 pc. 23″ x 30″ — bottom.

    2 pc. 15″ x 23⅞″ — doors.

    1 pc. 25″ x 30″ — counter. (This can be continuous with adjoining cabinets.)

2″ x 2″ (nom.) stock to make—

  2 pc. 35″ long — rear posts.

1″ x 6″ (nom.) stock to make—

  1 pc. 30″ long — apron.

  2 pc. 3″ x 5″ — apron cleats.

1″ x 2″ (nom.) stock to make—

  1 pc. 30″ long — horizontal face strip. (This can be continuous with the adjoining cabinets.)

1/4″ plywood to make—

  1 pc. 30″ x 35″ — cabinet back.

RACK:

1″ (nom.) stock to make—

  2 pc. 4½″ x 8″

  1 pc. 3½″ x 10½″

2 pc. 1/4″ x 1½″ x 12″ plywood.

GARBAGE PAIL HOLDER:

1″ (nom.) stock or 3/4″ plywood to make parts to suit the size of the pail used.

Pointers for Building

The cabinet is built as part of the two adjoining ones. The base is common to all. The sink cabinet itself has no framing other than the two sink-supporting posts at the rear corners. The plywood bottom is notched to allow these to continue to the kitchen floor. They are set forward enough to allow the 1/4″ plywood back to be recessed as shown in the detail drawing. The horizontal facing strip at the top is a continuation of the one used on the adjoining cabinets. The doors are attached to the vertical facing strips at the ends of the other cabinets.

  Cleats hold the apron in position between these vertical strips. Louvers can be cut in this board to ventilate the cabinet. As suggested alternatively in the drawing, you might also want to use a metal grille here for ventilation and to add a decorative note. A grille

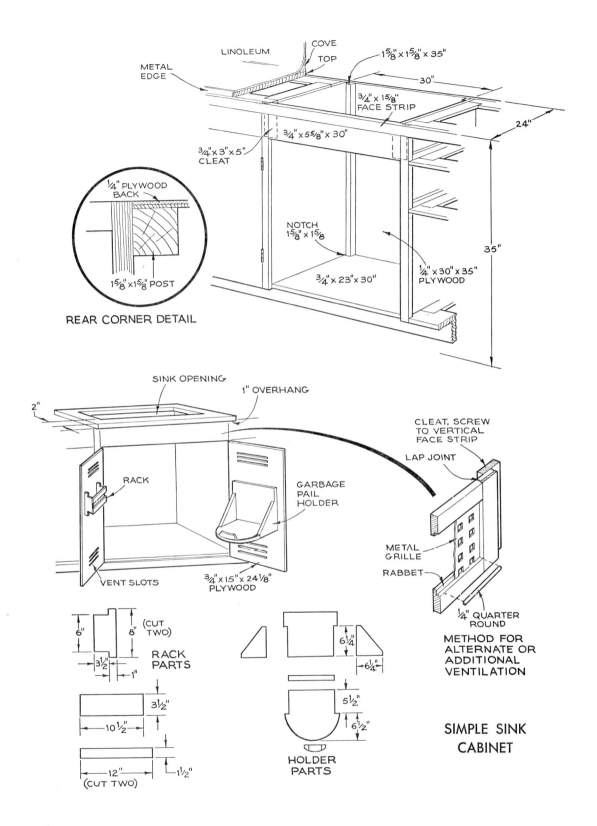

LINOLEUM COVE TOP
$1\frac{5}{8}" \times 1\frac{5}{8}" \times 35"$
METAL EDGE
30"
$\frac{3}{4}" \times 1\frac{5}{8}"$ FACE STRIP
24"
$\frac{3}{4}" \times 5\frac{5}{8}" \times 30"$
$\frac{3}{4}" \times 3" \times 5"$ CLEAT
35"
NOTCH $1\frac{5}{8}" \times 1\frac{5}{8}"$
$\frac{1}{4}" \times 30" \times 35"$ PLYWOOD
$\frac{3}{4}" \times 23" \times 30"$

$\frac{1}{4}"$ PLYWOOD BACK
$1\frac{5}{8}" \times 1\frac{5}{8}"$ POST
REAR CORNER DETAIL

SINK OPENING 1" OVERHANG
2"
CLEAT. SCREW TO VERTICAL FACE STRIP
LAP JOINT
RACK
GARBAGE PAIL HOLDER
METAL GRILLE
RABBET
VENT SLOTS
$\frac{3}{4}" \times 15" \times 24\frac{1}{8}"$ PLYWOOD
$\frac{1}{4}"$ QUARTER ROUND
METHOD FOR ALTERNATE OR ADDITIONAL VENTILATION

6" 8" (CUT TWO)
$3\frac{1}{2}"$
1"
RACK PARTS

$6\frac{1}{4}"$
$6\frac{1}{4}"$

$3\frac{1}{2}"$
$10\frac{1}{2}"$

$5\frac{1}{2}"$
$6\frac{1}{2}"$
HOLDER PARTS

$1\frac{1}{2}"$
12"
(CUT TWO)

SIMPLE SINK CABINET

such as the type designed for radiator enclosures is one possibility.

Building the rack and holder is simply a matter of sawing your stock as shown and assembling the parts with screws. Adjust the size of the holder base to fit the garbage pail you will use.

SINK STOOL AND SOAP TRAY

Uses

Dead storage wall cabinets too high for easy reach usually require a step-stool for access. What better place could you store this bulky piece of equipment than under the kitchen sink? The back of the stool shown here serves also as the cabinet front, disguising the fact that it actually is a stool. Pulled out, the stool can have a secondary use as a work seat beside a pull-out board located adjoining the sink. The stool need not be any wider than 18". But it can be adapted to a sink recess of any width by projecting the front board and toe-recess members equally on either side to make a full enclosure.

Besides soap, the hinged tray will hold boxes of cleanser, polish, and similar materials. The keyhole openings make it possible to lift the tray off its retaining screws for cleaning.

Materials

(FOR A SINK RECESS 24" WIDE)

$3/4$" plywood (4' x 4' panel) to make—

1 pc. $19\frac{5}{8}$" x 24" — front.

2 pc. $19\frac{1}{2}$" x $22\frac{1}{2}$" — stool sides.

1 pc. $8\frac{1}{2}$" x 24" (or 1" x 9" (nom.) stock) — soap tray front.

1" x 8" (nom.) stock (10 linear feet) to make—

6 pc. 18" long — treads and risers.

1" x 4" (nom.) stock (4 linear feet) to make—

2 pc. 24" long — toe recess.

1" x 2" (nom.) stock (4 linear feet) to make—

2 pc. 24" long — horizontal framing.

1 pc. 11" x 18" sheet metal.

Pointers for Building

Before you set out to build this stool and soap tray, be sure your sink installation allows space for them. If the sink is too far forward, you may not be able to put in the tray. If the plumbing comes down too far, you will find it impossible to slide a stool of this height into the recess. The sink itself can be supported on the counter spanning the two adjoining base cabinets. No framing or additional support should be needed if you use a steel sink or can place the adjoining cabinets close enough together so they help bear the weight of the sink. The adjoining cabinets should have full ends to the floor, and the kitchen floor covering should be laid back into the recess.

For a work counter 36″ high, the indicated dimensions allow for a horizontal facing strip of 1″ x 2″ just under the counter and a similar strip below to which the soap tray can be hinged.

After cutting the stool parts to size, assemble them with flat-head wood screws. If you use enough screws and set them well, no interior bracing should be required to make the stool fully safe. Triangular openings cut in each side of the stool will lighten it a bit without detracting materially from the strength. At the same time, these openings will provide passage for ventilating air that enters through two or three louvers cut in the face board. Two vertical lines of ½″ holes bored in the soap-tray facing board will help do the ventilating job above.

Strips of ¾″ half round attached to the bottom edges of the stool sides with finishing nails should make the stool easier to slide in and out. Set the nails and sand the strips smooth. The strips will serve as runners if you leave a clearance of about $\frac{1}{32}$″ between the floor and the bottom edges of the first riser and the toe board. After the finish coat has been applied, coat the runners with wax.

Plywood scraps left over from the stool can be used as end pieces for the soap tray. If available, a piece of sheet stainless steel would be ideal for the tray itself. Otherwise, use galvanized sheet, or sheet aluminum. Bend the metal to fit the wood ends, cut two keyhole openings for mounting, and tack the metal to the wood ends. After the tray facing board has been hinged to its crosspiece, adjust a metal elbow stop or a light chain so the tray won't open far enough to spill its contents on the floor.

Sink Cabinets

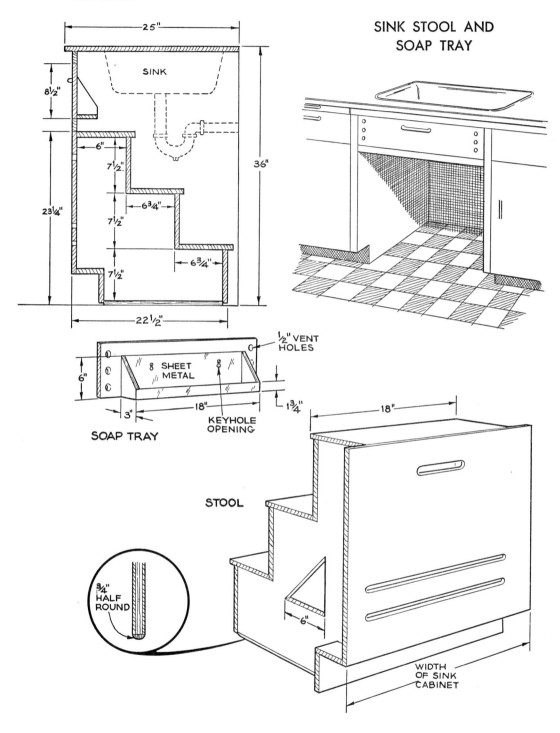

SINK STOOL AND
SOAP TRAY

25"

SINK

8½"

23¼"

36"

6"

7½"

6¾"

7½"

6¾"

7½"

22½"

½" VENT
HOLES

6"

8 SHEET
METAL

3"

18"

1¾"

KEYHOLE
OPENING

SOAP TRAY

STOOL

18"

¾"
HALF
ROUND

6"

WIDTH
OF SINK
CABINET

ENCLOSING AN OLD SINK

Since this construction job would vary widely, depending on the type, size, and shape of the sink, procedures only can be suggested. Unless it is necessary to move the sink, the original wall or leg supports might be retained, although these, especially a leg or legs, may rob you of useful cabinet space. The cabinets below will do the supporting job without other help.

Practically all old-fashioned sinks are of the roll-rim type, either with or without an apron, and more than likely having a drainboard. The drawings suggest how to proceed when the sink either has or lacks an apron. These plans propose that the upper edges of all four cabinet walls fit inside the recess formed by the roll rim. This will allow the rim or apron to overlap the cabinet on all sides. However, if you increase the cabinet width and length slightly, the

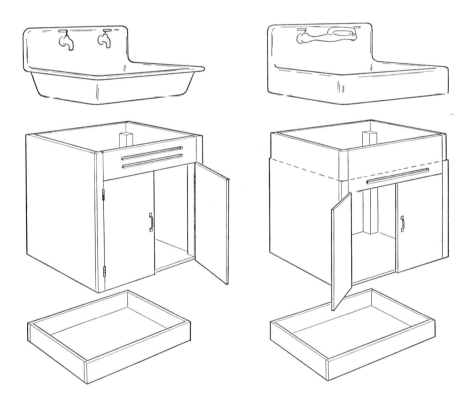

sink can be made to rest on the bottom edge of the rim or apron as the case may be.

If the cabinet is to provide full sink support, it would be advisable to use ¾″ plywood for all four sides. Otherwise, you might choose lesser material. Use nom. 1″ x 4″ pine for the base and nom. 1″ x 2″ and nom. 2″ x 2″ for the framing. The drawing at the right suggests rounding off the corners to allow the cabinet to slip under the sink apron.

SINK IDEAS

Diagonal Corner Sink

A sink placed across a corner will sometimes improve kitchen working arrangement, besides creating a novel effect. Located at 45 degrees across the inside of the corner formed by the line of base cabinets, the front of the sink cabinet tends to round and smooth the flow of the cabinet fronts. A deep corner cabinet is required for the sink. For its shape, see the sketch of the diagonal corner cabinet, page 151 of Chapter 8—Corner Cabinets.

In general, a single bowl is most suitable for corner sink installation. Most double bowls would increase the length of the sink front so much, at the same time boosting depth, that it would become impossible to utilize the space at the far back corner inside the cabinet. If the sink front is limited to about 24″, the housewife will be able to use most of the cabinet space—with a little reaching, of course. Installation of one or two sliding shelves will improve the utility of such a cabinet. These can be mounted between hardwood guides or on metal slides as suggested for the sliding shelf cabinet in the chapter on base cabinets. In the case of the corner sink cabinet, the shelves could be given a 90-degree point at the rear to fit into the corner. Stationary shelves could fill the cabinet space on either side of the sliding shelves—at the same level. A lip an inch or two high on the rear edges of the sliding shelves would keep stored articles from falling off to the rear when the shelves are pulled out for access to the stored articles.

The triangular space on the counter behind a diagonal sink can be utilized in various ways. If wall cabinets are placed in the corner above the sink, the space between them and the counter could be filled with shallow shelves for additional storage. The rear corner of the counter might also be devoted to a lift-up cover, opening into a disposal chute for cans, bottles, and such refuse. The chute could lead to a basement receptacle through the rear corner of the sink cabinet.

A more attractive kitchen would result, however, if windows are installed in the corner behind the sink. In new construction, this might be a single window or line of windows paralleling the sink lengthwise; that is, an exterior corner of the house would be chopped off at a 45-degree angle. If the sink faces into a corner formed by two exterior walls (that is, if one of them isn't just a partition between the kitchen and another room), windows can be installed in both walls—forming a right angle of illumination and visibility for the worker at the sink. A triangular plant box behind the sink would offer a bright note of growing green and blooming color the year round. If one of the facing walls is a partition, windows in the other still would offer the sink worker a view outside. In this case, the partition wall might be decorated with hanging planters. When windows are placed behind a corner sink, wall cabinets should stop approximately on a line with the corners of the sink front. A sink light could go behind a decorative cornice placed diagonally from the end wall cabinet on one wall to the end one on the other. The light could also be recessed in a soffit board installed across the corner.

Peninsula Sink

A kitchen sink doesn't always have to be backed up by a wall. For a more efficient working layout, it sometimes is located in a "peninsula" of cabinets jutting from the wall or in an "island" in the middle of the room—with walking space all around. Your basic kitchen plan will help you determine whether such a location is desirable. Any against-the-wall type of sink cabinet can be used. It will of course need its own back. But before placing a sink in such a location, be sure that piping the water there and installing the drain will present no difficulty or costly plumbing problems.

INSTALLING SINKS AND COUNTERS

Roll-rim sinks rest on a supporting framework built to suit them. There are no down cracks in the sink itself to allow water seepage, but making a waterproof and dustproof joint between the ends of the sink and adjacent work counters sometimes is a problem. Some sink manufacturers make a filler strip especially for the purpose.

Methods available for installing flat-rim sinks employ metal rims (usually aluminum) made to fit the specific sink. Each ordinarily requires a counter opening with dimensions less than the inside length and width of the sink cabinet although the sink lip might extend beyond the cabinet ends.

One method, and the most common, requires a counter opening of the exact dimensions of the sink at the point where the lip begins to flare. By careful layout, you can achieve this by cutting an opening in a single sheet of $3/4''$ plywood. But it is easier, and just as satisfactory, to butt a section of counter material against each end of the sink, and join these, front and back, with strips of the proper width. The edges of the opening should then be rabbeted to the depth and width of the sink lip so as to bring the upper surface of the lip flush with the counter as illustrated in the accompanying sketch. When everything is snug, it is a good idea to embed the sink edge in a cement such as Pliobond. The aluminum sink rim is then screwed down around the sink edge, the covering is cut to fit, and the inside edge of the rim is turned back over the edge of the covering. Typical rims supplied with flat-rim sinks have a $1/4''$ lip, a $11/2''$ flange. Turned back, the lip forms an effective seal.

You can also install flat-rim sinks with a clamp rim, a far easier procedure. No careful fitting of the sink or rabbeting of the edge is needed, just a counter opening roughly to the dimensions of the sink. After the counter and covering are in place, the rim and sink are put into place and drawn snug with clamp screws located out of sight below the counter surface. Another type of clamp frame has two sets of tapered tongues. One set is twisted to lock the frame to the sink flange. The other (manipulated from underneath the counter) locks the sink and rim assembly to the counter.

For sink and all other base cabinets, ¾″ plywood is the most convenient-to-install material for the counter. Allow sufficient width (front to back) for a 1″ overhang at the front. Used full length, a single plywood panel will usually span at least two cabinets. If a joint naturally falls midway in the width of a cabinet, material could be saved by installing an extra framing member from front to back in the top of the cabinet and butting the two lengths of plywood snugly above it. The covering will hide the joint.

Linoleum is the most widely used counter covering, and special damp-proof cement is available for applying it. But there are other materials to be considered, too. These, however, may give a lesser run without a joint than you can get with linoleum. They also are apt to be more expensive.

For instance, you can get a plastic counter top, with a rear splash board and a down-sweeping front edging molded in. This has the advantage of giving a counter totally without cracks or crevices. A raised lip at front keeps liquids from dripping down the fronts of the cabinets. Whatever sort of covering you use, a raised lip should be a feature of the molding along the front edge.

Linoleum or Formica already bonded to ¾″ plywood are other possibilities. These can be ordered in lengths up to eight feet. The width is $23^{15}\!/_{16}''$. Matching splash boards are also available. Vinyl plastic in rolls is still another available covering.

For a sink, a splash board is always desirable. Roll-rim types have them cast in. For flat-rim sinks, you can install the splash board and seal the joint with a special metal cove molding. Better still, perhaps, you can set a wood cove in the rear corner and run linoleum or other covering in an unbroken sweep from the front edge of the counter to the top of the back board, capping it with metal molding made for the purpose.

The careful craftsman might also use stainless steel, .018″ or .025″ annealed sheet. Cement the sheet to the plywood backing and then trim it to size. Using 1″ pipe, you can form the sheet to sweep up the back board. A sink rim and stainless steel or aluminum molding can be used to finish off such a counter.

In addition to buying a counter top to which a hard-pressed sheet plastic (Formica or Micarta, for instance) is bonded, the home builder also could attempt the cutting and bonding job himself. A hack saw will cut these plastic sheets, and a rasp or file will smooth the edges. Contact bond cements will attach the sheets to the wood or plywood backing.

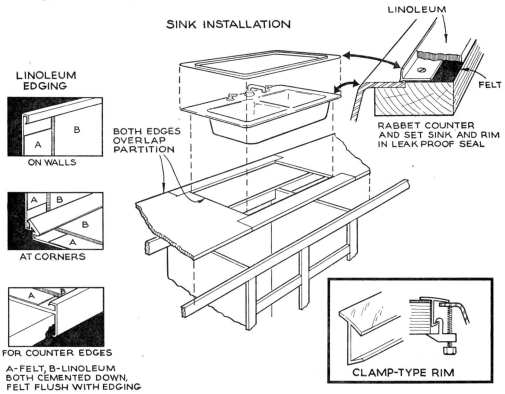

SINK INSTALLATION

LINOLEUM
EDGING

ON WALLS

AT CORNERS

FOR COUNTER EDGES
A-FELT, B-LINOLEUM
BOTH CEMENTED DOWN,
FELT FLUSH WITH EDGING

BOTH EDGES
OVERLAP
PARTITION

LINOLEUM

FELT

RABBET COUNTER
AND SET SINK AND RIM
IN LEAK PROOF SEAL

CLAMP-TYPE RIM

INSTALLING SINKS AND COUNTERS

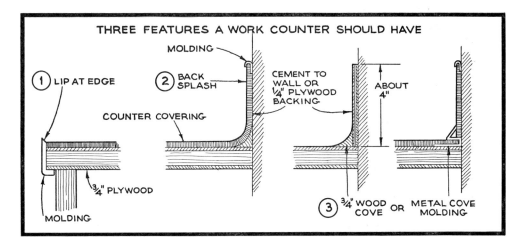

THREE FEATURES A WORK COUNTER SHOULD HAVE

① LIP AT EDGE

② BACK SPLASH

MOLDING

CEMENT TO
WALL OR
¼" PLYWOOD
BACKING

ABOUT
4"

COUNTER COVERING

¾" PLYWOOD

MOLDING

③ ¾" WOOD
COVE   OR   METAL COVE
MOLDING

6

Special-Purpose
Base Cabinets

Base cabinets are the work horses of the kitchen. Their tops provide a convenient work space for the many activities that go on in a kitchen. Their drawers and shelves store the bulk of the equipment required for these activities.

Modern base cabinets should not be confused, however, with old-fashioned cupboards. Inside the modern cabinets you will find far more than mere shelves and drawers. A shelf, strangely enough, no longer means just a fixed board in a fixed position between two uprights. Not only may today's shelf adjust up and down; it may in some base cabinets slide forward and out to display its stored wares for the housewife's ready selection. Shelves sometimes stand on end, too, sliding out of the cabinet (on rollers perhaps) and bringing into the light an array of kitchen tools and pots and pans supported on hooks.

Drawers also are in step with the times. They no longer are just catch-all boxes. Instead, some drawers lead an extremely specialized life, designed and fitted to do only one job. But they do this one job well.

Examples will be found on the following pages for your selection.

SLIDING SHELF CABINET

Uses

If you have known the annoyance of sorting through a cluttered bottom cupboard shelf and finally, perhaps, removing the contents to reach an article stored at the rear, you must have wished for a better method of storage. You can have it by installing shelves that slide forward and out. You then can see and reach anything, anywhere on the shelf.

Sliding shelves have become an important feature of modern kitchens. They serve a variety of purposes. With egg-crate divisions they store bottles nicely. Most commercial pull-out shelves have a surrounding lip to keep the contents from sliding off. These can be kept low, an inch or so above the shelf surface if you wish. How high you make the lip depends on what you plan to store on the shelf.

The simplest form of pull-out shelf is sketched at the bottom right on the accompanying page of drawings. This is simply a board with a rear ledge. The sliding shelf rests on the bottom shelf of an existing cabinet. Whatever the base cupboards you have, adding pull-out shelves like this one would make a big hit with the housewife. In some cases a breadboard of the right size might be used.

Materials

1″ x 2″ (nom.) stock (45 linear feet) — framing.

1″ x 3″ (nom.) stock (30 linear feet) — framing.

1″ x 4″ (nom.) stock (8 linear feet) — base.

⅝″ plywood (2′ x 4′ panel) to make—

    1 pc. 21⅛″ x 23″ — shelf.   1 pc. 21″ x 23″ — shelf.

    Strips of desired width around shelves, drawer sides, and back.

¾″ plywood (3′ x 4′ panel) to make—

    1 pc. 21¾″ x 25″ — door.   1 pc. 24¾″ x 25″ — counter.

    1 pc. 5″ x 21½″ — drawer front.

¼″ x 21½″ x 23″ plywood — drawer bottom.

Ball-bearing pull-out slides if available or desired.

⅛″ material for egg-crate construction for bottle tray.

SLIDING SHELF CABINET

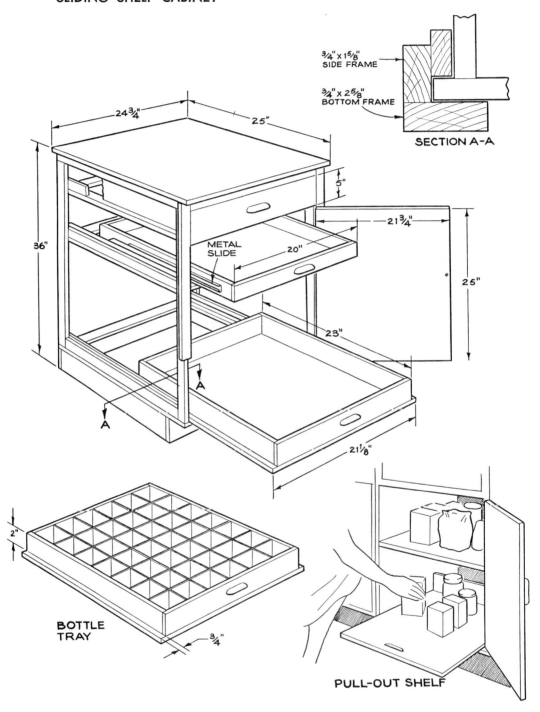

3/4" x 1 5/8"
SIDE FRAME

3/4" x 2 5/8"
BOTTOM FRAME

SECTION A-A

24 3/4"

25"

36"

5"

METAL
SLIDE

20"

21 3/4"

25"

23"

21 1/8"

A

A

2"

BOTTLE
TRAY

3/4"

PULL-OUT SHELF

Pointers for Building

Because of the variations suggested in the project, a hard-and-fast construction procedure is impossible. However, the cabinet itself can be built about the same in any case.

Make three 24″ x 24″ frames of 1″ x 3″ (nom.) material—for use under the two pull-out shelves and the drawer. Make another frame of 1″ x 2″ (nom.) stock for use just under the counter. Notch the front corners of this frame ¾″ x ¾″ to inset the vertical facing strips. Attach these horizontal frames between vertical side frames made of 1″ x 2″ (nom.) stock. Install 1″ x 2″ (nom.) strips on the side frames as guides for the drawer and the sliding shelves.

As shown, the cabinet sides can be enclosed with ¾″ material. The counter and vertical facing strips overhang for that reason. However, the cabinet probably will be located between others. In that case no partitions will be needed.

Two slide possibilities are shown. It is sometimes possible to buy suitable metal slides, originally intended for pull-out record players. Accordingly, you may find them at an establishment dealing in the components for home assembly of such musical instruments.

For the wood slides, smooth the sliding surface with extra care. Use progressively finer paper and wind up if possible with the finest steel wool. Allow clearance when making the assembly, but not too much or the shelf will twist and bind in the groove.

WIRE VEGETABLE BIN

This makes use of a ready-made wire basket—an accessory storage container such as sold by Sears Roebuck and others for home freezers. The mesh is small enough to hold all except the smallest fruits and vegetables. An overall length of 22¾″ makes the basket exactly right for installation behind a door in cabinets that have a 25″ work counter with a 1″ overhang. Close fitting would also put the basket into a cabinet that is 1″ less from front to back. A 12″ opening in the cabinet front will take the basket and a suitable mounting frame.

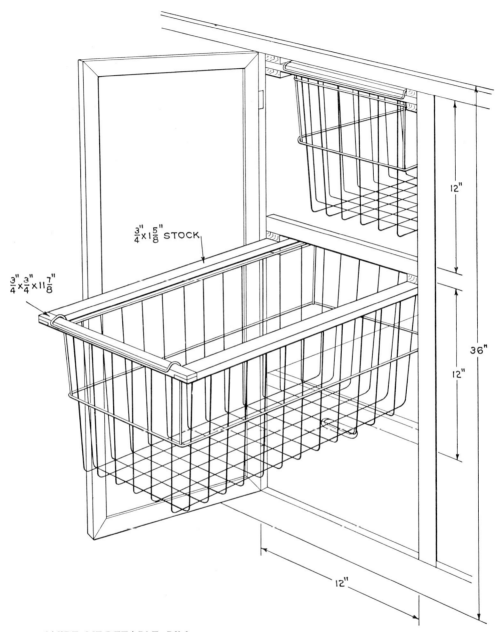

WIRE VEGETABLE BIN

Since the basket is 9″ deep, you can easily stack in two plus a conventional drawer. Three would go into a standard cabinet 36″ high, if your household needs this much vegetable and fruit storage.

The drawing suggests one way of mounting the baskets so they will slide out for easy access. A rectangular wood frame is fitted around the basket and the frame slides in parallel guides screwed to the sides of the cabinet or cabinet frame. Hardwood is best for such a sliding assembly. Sand the sliding members mirror-smooth and apply a hard wax. As shown, the basket simply sits in the frame. If she wishes, the housewife can lift it out. A stop to limit the outward travel of the basket should be installed.

A door with a panel of masonite peg board will provide ventilation for the stored supplies.

SWINGING BIN CABINET

Uses

You'll never find a much easier way of keeping vegetables and fruit within reach than these swinging bins. You can buy such bins from some building supply dealers or, if they are hard to find, you can make them or have them made. Despite the space the bins take, there's still room at the back of the shelves to store a lot of other supplies.

Materials

1″ x 2″ (nom.) stock (26 linear feet) — framing.

1″ x 4″ (nom.) stock (8 linear feet)— base.

¾″ plywood (4′ x 5′ panel) to make—

   1 pc. 20″ x 25″ — top.

   2 pc. 23¼″ x 31¼″ — sides.

   2 pc. 14$\frac{1}{16}$″ x 17″ — doors.

⅜″ plywood (2′ x 4′ panel) to make—

   1 pc. 18½″ x 24″ — middle shelf.

   1 pc. 18½″ x 23¼″ — bottom shelf.

¼″ x 20″ x 31⅝″ plywood or hardboard — back (optional).

1 16$\frac{11}{16}$″ x 22″ breadboard, or hardwood to make same.

SWINGING BIN CABINET

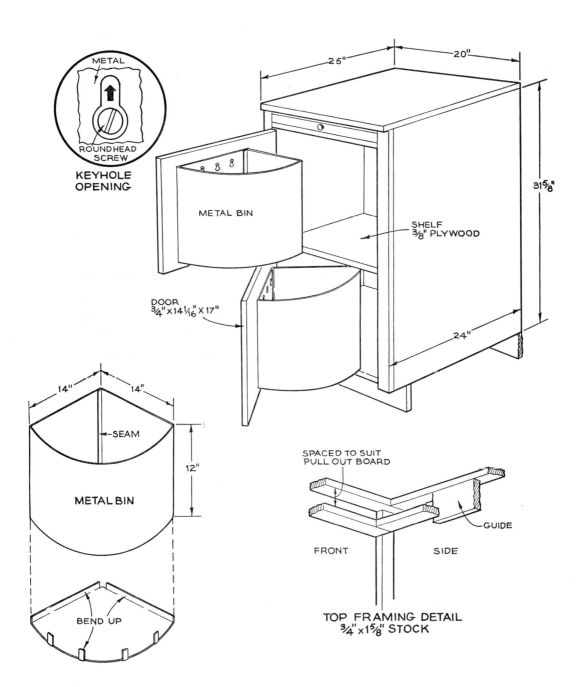

METAL

ROUNDHEAD
SCREW

**KEYHOLE
OPENING**

25"   20"

31⅝"

METAL BIN

SHELF
⅜" PLYWOOD

DOOR
¾"×14¹⁄₁₆"×17"

24"

14"   14"

SEAM

12"

METAL BIN

BEND UP

SPACED TO SUIT
PULL OUT BOARD

GUIDE

FRONT   SIDE

TOP FRAMING DETAIL
¾"×1⅝" STOCK

Pointers for Building

Make the top frame of 1″ x 2″ stock placed flat as shown in the detail. Below this, spacing to allow clearance for the pull-out board, mount a second frame, this one with the side members each moved inward 1⅝″—the width of the stock. These then will support the pull-out board. Under the top frame and butting against the edge of the side member below, place another strip of the framing stock to act as a guide. Do this on both sides.

Fit the stops into the under side of the pull-out board as shown in previous cabinets and install it in the same way. Locate the middle shelf at the proper height to serve as a stop for the top door.

If you can't buy suitable bins, you can make each one from two pieces of easily worked sheet metal as suggested in the drawing. Solder the seams. If you wish, the bottom of the bins might be made from wood.

In some kitchens it will be more convenient to have the cabinet doors hinged on the opposite edge. When that is the case, the keyhole mounts should be placed in the opposite edge of the bin.

TRAY AND BREAD CABINET

Uses

This combination unit could of course be separated and the two parts used in different parts of the kitchen. It is economical of material and effort, however, to put two such units into one. The stand-up rack holds trays neatly on end, making it easy to select the one you want. Keeping bread and pastries fresh no longer requires a container out in the open. The sketches suggest three things you can do to hide them. Building supply dealers, hardware stores, and mail-order houses can furnish insertable metal boxes to fit drawers of various depths, some with sliding tops, others with lift-up lids. Two sketches show how to use these types. A third indicates how you can adapt a deep drawer to a conventional shelf-type bread box. Cutting out or leaving off one side of the drawer will let the housewife keep the box endwise and open it from the side of the drawer. Such a box could also be kept on just a simple pull-out shelf.

Materials

1″ x 4″ (nom.) stock (12 linear feet) — base.

1″ x 2″ (nom.) stock (24 linear feet) — framing.

¾″ plywood (4′ x 8′ and 3′ x 4′ panels) to make—

    1 pc. 25″ x 33½″ — top.   2 pc. 23″ x 35¼″ — sides.

    1 pc. 14⅞″ x 30″ — door.

    2 pc. 15¾″ x 23″ — rack top and floor.

    2 pc. 13¾″ x 14¼″ — drawer fronts (or to suit).

¼″ plywood (4′ x 8′ and 3′ x 4′ panels) to make—

    1 pc. 33½″ x 35¼″ — back (optional).

    4 pc. 23″ x 30⅜″ — dividers.

    2 pc. 13″ x 22″ — drawer bottoms.

    2 pc. 13¾″ x 14¼″ — drawer backs.

2 pc. ⅝″ plywood 14¼″ x 22″ — drawer sides.

Insertable metal bread boxes.

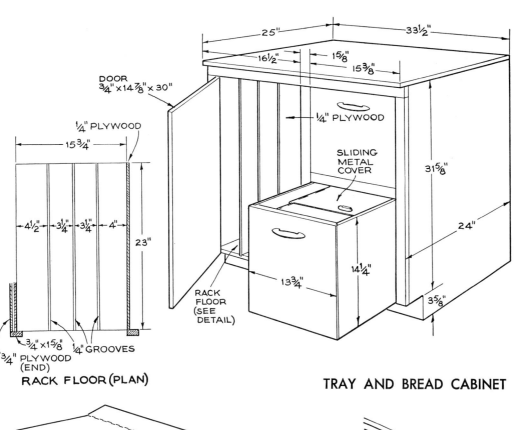

DOOR
3/4" x 14 7/8" x 30"

1/4" PLYWOOD

15 3/4"

4 1/2" 3 1/4" 3 1/4" 4"

23"

3/4" x 15/8"   1/4" GROOVES

3/4" PLYWOOD
(END)

RACK FLOOR (PLAN)

25"   33 1/2"

16 1/2"   15/8"
15 3/8"

1/4" PLYWOOD

SLIDING
METAL
COVER

31 5/8"

24"

14 1/4"

13 3/4"

RACK
FLOOR
(SEE
DETAIL)

3 5/8"

TRAY AND BREAD CABINET

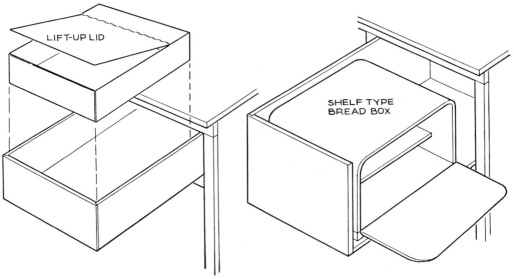

LIFT-UP LID

SHELF TYPE
BREAD BOX

Pointers for Building

Cut three $\frac{1}{4}''$ x $\frac{1}{4}''$ grooves lengthwise in the two $15\frac{3}{4}''$ x $23''$ pieces of $\frac{3}{4}''$ plywood that will support the tray rack partitions. Install one as the base of the cabinet. Attach the other under the counter with the dadoes facing downward. Glue the $\frac{1}{4}''$ partitions in place. One goes against the edge to separate the tray rack from the bread cabinet.

Adjust the size of the drawers you build to the bread box or boxes you intend to use. Make the boxes an easy fit so they can be removed from the drawers for cleaning.

FOOD PREPARATION BASE CABINET

Uses

The original of this base cabinet forms part of a food preparation and clearing center designed and tested by kitchen specialists in the U.S. Department of Agriculture. The complete center, shown in the accompanying sketch, consists of two base cabinets, two wall cabinets, and a sink cabinet. The center was designed to provide adequate work surfaces for food preparation and dishwashing, storage space for supplies and equipment for these jobs, and storage of everyday dishes.

Building plans for the sink cabinet and the right-hand wall cabinet have been presented earlier, the sink as the "Simple Sink Cabinet" in the chapter devoted to such units and the wall cabinet as the "Combination Wall Cabinet" in the wall cabinet chapter. (The opposite wall cabinet, designed for everyday dishes, can be a duplicate of the one for which plans are given.) Building plans for the base cabinet to the left of the sink are presented as the "Utensil Cabinet" that immediately follows. In the original kitchen, the short wall cabinets seen near the ceiling in the accompanying sketch, were used

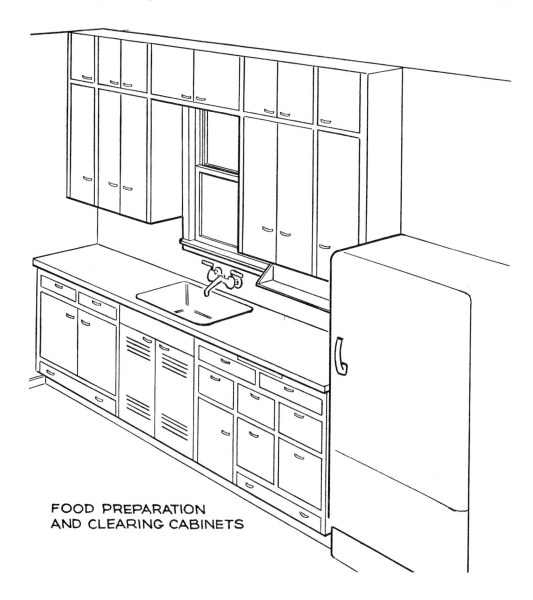

FOOD PREPARATION
AND CLEARING CABINETS

for storage of seldom-used items since they are located higher than a woman's normal reach.

Combined with the "Combination Wall Cabinet" and the simple spice rack shown, the food preparation base cabinet concentrates a sizable part of the housewife's work into one step-saving area. The two metal-lined drawers were designed originally for storage of sugar and flour. Experience showed, however, that these two household commodities are seldom stored in such quantity. Hence the builder should consider the requirements of the particular household before installing the metal drawer inserts.

A handy feature of the cabinet is the pull-out board with self-locking stop that provides a surface slightly lower than the 36-inch counter for rolling, kneading, or mixing. The food grinder can also be clamped here. Tapping the stop with the fingers lets the board slip back into the cabinet.

Materials

FRAMING:

1″ x 2″ (nom.) stock (64 linear feet)
1″ x 3″ (nom.) stock (16 linear feet)

BASE:

1″ x 4″ (nom.) stock (12 linear feet)
¾″ plywood (4′ x 8′ panel and 4′ x 4′ panel) to make—
    2 pc. 23″ x 35″ — ends.
    1 pc. 23¾″ x 25½″ — drawer support.
    1 pc. 23¾″ x 40½″ — bottom.
    1 pc. 14¼″ x 18″ — shelf.
    1 pc. 23¾″ x 23⅞″ — vertical divider.
    1 pc. 5¼″ x 23¾″ — pull-out board support.
    1 pc. 13½″ x 16⅛″ — door.
    1 pc. 25″ x 42″ — counter top.
    1 pc. 7″ x 13⅜″ (A) ⎫
    1 pc. 7″ x 12″ (B)   ⎬
    1 pc. 7″ x 11⅞″ (C) ⎬
    2 pc. 4⅜″ x 19″ (D) ⎬ drawer fronts.
    1 pc. 11⅜″ x 12″ (E) ⎬
    1 pc. 11⅜″ x 11⅞″ (F) ⎬
    1 pc. 4″ x 24⅝″ (G) ⎭
½″ plywood (4′ x 8′) — drawer sides and backs.

$\frac{1}{4}''$ plywood (4' x 8' panel) to make—

1 pc. 13" x 23$\frac{3}{8}$" }
4 pc. 11$\frac{1}{2}$" x 23$\frac{3}{8}$" }
1 pc. 23$\frac{3}{8}$" x 24$\frac{1}{4}$" } drawer bottoms.
2 pc. 18$\frac{5}{8}$" x 23$\frac{3}{8}$" }

4 pc. 8" x 22$\frac{3}{4}$" — adjustable partitions (drawer E).

1 pc. 5" x 5$\frac{1}{2}$" }
1 pc. 5" x 22$\frac{1}{4}$" } dividers (drawer B).

2 pc. 2" x 14$\frac{3}{4}$" }
1 pc. 2" x 14$\frac{3}{8}$" }
1 pc. 2" x 17$\frac{1}{2}$" } dividers (drawer D).
1 pc. 2" x 18$\frac{1}{8}$" }

1 maple breadboard 1$\frac{1}{16}$" x 14" x 23".

2 pc. $\frac{1}{4}$" x 3" x 4" hardwood — board stops.

$\frac{3}{4}$" cove, metal counter edging, linoleum.

4 pc. $\frac{1}{4}$" x 1$\frac{1}{4}$" dowel — shelf pegs.

1 pr. 1$\frac{1}{2}$" x 1$\frac{1}{2}$" hinges.

1 door pull.

1 cabinet catch.

8 drawer pulls.

$\frac{1}{4}$" No. 8 wood screws.

$\frac{3}{4}$" No. 4 wood screws.

25 sq. ft. galvanized iron (28 ga.) or tin (10 lb.).

Pointers for Building

The frame consists of glued units assembled with screws, dowels, or metal braces. All individual framing units, as well as the supporting plywood ends, should be completed before you begin assembly. In addition to a frame for the counter top and pull-out board, four separate frame units below support the drawers and a vertical one serves as a separator and support.

Rather than make the pull-out board, the builder may prefer to buy one ready-made. Either the board itself can be cut down to the dimensions indicated or the recess in the counter top framing altered

102

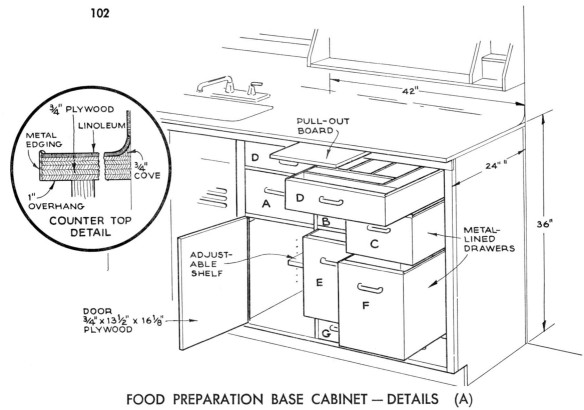

FOOD PREPARATION BASE CABINET — DETAILS (A)

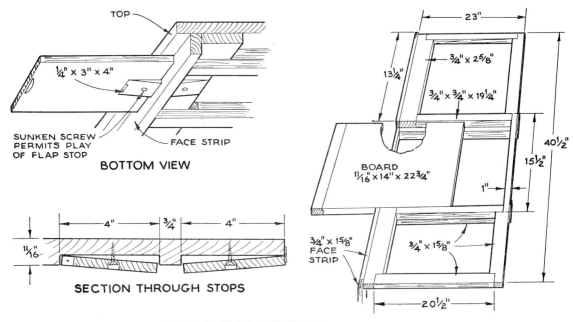

BOTTOM VIEW

SECTION THROUGH STOPS

PULL-OUT BOARD DETAIL

FOOD PREPARATION BASE CABINET — DETAILS (B)

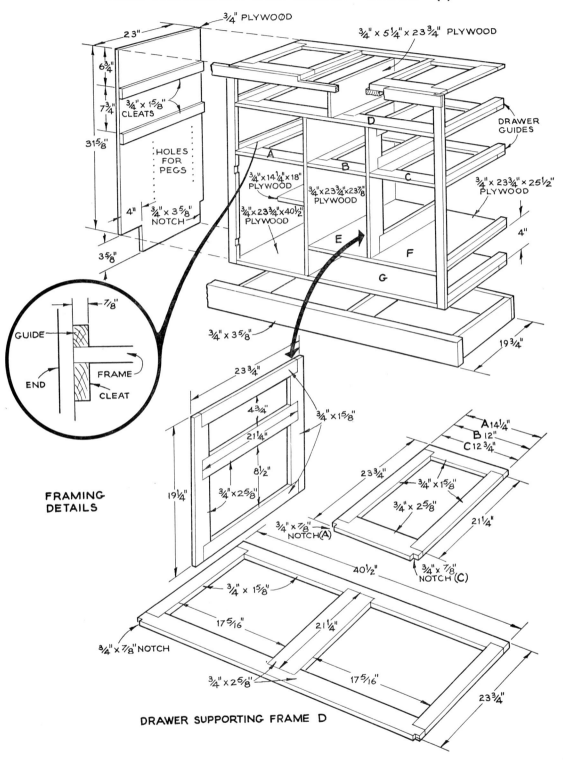

3/4" PLYWOOD

23"

6 3/4"

7 3/4"

3/4" x 1 5/8" CLEATS

31 5/8"

HOLES FOR PEGS

4"   3/4" x 3 5/8" NOTCH

3 5/8"

3/4" x 5 1/4" x 23 3/4" PLYWOOD

D

A

B

C

DRAWER GUIDES

3/4" x 14 1/4" x 18" PLYWOOD

3/4" x 23 3/4" x 23 7/8" PLYWOOD

3/4" x 23 3/4" x 40 1/2" PLYWOOD

3/4" x 23 3/4" x 25 1/2" PLYWOOD

E

F

G

3/4" x 3 5/8"

4"

19 3/4"

GUIDE

END

7/8"

FRAME

CLEAT

FRAMING DETAILS

23 3/4"

4 3/4"

21 1/4"

8 1/2"

3/4" x 1 5/8"

3/4" x 2 5/8"

19 1/4"

3/4" x 7/8" NOTCH (A)

A 14 1/4"
B 12"
C 12 3/4"

23 3/4"

3/4" x 1 5/8"

3/4" x 2 5/8"

21 1/4"

40 1/2"

3/4" x 7/8" NOTCH (C)

3/4" x 1 5/8"

3/4" x 7/8" NOTCH

3/4" x 2 5/8"

17 5/16"   21 1/4"

17 5/16"

23 3/4"

DRAWER SUPPORTING FRAME D

to suit. In either case, keep the $\frac{1}{16}''$ difference (clearance) between the thickness of the board ($1\frac{1}{16}''$) and the depth of the recess ($\frac{3}{4}''$) to assure proper operation. The stops under the board must work easily so that gravity will cause them to drop. As the drawing shows, the rear stop limits the position to which the board can be pulled out. The front one, pressed into its slot while the board is being withdrawn, automatically drops and locks the board. Pressing up this stop releases the board so it can be shoved in.

All framing units except the top one measure $23\frac{3}{4}''$ fore and aft, the top one and the two ends $23''$. The $\frac{3}{4}''$ difference allows the others to come out flush with the facing strips. Notches $\frac{3}{4}''$ x $\frac{7}{8}''$ are cut as indicated on the front corners to permit this. You should note, however, that the vertical framing unit and horizontal unit B do not require notches.

Bore pairs of $\frac{1}{4}''$ blind holes evenly spaced on the inside face of the left end to support the adjustable shelf. Corresponding holes also go on the $23\frac{3}{4}''$ by $23\frac{7}{8}''$ plywood framing member. A $\frac{3}{4}''$ by $3\frac{5}{8}''$ notch in the rear bottom corner of this end is needed to slip over the rear base member if the cabinet units continue to the left as suggested in the drawings. The right end fits over and hides the base. Drawer guides are needed at the ends of the cabinet to fill out the space behind the framing strips. For possible arrangement of the $\frac{1}{4}''$ dividers in the pair of top drawers, see the plan for the base cabinet that immediately follows this one. These drawers are $4\frac{3}{8}''$ deep, $19''$ wide, and $23\frac{3}{4}''$ long.

Since it would be difficult to make the metal boxes that fit into drawers C and F without a tinsmith's bending brake, the job is a good one for farming out to a shop that has the equipment. The upper lips of the guides for the sliding tops require two bends along the long edges of the boxes. A strip $\frac{3}{8}''$ wide is first bent back flat to make the upper part of the guide for the sliding top. Next, a 45-degree bend is made along the inside line thus formed. Then at a distance $\frac{3}{8}''$ below this corner, solder an L-shaped bottom guide similarly formed from a strip $1\frac{1}{8}''$ wide. The edges of the sliding top should be rolled to move easily within the guides.

To avoid a dust and dirt collecting corner, use a $\frac{3}{4}''$ cove at the rear of the counter and run linoleum or other covering up the wall to the wall cabinets or finish off its upper edge with metal molding.

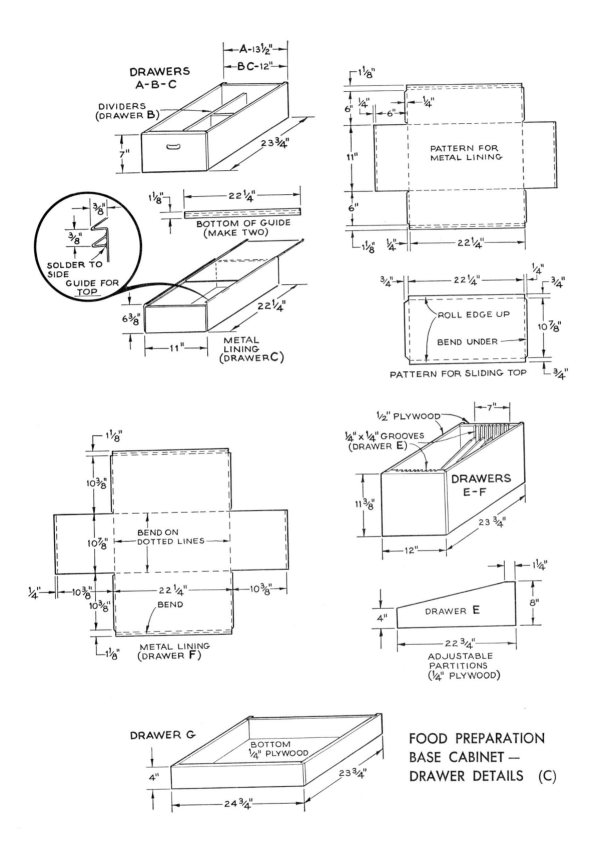

DRAWERS
A-B-C

A-13½"
BC-12"

DIVIDERS
(DRAWER B)

7"

23¾"

SOLDER TO
SIDE
GUIDE FOR
TOP

⅜"
⅜"

1⅛"

22¼"

BOTTOM OF GUIDE
(MAKE TWO)

6⅜"

22¼"

11"

METAL
LINING
(DRAWER C)

1⅛"

6" ¼"
¼"
6"

11"

6"

PATTERN FOR
METAL LINING

1⅛" ¼"
22¼"

¾" 22¼" ¼"
¾"

ROLL EDGE UP

BEND UNDER

10⅞"

PATTERN FOR SLIDING TOP ¾"

1⅛"

10⅜"

10⅞"

BEND ON
DOTTED LINES

¼" 10⅜" 22¼" 10⅜"

10⅜"

BEND

1⅛"

METAL LINING
(DRAWER F)

½" PLYWOOD

¼" x ¼" GROOVES
(DRAWER E)

7"

DRAWERS
E-F

11⅜"

23¾"

12"

1¼"

4"

DRAWER E

8"

22¾"

ADJUSTABLE
PARTITIONS
(¼" PLYWOOD)

DRAWER G

BOTTOM
¼" PLYWOOD

4"

23¾"

24¾"

FOOD PREPARATION
BASE CABINET —
DRAWER DETAILS (C)

UTENSIL CABINET

Uses

The space behind the two doors will hold the largest cooking utensils. The adjustable shelf, only 18″ wide, makes it possible to use the space to best advantage. The fact that the shelf is narrow enables the housewife to see and reach articles stored on the bottom of the cupboard.

Kitchen textiles, place mats, and the like can be kept in the shallow bottom drawer. Silver, serving spoons, and dish towels and cloths can go in the upper drawers. The plans show four possible arrangements of dividers for these drawers. One or more of these divider plans can also be used in the corresponding drawers of the food preparation cabinet.

Materials

FRAMING:

1″ x 2″ (nom.) stock (46 linear feet).

1″ x 3″ (nom.) stock (12 linear feet).

1″ x 4″ (nom.) stock (12 linear feet).

1″ x 5″ (nom.) stock (6 linear feet).

¾″ plywood (4′ x 8′ panel, 2′ x 4′ panel) to make—

   2 pc. 23″ x 35″ — ends.

   1 pc. 23¾″ x 40½″ — fixed shelf.

   1 pc. 18″ x 40½″ — adjustable shelf.

   2 pc. 19⅛″ x 19⅜″ — doors.

   1 pc. 25″ x 42″ — counter top.

   2 pc. 4⅜″ x 19″ — drawer fronts.

   1 pc. 4″ x 38¾″ — drawer front.

½″ plywood (4′ x 4′ panel) — drawer sides and back.

¼″ plywood (4′ x 4′ panel) to make—

   1 pc. 22½″ x 38¼″ ⎫
                     ⎬ drawer bottoms.
   2 pc. 18½″ x 22½″ ⎭

Drawer partitions as desired.

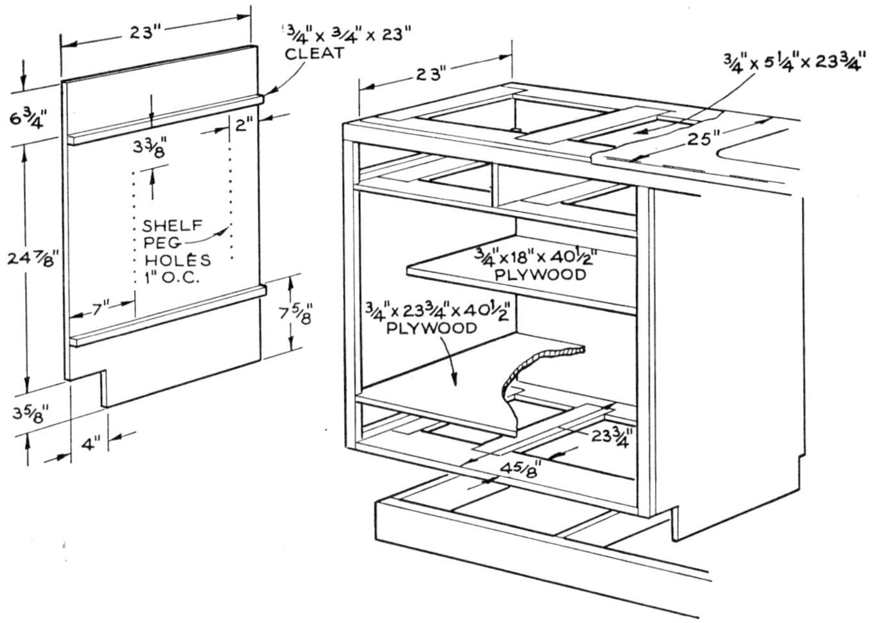
23"
3/4" x 3/4" x 23"
CLEAT
6 3/4"
2"
3 3/8"
SHELF
PEG
HOLES
1" O.C.
24 7/8"
7"
7 5/8"
3 5/8"
4"
23"
3/4" x 5 1/4" x 23 3/4"
25"
3/4" x 18" x 40 1/2"
PLYWOOD
3/4" x 23 3/4" x 40 1/2"
PLYWOOD
23 3/4"
4 5/8"

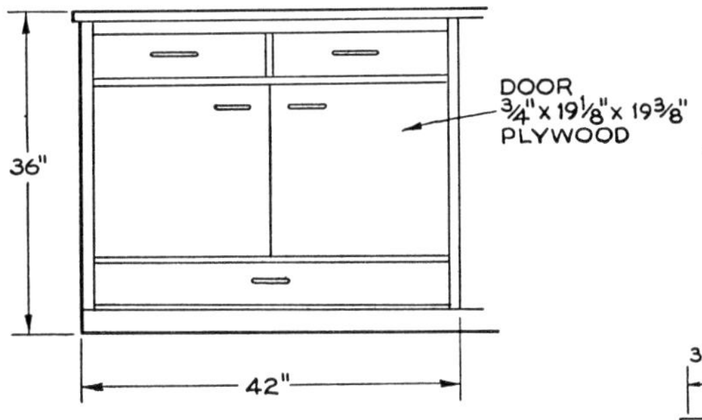
36"
DOOR
3/4" x 19 1/8" x 19 3/8"
PLYWOOD
42"

TOP DRAWER

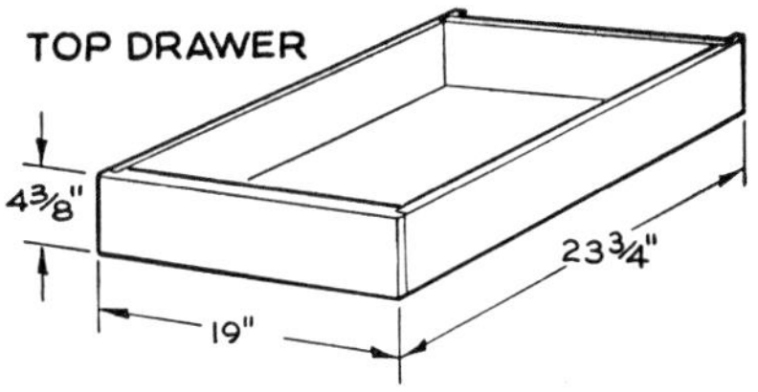
4 3/8"
23 3/4"
19"

UTENSIL CABINET

BOTTOM DRAWER

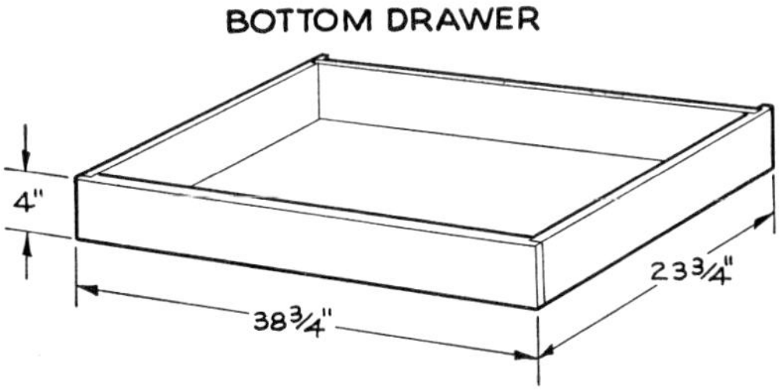
4"
23 3/4"
38 3/4"

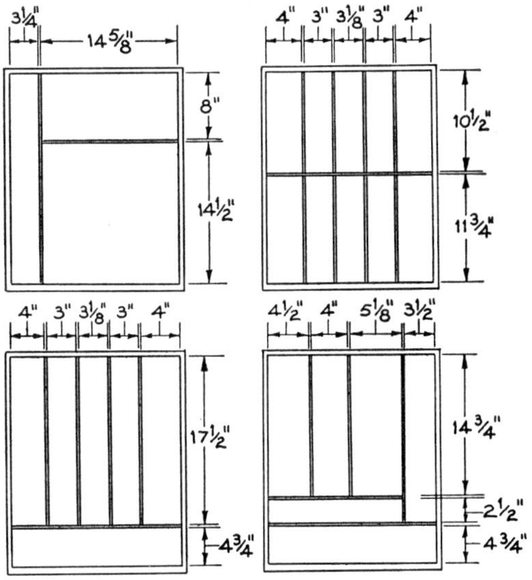
3 1/4"
14 5/8"
8"
14 1/2"
4" 3" 3 1/8" 3" 4"
10 1/2"
11 3/4"
4" 3" 3 1/8" 3" 4"
17 1/2"
4 3/4"
4 1/2" 4" 5 1/8" 3 1/2"
14 3/4"
2 1/2"
4 3/4"

DRAWER ARRANGEMENTS

Pointers for Building

The three supporting frames are built like those used in the food preparation cabinet. The overall length of each frame is 40½". The overall width of the top one is 23", the two below 23¾". Notches are cut in the front corners of the two wider frames, as well as the wide plywood shelf, to fit around the vertical facing strips. Use 1" x 2" (nom.) stock for the back and end members of the frames; 1" x 3" (nom.) stock for the front member and middle brace. In the bottom frame, however, 5" stock is needed to serve as the ceiling of the cabinet toe space.

Support the middle frame and fixed shelf on cleats cut from 1" x 2" stock. Above the two lower frames install drawer guides at each end of the cabinet. Use strips of ¼" plywood 2" wide for the drawer dividers.

SERVING CABINET

Uses

Located beside the range, this cabinet offers counter space for dishing up a meal, and the drawer and shelves below provide storage for utensils and equipment used in the job of cooking it. The shelves are adjustable to permit best use of the space.

Materials

1″ x 2″ (nom.) stock (14 linear feet) ⎱ framing.
1″ x 4″ (nom.) stock (12 linear feet) ⎰

¾″ plywood (4′ x 8′ panel) to make—

    2 pc. 23″ x 35″ — ends.

    2 pc. 10⅜″ x 24¼″ — doors.

    1 pc. 24″ x 25″ — counter.

    1 pc. 18″ x 22½″ — shelf.

    1 pc. 20″ x 22½″ — shelf.

    1 pc. 22½″ x 23″ — bottom.

    1 pc. 5″ x 20¾″ — drawer front.

½″ plywood (16″ x 24″ sheet) — drawer sides and back.

¼″ plywood (3′ x 4′ panel) to make—

    1 pc. 24″ x 35¼″ — back.

    1 pc. 20½″ x 23¼″ — drawer bottom.

8 pc. ¼″ x 1¼″ dowels — shelf pegs.

2 pr. 1½″ x 1½″ hinges.

2 door pulls.

1 drawer pull.

2 cabinet catches.

½ lb. 4d finishing nails.

1½ lb. 6d finishing nails.

1 doz. 1½″ No. 8 wood screws.

1 doz. 1¼″ No. 4 wood screws.

SERVING CABINET

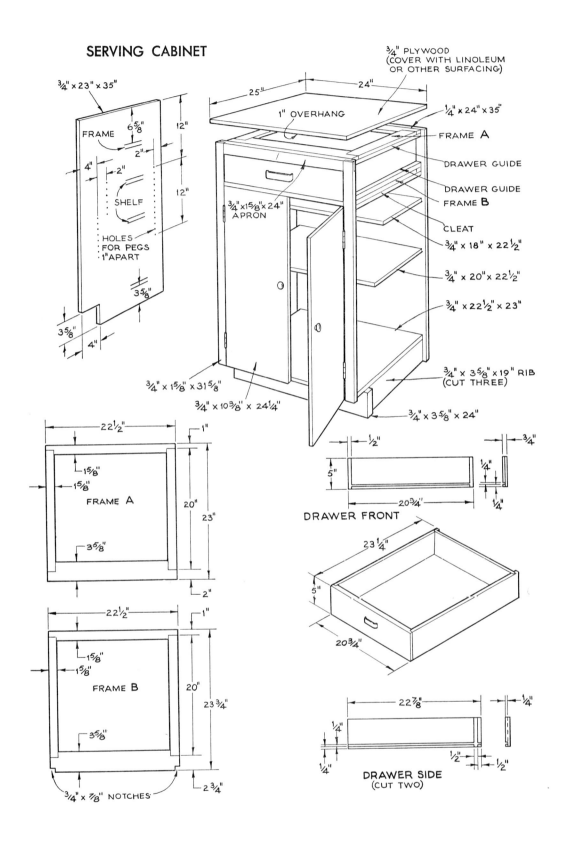

¾" × 23" × 35"

FRAME

6⅝"

12"

2"

4"

2"

SHELF

12"

HOLES
FOR PEGS
1" APART

3⅝"

3⅝"

4"

¾" PLYWOOD
(COVER WITH LINOLEUM
OR OTHER SURFACING)

25"

24"

1" OVERHANG

¼" × 24" × 35"

FRAME A

DRAWER GUIDE

DRAWER GUIDE

FRAME B

CLEAT

¾" × 18" × 22½"

¾" × 20" × 22½"

¾" × 22½" × 23"

¾" × 1⅝" × 24"
APRON

¾" × 3⅝" × 19" RIB
(CUT THREE)

¾" × 1⅝" × 31⅝"

¾" × 10⅜" × 24¼"

¾" × 3⅝" × 24"

FRAME A

22½"

1"

1⅝"

1⅝"

20"

23"

3⅝"

2"

FRAME B

22½"

1"

1⅝"

1⅝"

20"

23¾"

3⅝"

¾" × ⅞" NOTCHES

2¾"

DRAWER FRONT

½"

5"

¾"

¼"

¼"

20¾"

23¼"

5"

20¾"

DRAWER SIDE
(CUT TWO)

22⅞"

¼"

¼"

¼"

½"

½"

Pointers for Building

In construction procedure, this cabinet is a mate to the two just preceding. First, cut and assemble the two frames, Details A and B, using 1″ x 2″ and 1″ x 4″ (nom.) stock. Also cut a piece of ¾″ plywood to the same outer dimensions as Frame A. This is the bottom or floor of the cupboard.

Next, cut the two end pieces of ¾″ plywood and make matching layouts on each one for positioning the frames, floor, and shelf-supporting pegs. Complete the base, using 1″ x 4″ pine, put on the floor, and make a trial assembly of the main parts of the cabinet. Note that one end of the cabinet was omitted in the drawing so that inside parts could be shown. Here, as in many other cabinets described in this book, the vertical facing strips of 1″ x 2″ stock hide the forward edge of the ¾″ plywood ends and also serve for mounting the doors.

LAPBOARD CABINET

Uses

Kitchen authorities now urge the housewife to work sitting down when possible. A lapboard approximately 25″ from the floor, just high enough for working comfort while seated in a kitchen chair, will help her follow this advice. Seated relaxed with a good back rest and her feet flat on the floor, she can put the lapboard to excellent use in such long and tiresome jobs as making sandwiches, shelling peas and lima beans, paring apples, or preparing food for canning or freezing. Food supplies and utensils needed for a particular job can be placed on the counter above where they will be within easy reach.

The top of this cabinet is the work counter for the efficient mixing center in the step-saving U-kitchen developed by home economics experts in the United States Department of Agriculture. Besides the pull-out lapboard, the cabinet has two pull-out cutting boards just under the counter. The smaller board makes a sturdy base for attaching a food grinder. It also is handy for chopping small quantities of vegetables. The larger one can be used for larger quantities of food.

Below the two top pull-out boards are three drawers—one just deep enough for spoons, spatulas, and other mixing tools; a slightly deeper one for such things as a hand egg beater, can opener, and graters; and a deep drawer for refrigerator dishes and covers.

Below the lapboard are two tiers of drawers, with two drawers in each tier. The top one at the left might be devoted to such things as children's lunch-basket supplies and picnic things, the bottom one for seldom-used odds and ends of equipment that most kitchens include. At the top at the right, the housewife might keep her recipe books and cards. The dividers in the drawer below are for filing large, seldom-used baking utensils.

Materials

1″ x 4″ (nom.) stock (14 linear feet) — base.

1″ x 3″ (nom.) stock (20 linear feet) — frame, drawer guides.

1″ x 2″ (nom.) stock (78 linear feet) — frame, drawer guides, face strips.

¾″ plywood (4′ x 8′ panel) to make—

  2 pc. 23″ x 35″ — ends.

  1 pc. 25″ x 31¾″ — counter.

  1 pc. 22½″ x 28½″ — lapboard.

  2 pc. 11½″ x 13⅞″ (or 1″ x 12″ (nom.) stock) — drawer fronts.

  2 pc. 7⅝″ x 13⅞″ (or 1″ x 8″ (nom.) stock) — drawer fronts.

  1 pc. 7¼″ x 13⅞″ — drawer front.

  1 pc. 4⅝″ x 13⅞″ (or 1″ x 5″ (nom.) stock) — drawer front.

  1 pc. 2⅝″ x 13⅞″ (or 1″ x 3″ (nom.) stock) — drawer front.

½″ plywood (4′ x 8′ panel) — drawer sides and backs.

¼″ plywood (4′ x 5′ panel) to make—

  7 pc. 12⅜″ x 22″ drawer bottoms.

⅛″ material for drawer dividers.

1 10¼″ x 23¼″ breadboard.

1 18¼″ x 23¼″ breadboard.

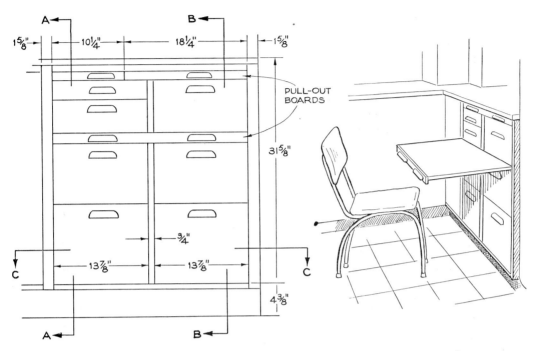

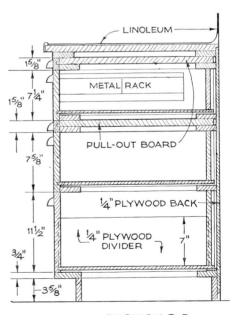

LAPBOARD CABINET (A)

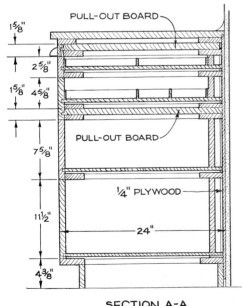

SECTION A-A

SECTION B-B

Pointers for Building

Supporting frames built of 1″ x 2″ and 1″ x 3″ stock are required. These can be similar to those in the food preparation base cabinet drawings presented previously in this chapter. Use the narrow stock where possible. But as a rule, the 1″ x 3″ material should be selected as the front frame member and as the center crosspiece (front to back) when the frame is the full width of the cabinet. An exception is the frame supporting the bottom drawers. Here the front member must be at least 1″ x 4″ nominal (3⅝″ actual) so you will have a closure at the top of the cabinet toe space. You will need five frames the full width of the cabinet, two sandwiching the upper pull-out boards, two sandwiching the lapboard, and one under the bottom drawer. You will also need three single-drawer width frames—each 14¾″ wide. The plans provide too for two vertical frames—one 7¼″ high and the other 19¼″—to separate the two tiers of drawers.

The pull-out boards are built like others previously described. You should note that in this case, however, the wide dimensions (2⅝″) of a piece of 1″ x 3″ (nom.) stock (the front part of the supporting frame) is indicated to serve as the member on which the automatic stops engage, whereas in a detail previously shown the engagement was on the narrow (¾″) dimension of 1″ x 2″ stock.

A strip of 1″ x 2″ clear pine can be used as the face of all three pull-out boards. To do this, groove the strip for a mating tongue cut on the edge of the pull-out board. The lapboard detail drawing makes this clear. Note that the face strip drops ¾″ below the under side of the pull-out and serves as a stop when the board is shoved in. Simple dowel stops are suggested at the rear of the lapboard. These are sufficient here since no sliding pressure will be exerted.

Notice that drawer guides, cut from 1″ x 2″ stock, will be needed at both ends of the cabinet to bring out a guiding surface flush with the inner edge of the 1⅝″-wide vertical facing strip. Make drawer dividers of ⅛″ material 1¼″ wide. These dividers can be assembled as a unit and then dropped into the two shallow drawers. The plans shown are only suggestions. You may want to alter them to suit the items you intend to store. Groove the front and rear of the deep drawer at the bottom for four ¼″ removable dividers 7″ wide. One of the plan sketches suggests where to locate the dividers.

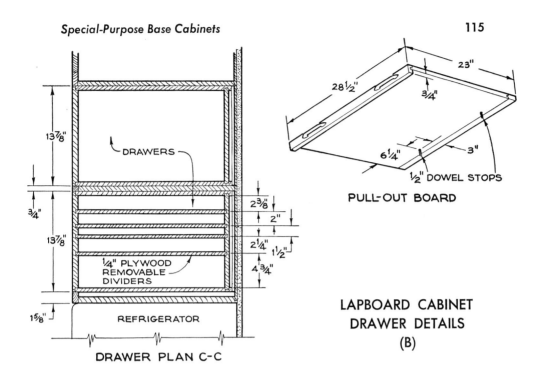

DRAWERS

$13\frac{7}{8}''$

$\frac{3}{4}''$

$13\frac{7}{8}''$

$\frac{1}{4}''$ PLYWOOD
REMOVABLE
DIVIDERS

$1\frac{5}{8}''$

REFRIGERATOR

$2\frac{3}{8}''$

$2''$

$2\frac{1}{4}''$ $1\frac{1}{2}''$

$4\frac{3}{4}''$

DRAWER PLAN C-C

$28\frac{1}{2}''$

$23''$

$\frac{3}{4}''$

$6\frac{1}{4}''$

$3''$

$\frac{1}{2}''$ DOWEL STOPS

PULL-OUT BOARD

**LAPBOARD CABINET
DRAWER DETAILS
(B)**

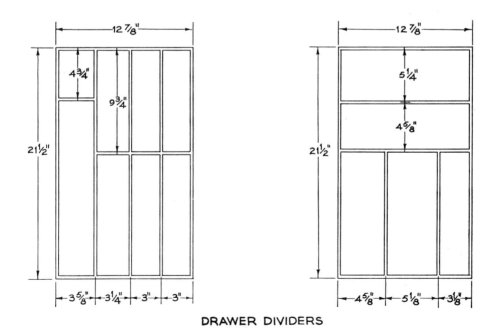

$12\frac{7}{8}''$

$4\frac{3}{4}''$

$9\frac{3}{4}''$

$21\frac{1}{2}''$

$3\frac{5}{8}''$ $3\frac{1}{4}''$ $3''$ $3''$

$12\frac{7}{8}''$

$5\frac{1}{4}''$

$4\frac{5}{8}''$

$21\frac{1}{2}''$

$4\frac{5}{8}''$ $5\frac{1}{8}''$ $3\frac{1}{8}''$

DRAWER DIVIDERS

PLATTER CABINET

Uses

In the step-saving U-kitchen designed by the Bureau of Human Nutrition and Home Economics, this cabinet adjoins the pull-out towel rack described in a later chapter and is located under the serving counter. (Sliding doors at the rear of the counter provide a pass-through opening to the dining room.) From top to bottom, the base cabinet includes a large breadboard, a drawer for small utensils used at the range (meat forks, basting spoons, potato masher, and other pieces), a metal-lined bread box big enough for four loaves and a pan or two of rolls, and a vertical file cupboard for trays, cooling racks, a turkey platter, and other large items most conveniently stored upright. The cabinet of course can be built as a separate unit and used at any desired location in the kitchen.

Materials

1″ x 2″ (nom.) stock (44 linear feet) — framing.

1″ x 4″ (nom.) stock (10 linear feet) — base.

16½″ x 22″ breadboard (or hardwood to make).

¾″ plywood (4′ x 6′ panel) to make—

    2 pc.   8¼″ x 16⅜″ — doors.

    1 pc.   7⅝″ x 16½″ (or 1″ x 8″ (nom.) stock) — drawer front.

    1 pc.   4⅝″ x 16½″ (or 1″ x 5″ (nom.) stock) — drawer front.

    2 pc. 23″ x 35″ — cabinet ends.

    1 pc. 20″ x 25″ — counter.

    1 pc. 17¼″ x 23″ — cabinet bottom.

    1 pc.   8″ x 17¼″ — backing for dividers.

½″ plywood (2′ x 4′ panel) to make—

    1 pc. 18¾″ x 35″ — cabinet back.

    7 pc. 12″ x 20½″ — dividers.

    2 pc. 16″ x 24″ — drawer bottoms.

⅛″ x 1¼″ plywood or hardboard strips (7 linear feet) — drawer dividers.

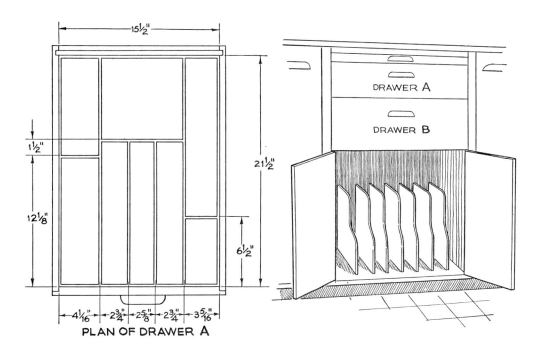

PLAN OF DRAWER A

PLATTER CABINET

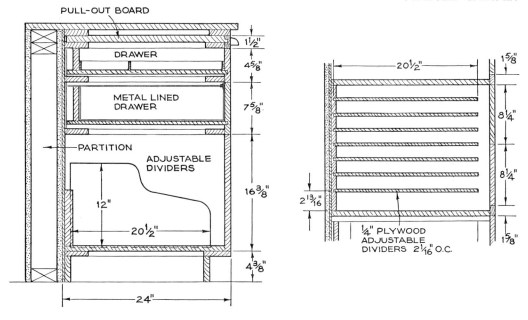

Pointers for Building

Cut the two ¾″ plywood sides for the cabinet and lay out on each the positions for the frames that will support the two drawers, the pull-out board, and the bottom of the cabinet. Cut and assemble these frames, using 1″ x 2″ stock or 1″ x 3″ if desired. Note, however, that a piece of 1″ x 4″ stock is required for the front piece of the bottom frame to enclose the toe space. Cut ¾″ x 1⅝″ notches in the front corners of this frame, as well as the counter-supporting frame at the top, to take the two 1″ x 2″ (nominal) vertical facing strips. Make the overall length of both of these frames 23¾″. Those that support the drawers and pull-out board are only 23″ long.

Build the two drawers by conventional methods, using the materials indicated. Install dividing strips ⅛″ thick in drawer A according to the plan given. The other deeper drawer (B) can be lined with metal according to procedures previously described. Or you may wish to change the dimensions to suit a box that you are able to buy ready-made. As suggested for other cabinets, you may find it most satisfactory to install a ready-made breadboard instead of assembling your own. A 1½″ strip screwed, glued or otherwise fastened to the forward edge as indicated in the drawings will provide a lip to butt against the frame in which the board slides. Install a locking stop in the board as described in previous projects. For the file compartment below, cut ¼″ grooves ¼″ deep in the bottom and backing pieces for the ¼″ plywood dividers. Space these grooves as shown in the plan.

BASE CABINET IDEAS

Basement Chute

A chute through the kitchen floor to a basement receptacle offers a convenient way of disposing of cans, bottles, papers, or laundry. You can hide the chute in a base cabinet in one of several ways.

The use to which you plan to devote it will determine what size you should make the chute in cross section. For cans, bottles, and such trash you normally could have a smaller chute than one for laundry or papers. Since the chute will not require the full cabinet depth, you will want to plan its location so as not to waste space. If a line of cabinets has access space at the end, such as at a door, a good spot for the chute might be at the rear corner adjoining the wall—behind a narrow tilt-out door in the end cabinet. A more convenient location, however, would be under the sink or immediately adjoining it. Here, the chute area might be set off from the rest of the cabinet interior by a three-wall enclosure. The space at the rear then could be utilized for storage, accessible by reaching behind the chute enclosure. The top would serve as a shelf.

A piano hinge can be used to attach a tilt-down door closing off the chute. Sideboards mounted on the inside face of such a door will allow it to serve a second function of inclined chute when opened.

Tempered hardboard would be suitable material for a chute that is square or rectangular in section, or it could be formed from aluminum sheet. In the basement, the chute could lead falling trash into a barrel, basket, or box. A collecting bag suspended on the chute is another possibility.

For disposal of cans only, you could locate a simple circular chute behind the door of the sink cabinet by cutting a hole through the kitchen floor or the cabinet floor and the kitchen floor. Insert a length of small diameter stove pipe in the hole so that the upper end is flush with the floor surface. A hinged trap door could be used to close the opening. If a chute like this is located in the kitchen floor, kitchen sweepings could be brushed down the opening.

Cabinet End Storage

Where a line of base cabinets comes to an end, perhaps at a door, you can set aside a narrow space adjoining the wall in the end cabinet for storage of large baking sheets, trays, and similar flat utensils. The depth of the drawers or cupboard shelves at the front of this cabinet of course will have to be reduced by the width devoted to the end recess. Fit a narrow door to the recess.

Curved shelves at the corner would provide a freer passageway past the end of the cabinet. The shelves might be utilized either for decorative knickknacks or such practical items as a toaster or mixer. Triangular shelves could be used too.

Laundry Hamper

The kitchen-cabinet builder can make provision in various ways for storage of soiled laundry.

A metal-lined chute behind a base-cabinet door is a big time saver if laundry is done in the basement. An entire base cabinet can also be devoted to temporary storage by hinging its door to swing downward. If a 6″ or 8″ strip of the upper end is separately hinged to the door itself, opening the strip will allow laundry to be stuffed into the cabinet. The entire door need be opened only when the laundry is to be removed on wash day.

A tilt-out hamper installed in a cabinet is one of the most favored storage devices. For a bin occupying the full base-cabinet height, curve the upper edges to a radius slightly less than the height of the front, with the bottom hinge as the pivot point. Make the front-to-back dimension about 1″ less than the cabinet depth. If the bin is made removable, the load can be carried direct to the washer. One way of doing this: Cut key-hole slots in the bin face, with the large ends down, and suspend it on roundhead screws driven part way into the rear surface of the door. A limit chain or other stop device can be used to keep the door from swinging down too far when opened.

Better than a removable bin in many ways, however, would be a laundry cart—a hamper on wheels. On all days except wash days, this can remain under the kitchen work counter, its face flush with the cabinet fronts but quickly rolled out so laundry can be put into its open top. Drawings for the utility cart in Chapter 13—Handy and Decorative Accessories, and for the rolling vegetable bin in Chapter 7 —Vertical Pull-out Racks will show the builder how to make it.

Screen-Bottom Vegetable Drawers

Stored fruits and vegetables should be well ventilated. Drawers with wire screen bottoms in a base cabinet offer one convenient way of providing ventilation. Frame and build the cabinet in the usual way. On the face just below the counter, leave an opening about 3″ wide and almost as long as the cabinet is wide. Fill this with a metal grill, or perhaps wood lattice work. Also screen a narrow opening in the ceiling of the cabinet toe space. Air entering there will sweep up through the screen bottoms of the drawers and out the upper vent. You could have either two or three drawers. Heavy, rust-resistant mesh would be best for the drawer bottoms, but ordinary copper or aluminum window screening could be used if supported by wood strips spaced at intervals across the drawer bottom.

Pop-Up Mixer Shelf

Some commercial cabinets are equipped with a spring-loaded shelf that raises an electric mixer up and forward into position for use— like the typewriter-raising mechanism in office desks. Few home builders would find it profitable to fabricate such a complicated mechanism from scratch, but if one can be bought ready-made— possibly from a dealer in kitchen cabinets or office furniture—there should be little difficulty in fitting it into a homemade cabinet. This would require about the upper two-thirds of the cabinet. A shelf or drawer could go in the space below.

Pull-Out Step Board

When the top shelves of wall cabinets are above the housewife's normal reach, pull-out step boards in the base cabinets will add to her reach. Properly installed, these are as safe as a step stool—and much more convenient. A step board can be built into a cabinet in the same manner as the pull-out lapboard and cutting boards described earlier in this chapter. Position the board above the bottom drawer— say about 12″ from the floor. For added strength, it would be best to locate the automatic stop so the step board pulls out only about 10″. Pad the step with a rubber stair tread for better footing. If wall cabinets are run to a high ceiling all around the kitchen, a line of these boards in several of the base cabinets will save a lot of step-stool carrying.

Sliding Doors

Some builders may want to install sliding doors on their base cabinets, especially where a walkway or limited space makes swinging doors impractical or inconvenient. This can be done by utilizing the same principles outlined for the sliding-door wall cabinet in the chapter on wall cabinets.

Heated Towel Dryer

There are several ways an ingenious builder might speed the drying of kitchen towels stored on rods inside a base cabinet.

For instance, why not make use of the heat source that warms the kitchen? If this is a steam or hot-water radiator, simply locating the cabinet beside it, or perhaps above, could be considered. If an unsightly old-fashioned radiator is to be hidden behind a perforated enclosure, it may be possible to combine a towel storage unit with it. If a warm-air system sends heat into the kitchen through a wall or floor register, the drying cabinet might go in front of or above the register, with a decorative grill in the cabinet door to pass the stream of heat on into the kitchen after it has passed around the towels. All such heating-source methods, of course, have a major drawback. They'll only help dry towels during the house-heating season. For all-year use, they might be combined with electrical heat that the housewife could switch on and off as desired. Such a combination would help hold down the electric bill.

Electrical units suitable for installation in a towel cabinet—a fan-heater, a hair dryer, a glass panel heater—all are likely to cost too much if devoted to towel drying alone. But this can be avoided by retaining the unit *for its original use* and merely *storing* it in the towel cabinet in a way that it can be used there, but withdrawn when desired. An ordinary cooling fan might also be put to use the same way. A pilot light mounted outside the towel cabinet will guard against forgetting that the dryer is on.

If a timer is available on the kitchen range, it might be wired into the circuit to turn off an electric heater automatically after the desired drying interval.

Aluminum-Foil Bread Box

Using household aluminum foil, you can convert a base-cabinet drawer into a bread box that offers storage protection equal to a metal box. Use the heavy foil designed for wrapping frozen foods.

If you build the drawer from scratch, you could use a separate piece of foil on the inside surface of each piece of the drawer, cutting the foil slightly larger than the drawer part and then wedging the edges into the joints when you assemble the drawer. Tape designed for use on foil will seal the joints. In the case of a finished drawer, you can cut and fold the foil to line the interior. Again seal the foil joints with tape.

Install a hinged cover on the drawer. Brad small cleats to the inner surfaces of the sides, front and back, locating them $1/2''$ below the upper edges. Cut a cover from $3/8''$ stock to fit down snugly on the cleats. Then saw the cover crosswise at a point about two-thirds of the way to the rear. Face the cover pieces with foil flapped over the edges. After hinging the two parts together, brad the rear piece permanently down on the cleats. Punch several ventilation holes through the cover and install a flat knob or other finger pull for opening the lid when the drawer has been withdrawn from the cabinet part way.

Sliding-Shelf Mixer Cabinet

A narrow-base cabinet designed just for storage of the mixer may be preferred by some home owners, the mixer being removed and used on the counter top. A compartment with an inside width of about $14''$ is sufficient for such storage. Since the mixer does not require the full cabinet depth (front to back), a sliding shelf to carry it to the rear and bring it out again easily will make it possible to install shelves on the inside of the door—and thus utilize some of the space that would be lost at the rear if the mixer were stored at the front of a stationary shelf. Locate the sliding shelf at the height where the top of the mixer will just clear the top of the door opening. Use the area below this shelf for storage of mixing bowls and related equipment.

7

Vertical Pull-Out Racks

Vertical pull-out racks in base cabinets are a comparatively new type of kitchen storage device. They take a variety of forms, each designed for a special job. They are divided into two general classes—those that slide on a raised floor in the cabinet (perhaps on rollers or special bearings) and those that have their own rubber-tired casters to roll out from under the work counter on the kitchen floor.

Sliding racks generally are of greatest value for storage of bulky lightweight materials. If heavy articles are introduced, slides with roller bearings become necessary. In this respect, it is interesting to note that some home cabinet builders have put skate wheels to excellent use. Mounted on large rubber-tired caster wheels (about 2″ diameter) the roll-out racks will move easily even with quite a heavy load.

Home economics research workers at the Oregon State College, Corvallis, Oregon, have made an extensive exploration of the possibilities of pull-out racks in the modern kitchen. Bulletin No. 482 of the Oregon Agricultural Experiment Station makes these recommendations about designing racks for specific purposes:

"Use the following method of determining the height of the available storage space: Determine the construction allowances for: (1)

distance from top of cabinet to bottom of apron, (2) top of base to floor. Add these two figures and subtract the sum from the overall height of the cabinet. This gives you the overall height of the pull-out rack. To determine the width of the available storage space, add the widths of the facing strips and subtract the sum from the overall width of the cabinet.

"Draw a sketch of the face of the cabinet and draw lines to indicate the construction allowances. After you have decided how to utilize the available storage space enter the measurements on your sketch.

"If you are planning a rack with shelves, cut pieces of paper the width and depth of the available space. Arrange your utensils and supplies and determine the number of shelves, the distances between them and the minimum overall width of the rack. Remember to allow clearances for handling contents, also thickness of materials used in the rack itself.

"If you are planning a rack for hanging utensils, cut pieces of paper the height and depth of this space and arrange the utensils with handle holes in a row at the top. After you have decided how to utilize the storage space, complete your sketch, entering dimensions and proposed use."

BESIDE-THE-RANGE TOWEL RACK

Uses

This pull-out towel rack draws heat from the range to dry tea towels placed on the four ½″ rods staggered across its width at varying heights. This is probably the best location in the kitchen for such a rack. Safety requirements are met by placing a sheet of asbestos board on the side next to the range, and holes bored in the asbestos and toe board and near the top of the front panel provide a flow of warm air to dry the towels. The rack slides out on the mating parts of a hardwood slide. A stop limits its travel, yet turns to allow the rack to be removed from the cabinet and placed beside a register or other source of heat to dry the towels faster.

Materials

1″ x 2″ (nom.) stock (18 linear feet) — framing.

1″ x 4″ (nom.) stock (4 linear feet) — base.

¾″ plywood (4′ x 4′ panel) to make—
    1 pc. 8½″ x 33½″ (or 1″ x 9″ (nom.) stock) — rack front.
    1 pc. 7⅝″ x 33½″ (or 1″ x 8″ (nom.) stock) — rack back.
    1 pc. 7⅝″ x 20¾″ (or 1″ x 8″ (nom.) stock) — rack base.
    1 pc. 24″ x 35¼″ — cabinet side.
    1 pc. 9½″ x 23″ (or 1″ x 10″ (nom.) stock) — cabinet bottom.
1 sheet ⅛″ asbestos 24″ x 35¼″.
2 pc. ¾″ x ¾″ x 19¼″ hardwood — bottom rack guides.
1 pc. ⅜″ x ⅜″ x 19″ hardwood — center rack track.
2 pc. ¾″ x 1³⁄₁₆″ x 23″ hardwood — rack slide.
4 rods ½″ x 20¾″.
2 corner blocks 1⅝″ x 1⅝″ x 7¾″.
1 pc. ½″ x ⅝″ x 21½″ — stop.
1 pc. ⅛″ x 3″ x 9¼″.

Pointers for Building

As shown, this cabinet is framed as part of the vertical filing cabinet described in the base cabinet chapter and the builder would conserve material and effort by building the two as a unit.

The top frame consists of pieces of 1″ x 2″ stock placed flat. The same material is used to form a framework on the range side to support the sheet of ⅛″ asbestos. The other side of the cabinet can be a piece of ¾″ plywood. Two vertical facing strips of 1″ x 2″ stock also are needed at the front.

If the rack is to have a smooth, trouble-free action, you must give close attention to the guides and side slide. One ¾″ x ¾″ guide goes behind the framing members on the range side. The other fills the bottom corner at the right and the rack face board butts against its end when the rack is closed. The bottom of the rack has a ⅜″ x ⅜″ groove centered through its full length underneath. By means of this groove, the rack then rides on a ⅜″ x ⅜″ hardwood single track glued to the bottom of the cabinet. One member of the side guide

BESIDE-THE-RANGE TOWEL RACK

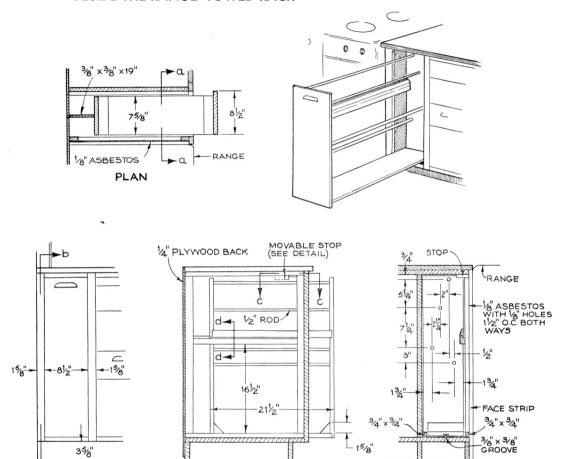

$\frac{3}{8}$" x $\frac{3}{8}$" x 19"

7$\frac{5}{8}$"

8$\frac{1}{2}$"

$\frac{1}{8}$" ASBESTOS

RANGE

PLAN

$\frac{1}{4}$" PLYWOOD BACK

MOVABLE STOP (SEE DETAIL)

$\frac{1}{2}$" ROD

16$\frac{1}{2}$"

21$\frac{1}{2}$"

1$\frac{5}{8}$"

1$\frac{5}{8}$" — 8$\frac{1}{2}$" — 1$\frac{5}{8}$"

3$\frac{5}{8}$"

SECTION b-b

$\frac{3}{4}$" STOP

RANGE

5$\frac{1}{4}$"

2"

7$\frac{1}{4}$"

2$\frac{1}{4}$"

$\frac{1}{8}$" ASBESTOS WITH $\frac{1}{8}$" HOLES 1$\frac{1}{2}$" O.C. BOTH WAYS

3"

$\frac{1}{2}$"

1$\frac{3}{4}$"

1$\frac{3}{4}$"

FACE STRIP

$\frac{3}{4}$" x $\frac{3}{4}$"

$\frac{3}{4}$" x $\frac{3}{4}$"

$\frac{3}{8}$" x $\frac{3}{8}$" GROOVE

SECTION a-a

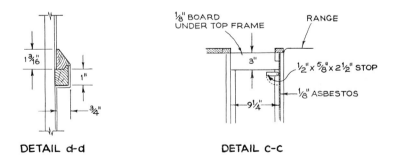

1$\frac{3}{16}$"

1"

$\frac{3}{4}$"

DETAIL d-d

$\frac{1}{8}$" BOARD UNDER TOP FRAME

RANGE

3"

$\frac{1}{2}$" x $\frac{5}{8}$" x 2$\frac{1}{2}$" STOP

$\frac{1}{8}$" ASBESTOS

9$\frac{1}{4}$"

DETAIL c-c

must overlap the other as shown in the detail sketch. If shaping this slide is beyond your capabilities or shop equipment, a shop specializing in such work can do it for you. Sand all the guide members glass smooth, apply a coating of wax, and rub it hard.

The drawings show where to locate the towel rods in the front and rear of the rack. Bore $\frac{1}{2}''$ blind holes at the points indicated and make the assembly with glue. If desired, metal or plastic rods could be used, the rack ends holding them captive when the assembly is complete. Pivot the stop so it will allow the rack to be drawn out when pushed back against the cabinet side.

RANGE RACK

Uses

The range rack is designed for storage of part of the equipment and supplies needed at the range. Lids for sauce pans can go in the slots on the bottom shelf. Frying pans, skillets, ladles, and other bulky but flat equipment go on hooks turned into the vertical storage board. Salt, pepper, sugar, and cereals that require cooking are among the staples that can be kept on the shelves.

Materials

$\frac{1}{4}''$ plywood (2' x 4' panel) to make—
    3 pc. 12" x 12" — shelf dividers.
    3 pc. $1\frac{1}{2}''$ x $22\frac{1}{4}''$ — shelf edging.
$\frac{3}{4}''$ plywood (4' x 6' panel) to make—
    1 pc. 17" x 30" — front.
    1 pc. $12\frac{1}{4}''$ x $29\frac{1}{4}''$ — back.
    1 pc. 17" x 23" — base.
    2 pc. $12\frac{1}{4}''$ x 23" — shelves.
    1 pc. 23" x $29\frac{1}{4}''$ — partition.
1" x 4" (nom.) stock 17" long — toe board.
Casters.

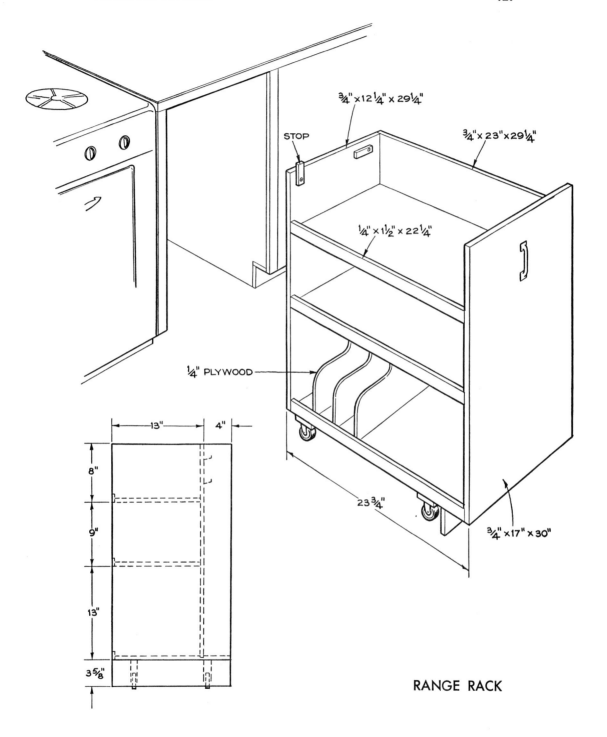

STOP

¾" × 12¼" × 29¼"

¾" × 23" × 29¼"

¼" × 1½" × 22¼"

¼" PLYWOOD

13" 4"

8"

9"

13"

3⅝"

23¾"

¾" × 17" × 30"

RANGE RACK

Pointers for Building

The counter part of a unit like the range rack is best approached as part of the job of building the adjoining cabinet or cabinets. Ends of adjoining cabinets can be enclosed with 3/4" plywood or by building frames of 1" x 2" stock and covering with 1/4" plywood or hardboard. Adjoining the range, a sheet of asbestos board may also be advisable. Build a 1" x 2" frame at the rear of the counter opening and surface this too with 1/4" material—plywood or composition board. The kitchen floor covering is carried back into the recess.

For strength, use dadoes and glue in joining the rack shelves to the ends. Butt joints secured with countersink screws and glue should do elsewhere.

Glue the 1/4" dividers into grooves cut in the base and the dividing boards. Install as many dividers as you have pan lids to store. The casters should project just far enough so there is about 1/32" clearance between the 3 5/8" toeboard and the floor. Shim the casters with wood blocks to achieve this clearance. Pivoted stops on the top of the rear upright will restrict normal outward movement of the racks by striking on the cabinet apron, yet these can be quickly turned to free the racks when this is desired.

ROLLING VEGETABLE BIN

(Drawing on page 133)

Uses

The vegetable bin has enough compartments to store current supplies of vegetables and fruit. Wire mesh bottoms in all compartments and mesh in the front provide necessary ventilation.

Rolling easily on the four large casters, the bin can be moved anywhere in the kitchen where the worker may prefer—to the sink, perhaps, or to the unloading counter where the grocery order is sorted and distributed.

Materials

1″ x 12″ (nom.) stock (10 linear feet) to make—
  2 pc. 22¾″ long — sides.
  6 pc. 10″ long — bottom bin partitions.
1″ x 5″ (nom.) stock 36″ long — top bin at front.
1″ x 4″ (nom.) stock (6 linear feet) to make—
  2 pc. 16½″ long — sides of top rear bin.
  1 pc. 8″ long — end of top rear bin.
  1 pc. 24″ long — toe board.
¾″ plywood (3′ x 4′ panel) to make—
  1 pc. 24″ x 30″ — front.
  1 pc. 22¾″ x 29″ — center partition.
Heavy wire mesh.
½″ half round or other molding.
4 ball-bearing casters (3″ wheels).

Pointers for Building

Cut a 4⅝″ x 5″ piece out of the upper corner of the 22¾″ x 29″ center partition to accommodate the shallow bin at the top front. The double rear bin is built around this center partition. Strengthen the assembly with corner blocks or corner irons. Corner blocks used in all four corners of the base will provide places to mount the casters. Staple the mesh across the bottom of all bins.

CANNED GOODS SHELVES

(Drawing on page 133)

Uses

Cans and jars of food can be placed on both sides of the centered partition of the canned goods shelves. The shelves are wide enough for the average can or jar without wasting space.

Materials

1″ x 9″ (nom.) stock (8 linear feet) to make—
  2 pc. 30″ long — front and back.
  1 pc. 21″ long — bottom.
1″ x 4″ (nom.) stock (12 linear feet) to make—
  6 pc. 21″ long — shelves.
¾″ x 21″ x 29¼″ plywood — middle partition.

Pointers for Building

There's nothing special to watch out for here. Follow the suggestions given for building similar cabinets.

PULL-OUT BOARD AND SLIDING RACK

Uses

These two units would serve practically the same purposes. Both are intended for the orderly hanging of long-handled utensils—ladles, stirring spoons, and such. In the width shown, they would also handle pans with an overall depth of less than 3″.

Materials (Pull-out Board)

1 pc. ¾″ x 22″ x 28¼″ plywood.   ½″ quarter round.

Materials (Rack)

1 pc. ¾″ x 21″ x 27″ plywood — center partition.
1″ x 8″ (nom.) stock (8 linear feet) to make—
  2 pc. 29¼″ long — front and back.   1 pc. 21″ long — bottom.

Pointers for Building

Smooth the quarter round and the bottom and top edges of the pull-out board thoroughly with sandpaper and then apply paste wax. Screw down the quarter round to the compartment floor and the top of the compartment with clearance for the board to slide smoothly.

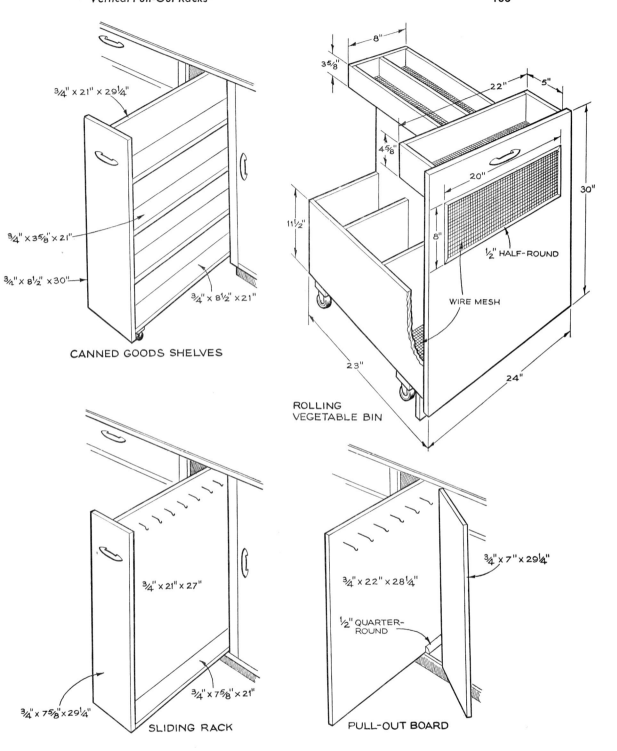

3/4" x 21" x 29 1/4"

3/4" x 3 5/8" x 21"

3/4" x 8 1/2" x 30"

3/4" x 8 1/2" x 21"

CANNED GOODS SHELVES

8"

3 5/8"

22"

5"

4 5/8"

20"

30"

11 1/2"

8"

1/2" HALF-ROUND

WIRE MESH

23"

24"

ROLLING
VEGETABLE BIN

3/4" x 21" x 27"

3/4" x 7 5/8" x 29 1/4"

3/4" x 7 5/8" x 21"

SLIDING RACK

3/4" x 22" x 28 1/4"

3/4" x 7" x 29 1/4"

1/2" QUARTER-
ROUND

PULL-OUT BOARD

SINK PULL-OUT RACKS

Uses

These two racks provide convenient and out-of-sight storage for dish towels, soaps, and washing powders. Potatoes and vegetables might also be stored in the five-inch-deep bins at the bottom of the racks. Ventilation openings help wet towels to dry.

The back ends of the racks are curved to avoid striking the pipes coming down from the sink. If you should choose to build the entire unit wider, an electric garbage-disposal unit might be mounted between the racks. The 18″ x 22″ opening in the counter can be adjusted to suit the sink you wish to use. The original installation, designed by the makers of Malarkey plywoods, has a recessed shelf built above the rear six inches or so of the counter. That explains why the cabinet is deeper (from front to back) than most others. In many cases it might be better to reduce this dimension to the usual 25″ and shorten the racks accordingly.

Materials

¾″ plywood (4′ x 8′ panel, 2′ x 4′ panel) to make—
    1 pc. 24″ x 31⅝″ — cabinet front.
    1 pc. 24″ x 31½″ — counter.
    2 pc. 29¾″ x 35¼″ — cabinet ends.
    1 pc. 22½″ x 29¾″ — cabinet floor.
⅜″ plywood (4′ x 4′ panel) to make—
    2 pc. 7¼″ x 28⅞″ — rack bottoms.
    2 pc. 23¼″ x 29¼″ — rack sides.
    2 pc. 5″ x 29¼″ — rack sides.
    2 pc. 8″ x 23¼″ — rack backs.
    1 pc. 5″ x 28⅞″ ⎱
    1 pc. 4″ x 28⅞″ ⎰ rack shelf.
    2 pc. 4″ x 5″ ⎰
1″ x 2″ (nom.) stock (34 linear feet) — frame.
1″ x 4″ (nom.) pine stock (10 linear feet) — base.
4 pc. ¾″ quarter round 22¾″ long.
4 pc. ¾″ quarter round 4½″ long.
3 towel rods.

SINK PULL-OUT RACKS

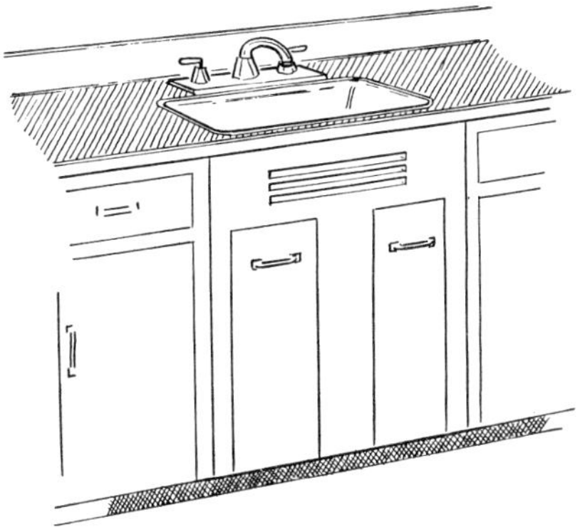

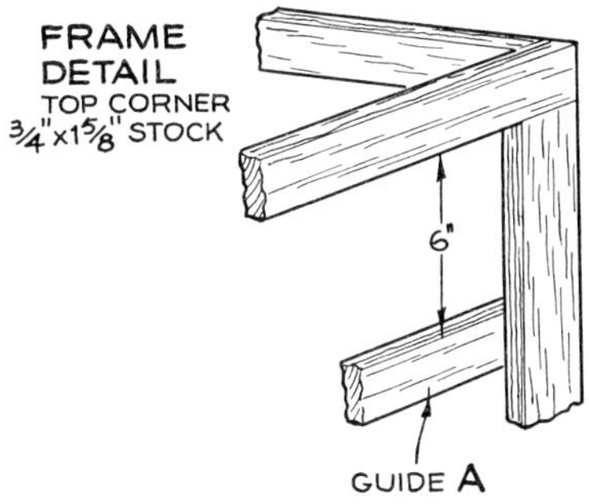
FRAME
DETAIL
TOP CORNER
3/4"x1 5/8" STOCK
6"
GUIDE A

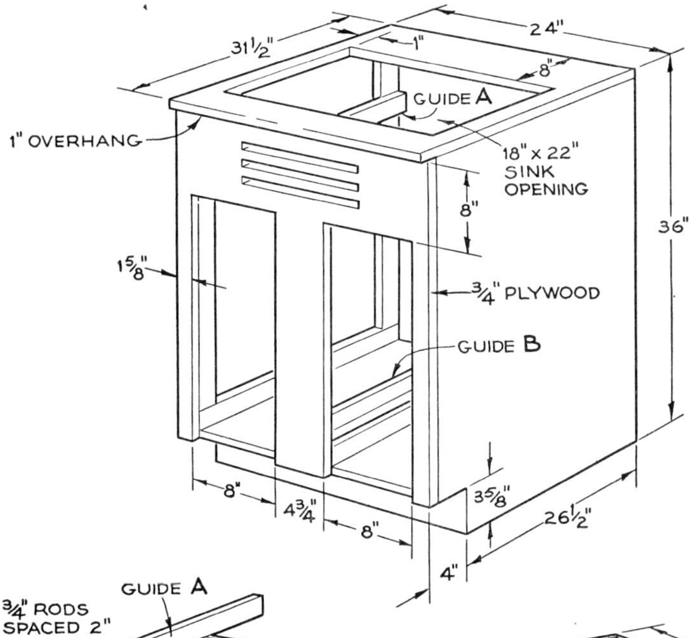
24"
31 1/2"
1"
8"
GUIDE A
1" OVERHANG
18" x 22"
SINK
OPENING
8"
36"
1 5/8"
3/4" PLYWOOD
GUIDE B
3 5/8"
8"
4 3/4"
8"
26 1/2"
4"

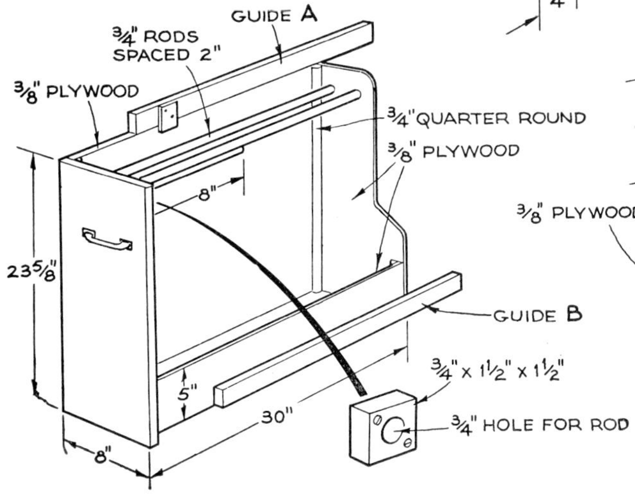
GUIDE A
3/4" RODS
SPACED 2"
3/8" PLYWOOD
3/4" QUARTER ROUND
3/8" PLYWOOD
8"
23 5/8"
GUIDE B
3/4" x 1 1/2" x 1 1/2"
5"
30"
3/4" HOLE FOR ROD
8"

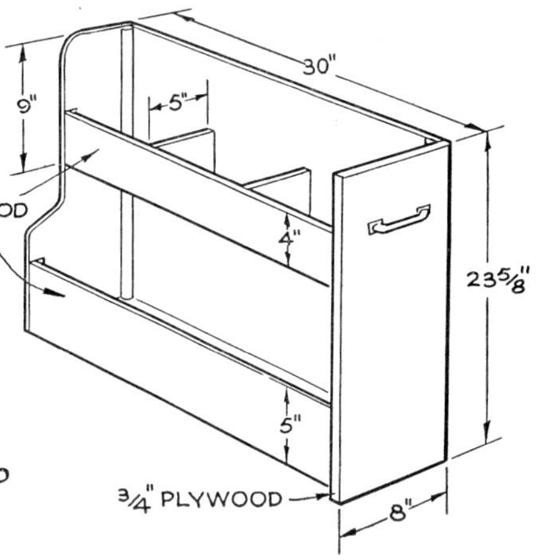
30"
9"
5"
3/8" PLYWOOD
4"
23 5/8"
5"
3/4" PLYWOOD
8"

Pointers for Building

Assemble the base first and put down the cabinet floor. Then cut the framing members from nominal 1″ x 2″ stock. Assemble these with lap or other joints. Notice that the frame length should be enough less than 24″ to allow the thickness of the two ¾″ plywood ends to make up the total 24″ dimension.

Careful use of the saw will yield fronts for the two racks and the cabinet itself from one 24″ x 32″ piece of ¾″ plywood. The cutouts become the rack fronts. Use a piece of vertical grain plywood for this. Install the cabinet front so that the horizontal frame member at the bottom of each end becomes a guide for its neighboring pull-out rack.

For greatest cabinet strength, use ¾″ plywood on the ends. The ends could, however, be of lesser thickness, especially if you take pains with the framing. Or they could be dispensed with entirely to save material if you don't mind side openings in the adjoining cabinets. A ¼″ back, of plywood, hardboard, or composition material, on the cabinet also is optional.

Curve the inside edges of the back ends of the racks so they do not strike the sink plumbing. Rabbet the rack sides to the front, but butt joints will do at the rear. Nailed, or perhaps screwed, in place, the pieces of ¾″ quarter round will help make the racks rigid. Either ¾″ dowel stock or metal rods might be used in the towel rack. Bored holes in blocks offer the easiest way to mount these, although the rods also could go into blind holes in the rack ends before the rack is assembled.

When the racks are complete, use them to position the four guides A and B in the cabinet. For these pieces, you might do better to use hardwood than the pine stock suggested. Highly polished before installation, the hardwood will allow the racks to slide with greater ease. In any case, treat all the guides, as well as the rubbing rack surfaces, with a hard wax.

8

Corner Cabinets

When rows of cabinets along adjacent walls meet in a corner, the question arises of how to use the corner space most efficiently. Wall cabinets offer no difficulty. But base cabinets do. The diagonal depth, from the point where the cabinet fronts form a right angle back to the far corner, no longer is an easy reach. The corner storage space in effect is blocked off. Access is sometimes gained by opening the door of the adjoining cabinet and reaching sideways into the corner. This, however, tends to make the space a dead storage catch-all, which it needn't be.

Various ways have been worked out to make corner space just as accessible and useful as the space in other base cabinets. Some of these ways are presented in the following pages for your selection. Merry-go-round corner shelves are a common way of using the space. But there are others too. When you consider that approximately 11 cubic feet of useful storage space is available in the standard base-cabinet corner, it is readily apparent that here at least is one corner you should not attempt to cut.

137

SLIDING-SHELF CABINET

Uses

This cabinet might serve its best purpose as the storage space for bulky utensils—roasters, large baking pans, perhaps an electric mixer. Seldom-used items could go on the floor, others that are needed more frequently on the sliding shelf. Opening the cabinet door not only brings the contents of the two swing shelves out into the open; it clears the way for the sliding shelf to be drawn to the left, making its contents more easily reached. The lip at the end keeps items from sliding off the pull shelf. Nearly 8″ of cabinet space available back of the swing shelves when the door is closed might be devoted to sacked supplies, especially the floor area up to the level of the sliding shelf. A pan or two could also be placed on hooks on the upper part of the back wall. But anything stored in the area might have to be removed before the sliding shelf could be drawn out.

Materials

FRAMING:

2″ x 2″ (nom.) stock 30⅛″ long — corner post.

1″ x 2″ (nom.) stock (32 linear feet).

1″ x 4″ (nom.) stock (14 linear feet) — base.

¾″ plywood (4′ x 8′ panel) to make—

  1 pc. 23″ x 31⅝″ — end.   1 pc. 23″ x 42½″ — floor.

  1 pc. 23″ x 25⅝″ — shelf.   1 pc. 16″ x 30″ — door.

  1 pc. 25″ x 43¼″ — counter.

½″ plywood to make—

  2 pc. 15″ x 15″ — swing shelves.

  1 pc. ¾″ x 16″ — swing shelf separator.

¼″ plywood (4′ x 6′ panel) to make—

  1 pc. 31⅝″ x 43¼″ — back.   1 pc. 24″ x 31⅝″ — end.

  1 pc. ¾″ x 20½″ — sliding shelf lip.

⅛″ plywood or hardboard ¾″ wide — shelf edging.

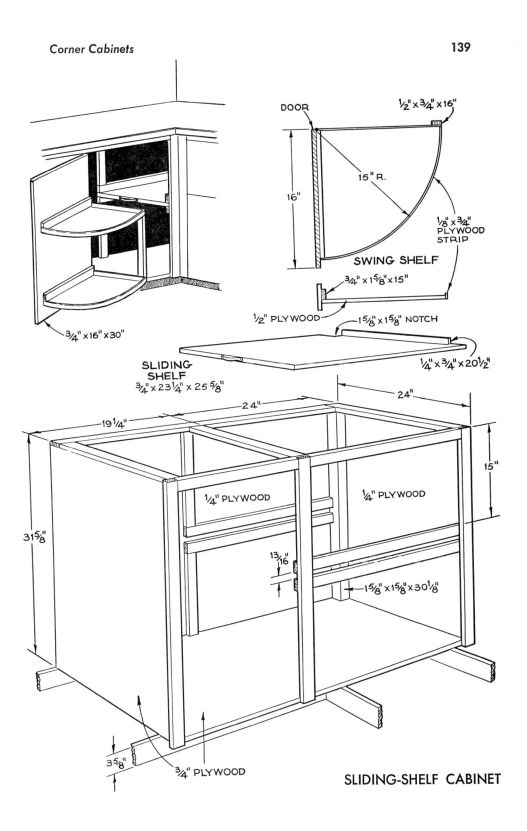

DOOR

½" x ¾" x 16"

15" R.

16"

⅛" x ¾" PLYWOOD STRIP

SWING SHELF

¾" x 1⅝" x 15"

½" PLYWOOD

1⅝" x 1⅝" NOTCH

¼" x ¾" x 20½"

SLIDING SHELF
¾" x 23¼" x 25⅝"

¾" x 16" x 30"

24"

19¼"

24"

¼" PLYWOOD

¼" PLYWOOD

15"

13/16"

1⅝" x 1⅝" x 30⅛"

31⅝"

3⅝"

¾" PLYWOOD

SLIDING-SHELF CABINET

Pointers for Building

Cut four pieces of the 1″ x 2″ stock 31⅝″ long for vertical framing members. Cut three pieces 24″ long to go across the top, front to back, and two 43¼″ pieces for the longitudinals. Four pieces 25⅛″ long are needed as the sliding shelf guides.

Put on the ¼″ plywood back and end after the frame and ¾″ plywood end and floor are in place atop the sub-framing. No enclosure is needed over the section at the right of the cabinet door since the end of the adjoining base cabinet will butt here. Install the two bottom guides first for the sliding shelf. Then slip the shelf into the cabinet framework and rest it on these two guides while fastening the upper ones with screws. You can provide for proper sliding clearance by inserting thin cardboard between the guides and shelf while positioning and attaching the upper ones. A drawer pull on the end of the shelf will make it easier to draw.

The swing shelves are quarters of a full circle, having a 15″ radius. Glue and screw each of these on the narrow edge of a 15″ length of 1″ x 2″ stock and screw the latter to the door. Locate the bottom shelf so it will just clear the cabinet floor when the door closes. Locating the other 16″ above probably will give best use of both shelves. A supporting strip of ½″ plywood located as shown in the drawing will make the assembly more rigid. Put this on after ⅛″ plywood or hardboard strips have been curved around the edges of the two shelves and nailed in place.

REVOLVING SHELF CORNER BASE CABINET 1

Uses

Shelves that revolve in Lazy Susan fashion make use of most of the space that otherwise is lost when two rows of cabinets come together in a corner. This one was designed for the U.S. Department of Agriculture's model U-kitchen, and plans were drawn by J. Robert Dodge, architect. Two are used in this kitchen—one in the left corner of the

U, one in the right. Mounted level with the revolving shelves, fixed shelves keep stored goods from falling down behind the revolving unit. But the toe board is made removable, in case items do fall. This also makes it possible to clean the unit easily. If used for seldom-needed supplies, the fixed shelves offer a tremendous expansion of available storage space.

Materials

1″ x 2″ (nom.) stock (8 linear feet) — facing strips, cleats.

1″ x 3″ (nom.) stock (18 linear feet) — top frame.

1″ x 4″ (nom.) stock (14 linear feet) — base.

1″ x 8″ (nom.) stock (6 linear feet) — bottom frame.

2″ x 2″ (nom.) stock 34½″ long — corner post.

2″ x 2″ (nom.) stock 27½″ long — center post.

¾″ plywood (two 4′ x 8′ panels) to make—

    2 pc. 23″ x 35¼″ — ends (optional).

    1 pc. 38″ x 38″ — counter.

    1 pc. 12⅜″ x 29⅞″ — door.

    1 pc. 13⅛″ x 29⅞″ — door.

    2 pc. 37″ x 37″ — circular and fill-in shelves.

    1 pc. 20″ x 20″ — circular shelf.

¼″ plywood or hardboard (4′ x 6′ panel) to make—

    2 pc. 35½″ x 38″ — back.

    1 pc. 9½″ x 36″ — bottom shelf reinforcing.

Pointers for Building

Find the center of the two 37″ x 37″ squares of ¾″ plywood by crossing lines from the corners. Then lay out on these centers circles of an 18⅛″ radius. Just outside, lay out other circles with a radius of 18¼″. Then saw out the larger circles, cutting outside the line and keeping the outer area intact. As the plan details show, this area becomes the fixed fill-in shelves that are placed inside the cabinet on the same level as the two large revolving shelves. Now reduce the

REVOLVING SHELF CORNER BASE CABINET 1 (A)

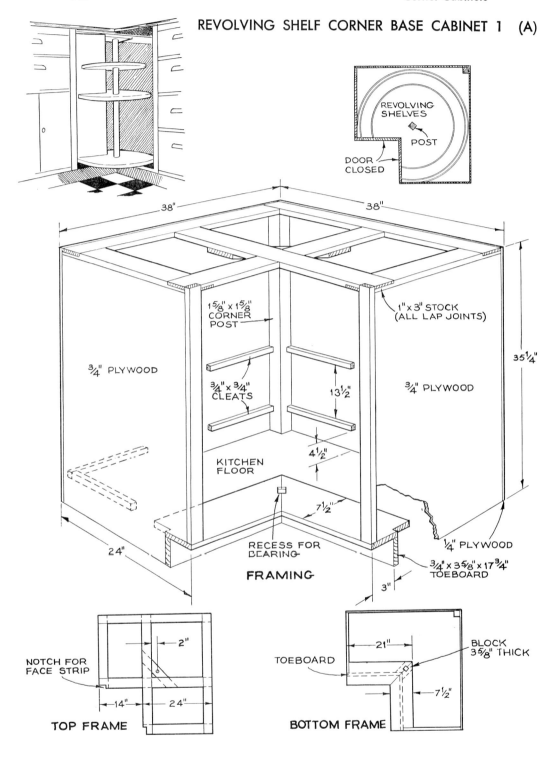

REVOLVING
SHELVES

POST

DOOR
CLOSED

38"   38"

1⁵⁄₈" x 1⁵⁄₈"
CORNER
POST

1" x 3" STOCK
(ALL LAP JOINTS)

¾" PLYWOOD

¾" x ¾"
CLEATS

13½"

¾" PLYWOOD

35¼"

4½"

KITCHEN
FLOOR

RECESS FOR
BEARING

7½"

¼" PLYWOOD

24"

FRAMING

3"

¾" x 3⁵⁄₈" x 17¾"
TOEBOARD

2"

NOTCH FOR
FACE STRIP

14"   24"

TOP FRAME

TOEBOARD

21"

BLOCK
3⁵⁄₈" THICK

7½"

BOTTOM FRAME

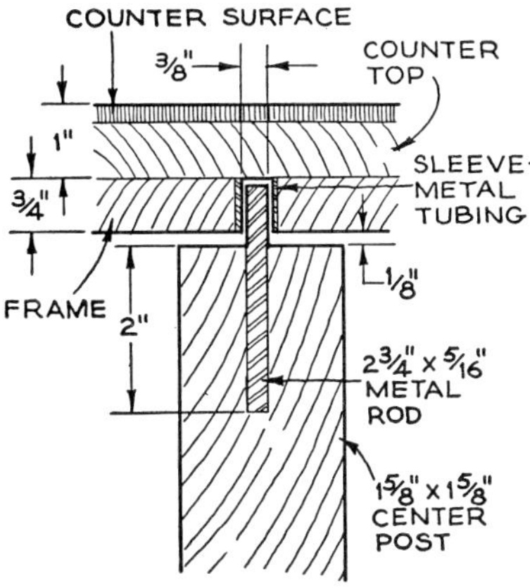
COUNTER SURFACE
3/8"
COUNTER TOP
1"
3/4"
SLEEVE-METAL TUBING
FRAME
2"
1/8"
2 3/4" x 5/16" METAL ROD
1 5/8" x 1 5/8" CENTER POST

PIVOT

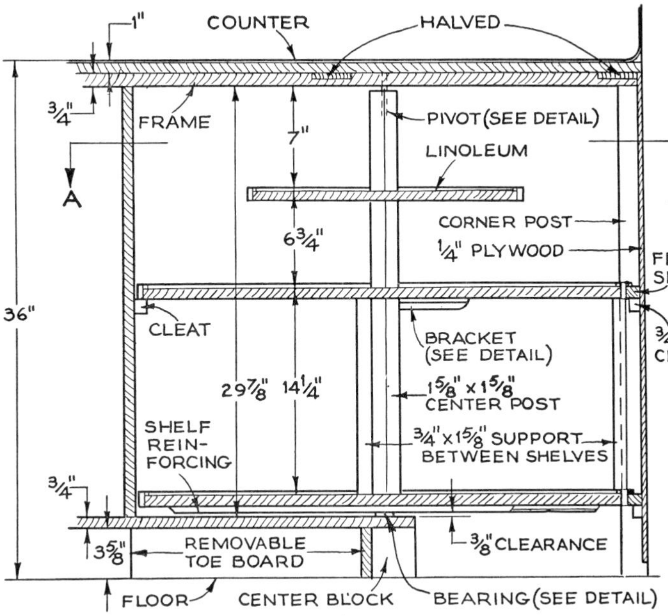
1"
COUNTER
HALVED
3/4"
FRAME
7"
PIVOT (SEE DETAIL)
LINOLEUM
A
A
6 3/4"
CORNER POST
1/4" PLYWOOD
FILL-IN SHELF
36"
CLEAT
BRACKET (SEE DETAIL)
3/4" x 3/4" CLEAT
29 7/8"
14 1/4"
1 5/8" x 1 5/8" CENTER POST
SHELF REIN-FORCING
3/4" x 1 5/8" SUPPORT BETWEEN SHELVES
3/4"
3 5/8"
REMOVABLE TOE BOARD
3/8" CLEARANCE
FLOOR
CENTER BLOCK
BEARING (SEE DETAIL)

SECTION B-B

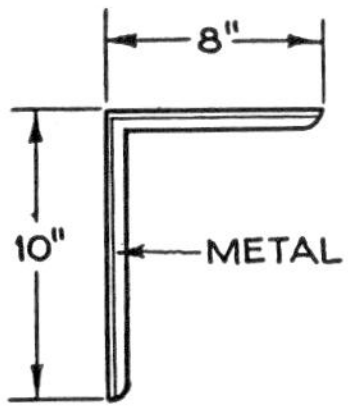
8"
10"
METAL

SHELF BRACKET

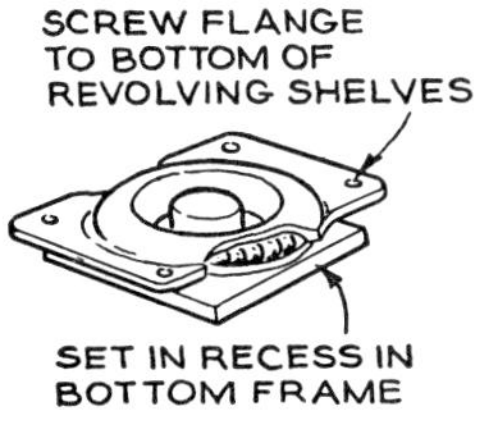
SCREW FLANGE TO BOTTOM OF REVOLVING SHELVES
SET IN RECESS IN BOTTOM FRAME

BEARING

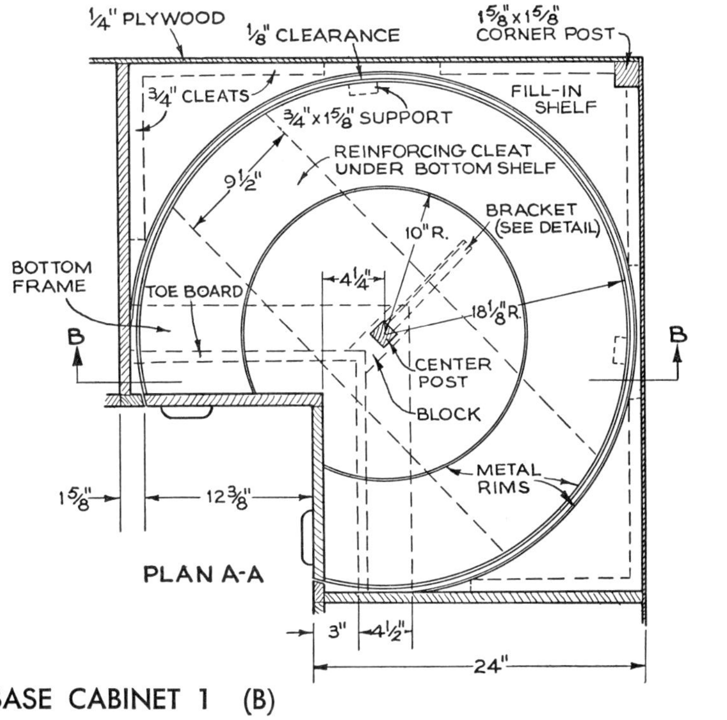
1/4" PLYWOOD
1/8" CLEARANCE
1 5/8" x 1 5/8" CORNER POST
3/4" CLEATS
3/4" x 1 5/8" SUPPORT
FILL-IN SHELF
9 1/2"
REINFORCING CLEAT UNDER BOTTOM SHELF
BRACKET (SEE DETAIL)
10" R.
BOTTOM FRAME
4 1/4"
TOE BOARD
18 1/8" R.
B
B
CENTER POST
BLOCK
METAL RIMS
1 5/8"
12 3/8"
3"
4 1/2"
24"

PLAN A-A

REVOLVING SHELF CORNER BASE CABINET 1 (B)

diameter of each disk by cutting on the inner lines. Smooth the edges of each disk and apply copper or aluminum edging around it. Also apply edging on the fill-in shelves. This will then allow the two larger shelves to revolve without spilling their contents. The fill-in shelves are held by $3/4''$ x $3/4''$ cleats.

Cut openings in the two upper circular shelves for the center post. Make the openings a drive fit if possible. Mount the shelves to the post with metal brackets and glue. Two $1''$ x $2''$ posts between the two larger shelves also help keep the assembly rigid.

Form the bottom bearing from a furniture caster as shown by the sketch. Screw it to the $1/4''$ reinforcement piece under the bottom shelf. The bottom of the bearing simply slips snugly in a recess cut for it on the upper face of the bottom frame. After the cabinet framing has been built around the revolving assembly, keep the latter captive by slipping down the triangular framing piece on top that contains the metal sleeve for the upper pivot.

REVOLVING SHELF CORNER BASE CABINET 2

Uses

This example has two shallow drawers at the top. In the original, a design by the makers of Malarkey plywoods, one of these drawers is devoted to sharp knives and the counter above has a hardwood chopping block. Details of these are given in the chapter on kitchen accessories.

Materials

1″ x 4″ (nom.) stock (22 linear feet) — base.

1″ x 2″ (nom.) stock (50 linear feet) — framing.

1 pc. 2″ x 2″ (nom.) stock 12″ long — top flange mount.

2 pc. 2″ x 2″ (nom.) stock 14″ long — shelf separators.

⅝″ or ¾″ plywood (two 4′ x 8′ panels) to make—

    2 pc. 23″ x 35¼″ — ends (optional).

    1 pc. 18″ x 25″ — door.

    1 pc. 18¾″ x 25″ — door.

    2 pc. 38″ x 38″ — circular shelves.

    1 pc. 43⅝″ x 43⅝″ — counter.

¼″ plywood or ⅛″ hardboard (4′ x 8′ panel) to make—

    2 pc. 35¼″ x 42⅝″ — back.

    2″-wide bands around shelves.

1 pc. ¾″ pipe 34″ long — stanchion.

2 flanges for ¾″ pipe.

1 ball-bearing race.

2 flanges with setscrews.

REVOLVING SHELF CORNER
BASE CABINET 2

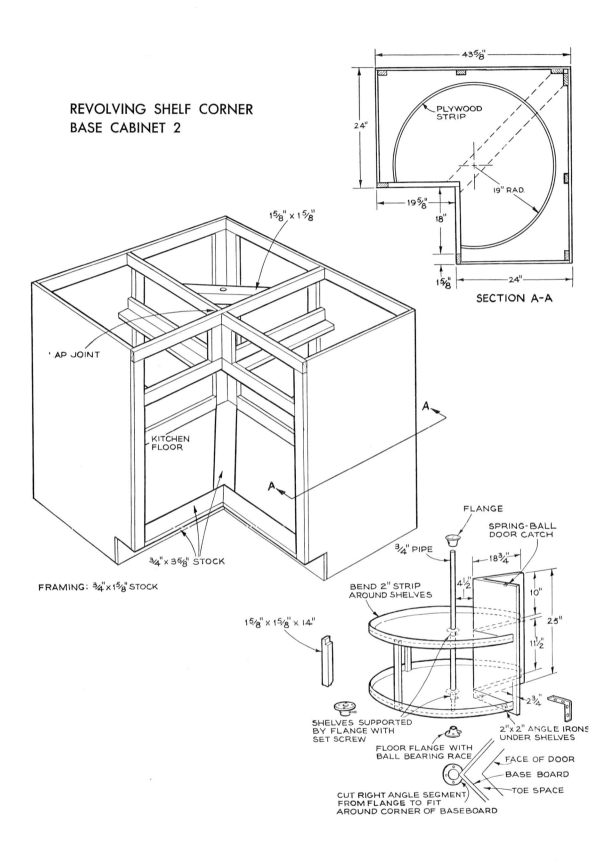

43⅝"

24"

PLYWOOD
STRIP

19⅝"

18"

19" RAD.

1⅝"

24"

SECTION A-A

1⅝" × 1⅝"

'AP JOINT

KITCHEN
FLOOR

A

A

¾"× 3⅝" STOCK

FRAMING: ¾"× 1⅝" STOCK

1⅝" × 1⅝" × 14"

FLANGE

SPRING-BALL
DOOR CATCH

¾" PIPE

18¾"

4½"

10"

BEND 2" STRIP
AROUND SHELVES

25"

11½"

2¾"

SHELVES SUPPORTED
BY FLANGE WITH
SET SCREW

2"× 2" ANGLE IRONS
UNDER SHELVES

FLOOR FLANGE WITH
BALL BEARING RACE

FACE OF DOOR

BASE BOARD

TOE SPACE

CUT RIGHT ANGLE SEGMENT
FROM FLANGE TO FIT
AROUND CORNER OF BASEBOARD

Pointers for Building

Since its dimensions make the revolving assembly a captive within the cabinet, this is a project you should build, or at least assemble, from the inside out.

If you are working by hand, the two circular shelves might be cut with a compass saw. Smooth the edges and apply the 2″ strips of ¼″ plywood by bending it gradually while progressively drawing it in with screws. If this gives you trouble, strips of ⅛″ hardboard will be easier and just as satisfactory. Two posts of 2″ x 2″ stock support the shelves at one edge, the doors do the job at the other. Drive nails through the doors into the edges of the shelves. Angle irons also help keep the assembly rigid. You will save time and energy by having the pipe stanchion cut to the correct length when you buy it. A hacksaw will cut the pie segment from the bottom flange.

Cut all parts of the cabinet and make a trial assembly before enclosing the revolving unit.

REVOLVING WALL CABINET

Uses

Two of these wall units are used in the Step-Saving U-Kitchen developed by the Bureau of Human Nutrition and Home Economics, one at each rear corner of the U. The one shown in the drawing is located at the immediate left of the mixing counter. Its small shelf is designed especially for spices. This cabinet is big enough so that staples in daily use can occupy the outer part of the shelves and yet leave room at the rear for reserves. The shelves extend down to the counter, providing storage at working level for the heaviest and most often used staples.

In the twin Lazy Susan on the wall of the opposite corner, heavy dishes and those most often used are on the lowest shelves. Ready-to-eat cereals are kept on the top shelf. Steps are saved when cereals and bowls are in the same cupboard. Shelves in this cabinet are all the same size.

Many wall Lazy Susans are cut off at the bottom even with adjoining flat wall cabinets. Where that would be preferred, the accompanying plans could be altered to suit and the shelves spaced accordingly.

Materials

1″ x 2″ (nom.) stock (8 linear feet) to make—

  2 pc. 51¾″ long — vertical facing strips.

  1 pc. 10½″ long — horizontal facing strip.

  1 pc. 11¼″ long — horizontal facing strip.

2 pc. 1″ x 12″ (nom.) stock 51″ long — cabinet sides.

2 pc. ¼″ plywood 22½″ x 51″ — back.

¾″ plywood (4′ x 6′ and 4′ x 5′ panels) to make—

  2 pc. 21½″ x 21½″ — base and top of cabinet.

  5 pc. 21″ x 21″ — large shelves.

  1 pc. 16″ x 16″ — small shelf.

  1 pc. 9″ x 49⅜″ (or 1″ x 10″ (nom.) stock) — door.

  1 pc. 9¾″ x 49⅜″ (or 1″ x 10″ (nom.) stock) — door.

2 4″ x 6″ shelf angles.

6 6″ x 6″ shelf angles.

Pointers for Building

Saw a 10″ x 10″ segment from one corner of each of the two 21½″ x 21½″ pieces of ¾″ plywood, cut the 1″ x 2″ stock to length, and you have all the parts for the cabinet frame. One notched square of plywood goes on the counter to form the cabinet base; the other can be placed under a drop ceiling in place of a soffit board. The 12″ pine stock connects these pieces on the sides while the two 51″ strips of 1″ x 2″ (nom.) form the vertical facing strips. Depending on the construction, the short horizontal facing strips might be dispensed with.

REVOLVING WALL CABINET

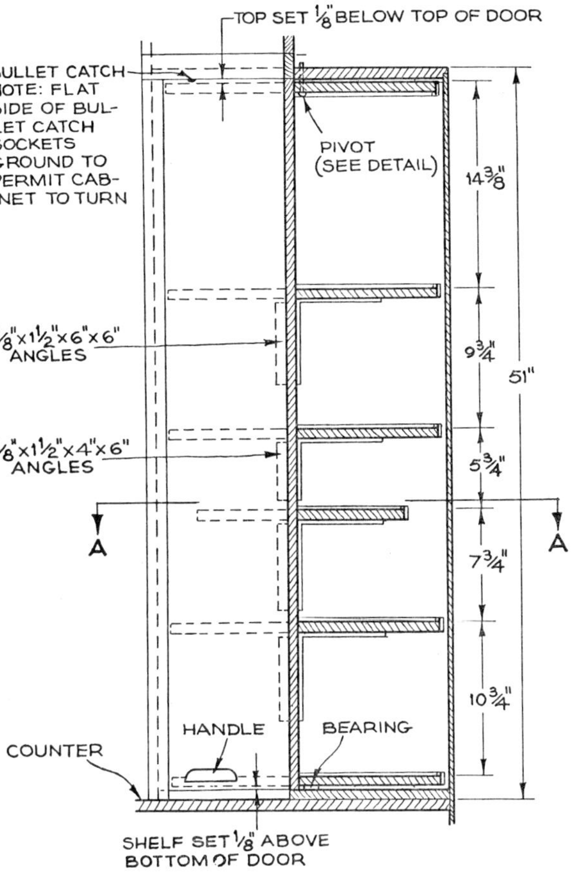
TOP SET 1/8" BELOW TOP OF DOOR
BULLET CATCH
NOTE: FLAT SIDE OF BULLET CATCH SOCKETS GROUND TO PERMIT CABINET TO TURN
PIVOT (SEE DETAIL)
14 3/8"
9 3/4"
51"
1/8"x1 1/2"x6"x6" ANGLES
1/8"x1 1/2"x4"x6" ANGLES
5 3/4"
A
A
7 3/4"
10 3/4"
HANDLE
BEARING
COUNTER
SHELF SET 1/8" ABOVE BOTTOM OF DOOR

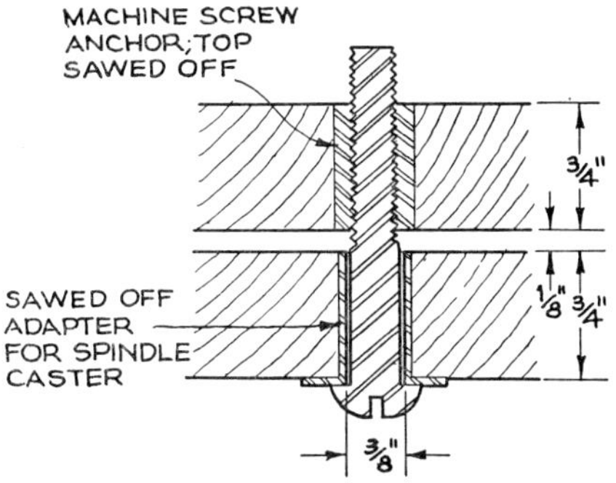
MACHINE SCREW ANCHOR; TOP SAWED OFF
3/4"
SAWED OFF ADAPTER FOR SPINDLE CASTER
1/8"
3/4"
3/8"

PIVOT DETAIL

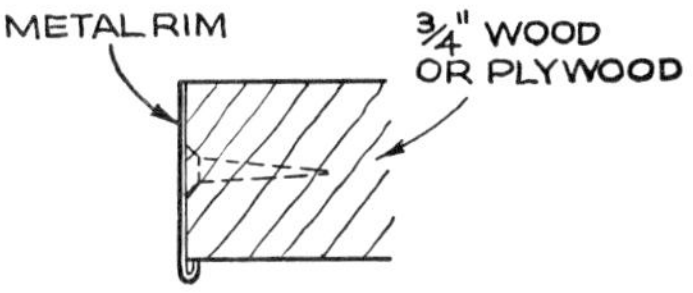
METAL RIM
3/4" WOOD OR PLYWOOD

TOP OF CABINET DETAIL

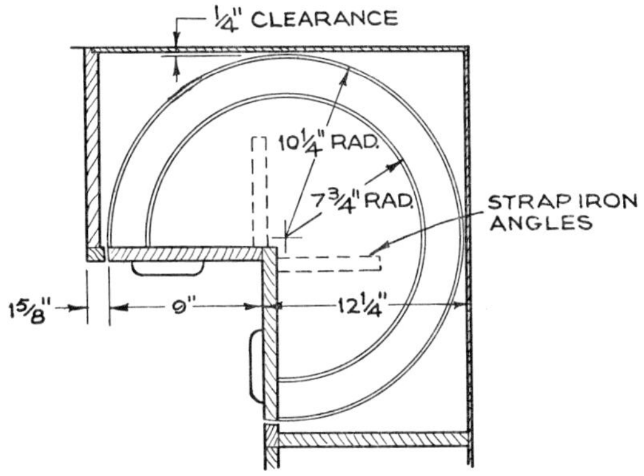
1/4" CLEARANCE
10 1/4" RAD.
7 3/4" RAD.
STRAP IRON ANGLES
1 5/8"
9"
12 1/4"

PLAN A-A

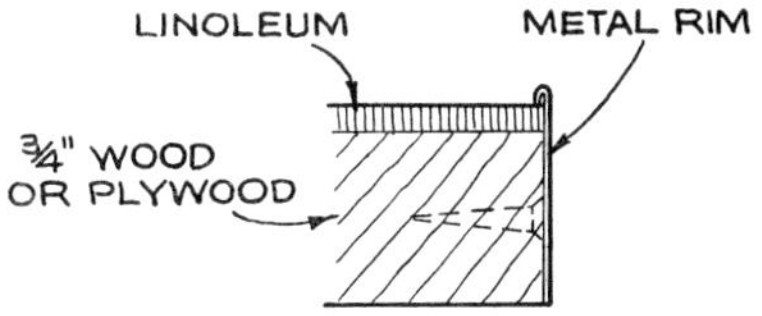
LINOLEUM
METAL RIM
3/4" WOOD OR PLYWOOD

SHELF DETAIL

If power equipment is available, you would do well to clamp or tack the five 21″ x 21″ shelf blanks together and saw the 20½″ diameter shelves in a single operation. If a ⅜″ center hole is bored through all the blanks, the assembly might be revolved in a jig while the cut is made. Also saw out the segments where the doors go before taking the finished shelves apart.

A cut-off ball-bearing furniture caster can be used as the bearing. This should be recessed in the top of the horizontal frame member that is fastened to the top of the counter and in a mating recess in the bottom surface of the first revolving shelf. Make the bearing a tight press fit. A hacksaw will enable you to cut the machine-screw anchor and the adapter for the spindle caster that are specified for the top pivot.

Locate the shelves as indicated along the doors, attaching them with countersunk wood screws run through the doors. Then apply the shelf brackets. Locate the top and bottom shelves so there will be revolving clearance. Sand the top and bottom edges of the doors until the unit revolves freely. For appearance, the metal rim is placed upside down on the top shelf as the detail sketch shows. Position the bullet catch so that the revolving shelves will stop with the doors in their closed position.

DIAGONAL-FRONT CABINETS

Uses

Diagonal-front cabinets can utilize corner space in a variety of ways. The shape is excellent for full-circle revolving shelves, either in a wall or base unit. As outlined in the sink chapter, a diagonal-front base cabinet will make a sink the conversation piece of a modern kitchen. If a trap door is installed in the back corner of the counter, space behind the sink may be utilized for a trash chute to the basement, or for a garbage compartment—with access to the container from outside the house through a small door in the wall.

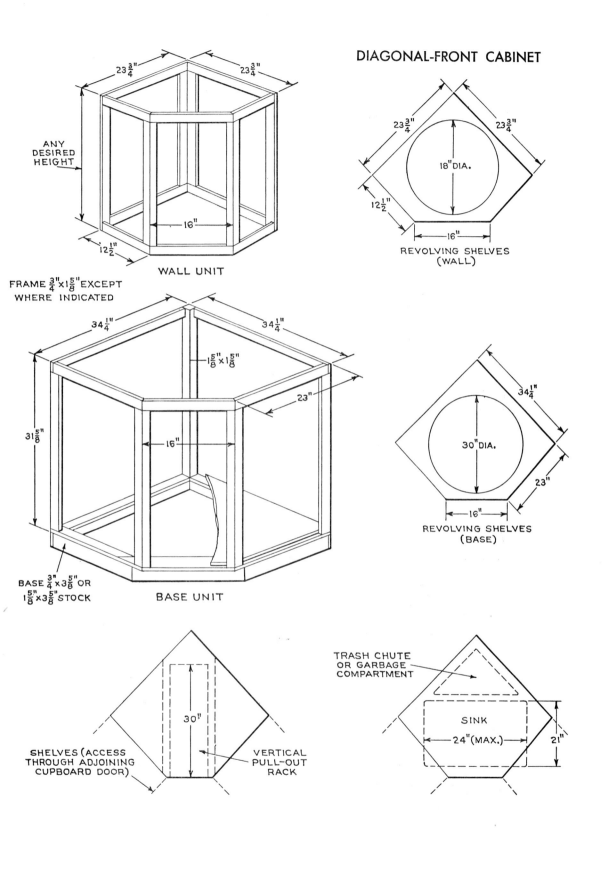

DIAGONAL-FRONT CABINET

WALL UNIT

23¾"   23¾"

ANY
DESIRED
HEIGHT

16"

12½"

FRAME ¾"×1⅝"EXCEPT
WHERE INDICATED

**REVOLVING SHELVES
(WALL)**

23¾"   23¾"

18"DIA.

12½"

16"

BASE UNIT

34¼"   34¼"

1⅝"×1⅝"

23"

31⅝"

16"

BASE ¾"×3⅝" OR
1⅝"×3⅝"STOCK

**REVOLVING SHELVES
(BASE)**

34¼"

30"DIA.

23"

16"

SHELVES (ACCESS
THROUGH ADJOINING
CUPBOARD DOOR)

30"

VERTICAL
PULL-OUT
RACK

TRASH CHUTE
OR GARBAGE
COMPARTMENT

SINK
24"(MAX.)

21"

Shelves, of course, are the most common storage device in these cabinets. In a wall unit, shelves offer easy access to the stored items. But in the base cabinet, the shelf depth and the comparatively narrow door lower the cabinet's efficiency.

A base cabinet is another possible location for one of the vertical pull-out racks described in the chapter devoted to these handy storage devices. In this case, the rack might have a 90-degree pointed end to fit fully into the cabinet corner. The head-on area directly behind the door could also be partitioned vertically for on-edge storage of large trays, etc. For this, a door might be omitted from the cabinet. Alternatively, a bank of drawers could go into the space.

Pull-out racks, partitions, and drawers, however, all have one drawback in common when used in a diagonal-front cabinet. They shut off the space remaining at the right and left. But this can be overcome in many cases by installing shelves in the space and providing access to them through the doors of cupboards on the right and left of the corner unit. The shelves actually would be extensions of those in the adjoining base units. Triangular shelves within the cabinet could be devoted to dead storage if a roll-out rack is used. The space offers many possibilities, too, for a secret compartment—accessible, perhaps, by removing a drawer from the corner cabinet or one of its neighbors.

Materials

A list is omitted because of the variations suggested.

Pointers for Building

Before starting work, the builder should consider whether the dimensions shown in the drawings will yield a cabinet to suit his needs and fit the adjoining cabinets, either wall or base. To illustrate, the 12½″ dimension of the wall cabinet may have to be adjusted to a different depth dimension that has been chosen for the other wall cabinets. If this must be increased, say to 14″, the width of the door will automatically decrease. The builder will then want to consider whether the lesser door width is acceptable. If not, the 23¾″ dimension along each wall should be increased to bring the door to the desired width.

The same principle applies of course to a base unit. If it is desirable to increase the door width, as might be the case when a sink is being installed, it will be necessary to increase the $34\frac{1}{4}''$ dimensions at the back. But such increases, it should be noted, produce a corresponding increase of the cabinet's diagonal depth from door to back corner.

Assemble the framing as for other cabinets, using the joint procedure you prefer, and make and install the door. The floor of the wall cabinet can be cut to fit on the top edges of the lower frame members. In the case of a wall unit, a door could be omitted and the shelves used for display or open storage. Another possibility is a door with one or two glass panels. Set the glass in rabbets cut in a glued-up wood frame.

Full-circle revolving shelves can be built like the revolving units shown previously. However, since the present ones lack the support that the doors provide the former, vertical supporting strips between the shelves probably will be needed at intervals around the rim of the unit, especially the base cabinet. Install an additional frame member across the top of the cabinet to take the bearing for the revolving unit.

A trash chute or garbage compartment and a work-counter access door can be built as described in the chapter on base cabinets. If a vertical pull-out rack is used, parallel guide strips will be required inside the cabinet.

CORNER CABINET IDEAS

Adjoining Room Cabinet

Straight-line access into a corner base cabinet can sometimes be provided through what normally would be one of the rear faces. This possibility may occur in two ways. First, one arm of the L formed by the cabinets may serve as a peninsula instead of being backed against the wall. Second, one arm may back against a wall separating the kitchen from another room. In either case, the corner cabinet can be fully utilized by providing access into it in the opposite direction from its companions in the peninsula or along the partitioning wall.

In a peninsula, the switch is simple. Just install drawers or doors on the side facing away from the kitchen. If the peninsula separates kitchen and dining area, this rear-facing cabinet might be used for table linen, mats, silver, dishes, and other items needed in the dining area.

When the cabinet backs against a partitioning wall, a hole must be cut through the wall at the proper spot and a frame of 2 x 4's installed to substitute for the wall studs that are cut. Again, either doors or drawers can be installed. The useful depth of the cabinet in this case will be increased by the thickness of the wall. If the cabinet opens into the dining room, it can be put to use as previously suggested. If it opens into the living room, a television set could be hidden inside or the space could be used for storage of phonograph records.

L-Shaped Cabinet

Storage space within a corner base cabinet can be made more accessible by extending the cabinet both ways along the meeting walls, omitting a vertical frame member from the near corner and enclosing the front with an L-shaped door. (Outwardly, the cabinet would resemble the two revolving-shelf base cabinets shown earlier in this chapter.) The lack of upright framing at the center corner of the face offers unobstructed access into the entire cabinet.

Shelves within such a cabinet can be single pieces of plywood cut to fit, or L-shaped assemblies of pine stock. A full-circle revolving-shelf unit also could go into the corner area with fixed shelves in the cabinet wings on either side. A two-part door could be used to enclose the cabinet. If desired, you could make the door a rigid, L-shaped unit, with hinges on one end and a latch on the other. You would have a more convenient arrangement, however, by hinging or pivoting the two door sections together. This would allow them to straighten out parallel to the front of the adjoining cabinet when the door is opened. When closed, the door parts would fold into the right-angle opening.

Drawers with 90-degree notched fronts also might be installed in such a cabinet frame, sliding in and out in a line toward the far corner. But these have the disadvantage of leaving waste space on either side. This space could be made accessible only through adjoining cabinets fitted with doors.

Lifting-Counter Cabinet

Hinging part or all of the counter so it can be swung up offers another way of utilizing space in a corner base unit. Government plans for modernizing a farm kitchen suggest locating garbage and trash containers there with a removable door on the outside of the house. The lower half of this corner space is occupied by a square container for paper. Above, occupying a quarter of the cabinet space, is a rectangular compartment with its end open at the outside access door. Garbage containers are kept in this compartment. Beside it, resting on cleats, is a square container for tin and glass that occupies one-eighth of the cabinet space. When this container is pushed along its cleats toward the outside door, an area is left free so that paper can be dropped from the counter opening into the large box at the bottom of the cabinet. Two hinged counter openings are suggested—one over the garbage box and one to serve both the paper receptacle and the tin and glass receptacle. Guides are installed in the cabinet so that from outside the house you can withdraw and replace the three containers like drawers.

A lift-up counter panel also would enable a housewife to use space in a corner base unit for storage of roasting pans and other bulky articles that are needed infrequently.

Corner Wall Shelves

Instead of joining two right-angle lines of wall cabinets with a corner cabinet, you might prefer simple open shelves in the corner. Stop the cupboard-type cabinets at equal distances from the corner—at a point equal to about one and one-half times their depth (front to back dimension). Then cut shelves with a diagonal front edge to fill the corner. Or, cut the front edges to a concave curve to improve the appearance.

Corner Mixer Cabinet

An electric mixer can be stored in a triangular corner cabinet installed between the counter and bottom of the wall cabinets. From $3/4''$ plywood cut a triangular base large enough so that no part of the mixer will protrude beyond its edges. Mount this base with brackets to the bottom edge of a door hinged to a simple frame mounted diagonally across the kitchen counter. When the door is opened, swung back against the wall and latched, the mixer rides into the open on the triangular base, ready for use. A matching diagonal-front corner unit can be located in the line of wall cabinets above.

If one end of the work counter butts against a floor-to-ceiling cabinet, a swing-out door shelf also might be located in the cabinet to carry the mixer to working position over the counter.

9

Peninsula Cabinets

A line of cabinets jutting out from the wall in a peninsula arrangement frequently improves the utility of a modern kitchen. Some peninsulas extend only a few feet. Others reach most of the way across the room. Base cabinets in a peninsula may or may not have wall-type cabinets suspended from the ceiling above them. Both base and wall cabinets may be accessible from either one or two sides.

Peninsulas take many forms and serve many functions. One of the simplest to build is just a counter, without cabinets under it, extending at right angles to the end of a line of base cabinets backed against the wall. A pipe or curtain-pole leg, or perhaps a tier of shelves, supports the free end of the counter, which is usually rounded. Because of its knee space, a counter peninsula is a convenient breakfast bar if stools are kept under it. It also may double as a serving counter between the range and dining table.

A peninsula has its major use, however, as one arm of a U-shaped kitchen plan. If a large kitchen is being remodeled, the peninsula is often chosen as a means of keeping the work area compact. In new

157

construction a peninsula may serve as a divider between kitchen and dining areas, or perhaps between kitchen and laundry. This saves the cost of a full wall. Also, it gives the open construction that many modern homeworkers prefer.

Either sink or range may go into the peninsula against a low backing wall. A narrow counter on top of or against the opposite side of the wall will then serve as a handy breakfast bar or as a stacking area for dishes being taken to the sink. A breakfast bar of this type will be found in the chapter devoted to kitchen tables. A dish washer or a home food freezer of the horizontal type might also go into a peninsula that bounds a kitchen.

Peninsula cabinets, both floor and ceiling-suspended types, may be exactly like those built for use against a wall. However, the builder has the opportunity of making the storage space accessible from either side. With the kitchen on one side and the dining area on the other, this double accessibility has obvious advantages. If a hanging cabinet has doors on both sides, dishes can be reached or stored from either the kitchen or dining area. Double-faced drawers put silverware, table mats, etc., at your fingertips no matter which area you are in. Peninsula cabinets usually are the same depth as standard base and wall types. But this can sometimes be varied if circumstances call for it. You should note that where a counter 24″ wide is used, with a 1″ overhang on each side, the depth (face-to-face) dimension of the basc cabinet will be only 22″ instead of the usual 23″.

At the corner where the peninsula joins the wall-backed cabinets, drawers or doors opening from the dining-room side offer the most direct and satisfactory use of the corner space, especially in the base units. Suggestions for other ways to use this corner space are given in Chapter 8—Corner Cabinets.

When a peninsula separates kitchen and dining areas, the space between upper and lower cabinets makes a convenient pass-through. Sliding doors are sometimes used here to close off the kitchen from the dining area. Rather than mount wall-type cabinets above a peninsula, however, some home owners have used open shelves, lattice work, bamboo curtains, and the like. Lattice work above a peninsula-located range might serve as a place to hang pots and pans, especially those with copper bottoms.

The free end of a peninsula base usually is rounded to improve its appearance and to remove the bumping hazard of square corners. This may consist simply of a rounded, overhanging extension of the counter, with two or more semicircular shelves below—perhaps supported by brackets or a wood or metal upright. These open shelves are commonly used for decorative display or for the more utilitarian storage of toaster and electric mixer. A novel and useful variation here would be a set of merry-go-round shelves on the post that supports the counter extension.

Island arrangement of cabinets is another possibility that the kitchen planner may want to consider. In this case, the range, sink, or several base cabinets are placed in the open, with walking space all around. Construction features would be similar to those required for a peninsula plan and you could use or adapt practically all of the ideas suggested for use in a peninsula arrangement.

CURVED-DOOR END CABINET

Uses

Here is the cabinet to place at the end of a peninsula if the builder wants all enclosed storage space. Shelves on the curved door have a usable length of a little more than 12″ and a depth of about 3″. A 1″ retaining strip rising above the shelf edges will keep stored items from sliding off. The two middle door shelves meet the middle cabinet shelves when the door is closed. The bottom shelf enters the cabinet above the rounded bottom shelf; the top one slips under the top cabinet framing. Articles stored in the main cabinet are all accessible through the one door, but a similar door could be placed on the opposite side if desired. You would build this like you do the door shown in the drawing on page 161.

Built without a door and enclosing wall, the cabinet offers convenient open shelving. In that case, the middle shelves should be cut to a full 11″ radius instead of being sliced off as indicated for the door version.

Materials

¾″ plywood (3′ x 4′ panel) to make—

   2 pc. 11⅞″ x 22″ — bottom shelf, top frame.

   1 pc. 20½″ x 31⅝″ — cabinet back.

½″ plywood (2′ x 4′ panel) to make—

   2 pc. 11⅛″ x 20½″ — middle shelves.

   4 pc. 3¾″ x 15½″ — door shelves.

1″ x 2″ (nom.) stock (12 linear feet) to make—

   3 pc. 31⅝″ long — cabinet frame.

   1 pc. 29⅝″ long — door frame.

2″ x 2″ (nom.) stock to make—

   2 pc. 28⅝″ long — door frame.

1 pc. 1″ x 4″ stock 16″ long and pine scrap — base frame.

1 4′ x 4′ panel ⅛″ tempered hardboard.

Pointers for Building

The top framing of the cabinet can be two or more pieces of stock cut and assembled as suggested in the sketch of the base frame. However, the builder may find it simpler to cut a full semicircle of ¾″ plywood to the same radius as the bottom shelf. In laying out these parts, be careful to allow a ⅞″ extension beyond the radius base line to reach the back piece. Notches are required in the corners of these pieces for the one-by-two vertical frame members, also another athwart the center line for the door mullion. After laying out the radius for the two middle shelves, draw a straight line between the points where the arc bisects the base and center lines. Saw along this to form the straight edges that face the door. Set these shelves in notches cut in the middle frame members. Assemble the cabinet with glue and screws. The shelves can be set in dadoes cut in the back piece if desired.

To lay out the door shelves, strike a quarter-circle arc on a 11″ radius. Measure in ¾″ on both the right angle lines. Connect these points with a straight line. This gives the shape for the top and bottom shelves since they are butted against the ends of the end frame

CURVED-DOOR END CABINET

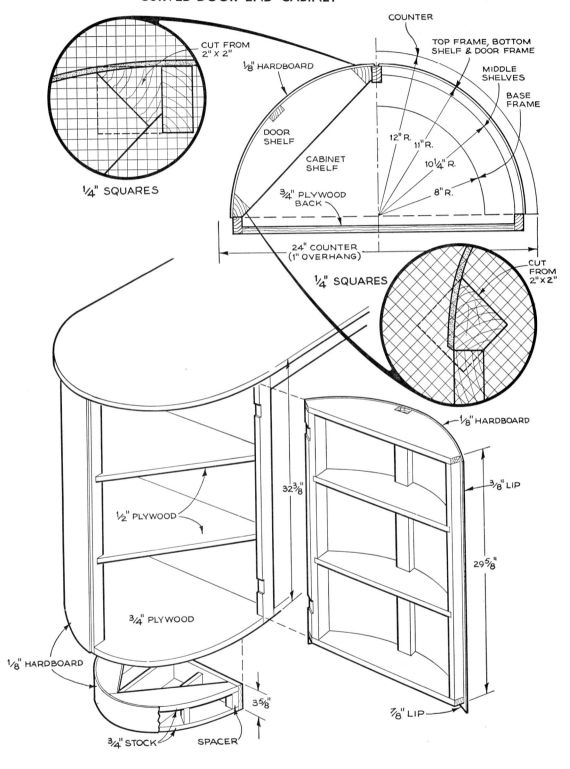

CUT FROM 2" X 2"

¼" SQUARES

COUNTER

TOP FRAME, BOTTOM SHELF & DOOR FRAME

MIDDLE SHELVES

BASE FRAME

⅛" HARDBOARD

DOOR SHELF

CABINET SHELF

12" R. 11" R.

10¼" R.

8" R.

¾" PLYWOOD BACK

24" COUNTER (1" OVERHANG)

¼" SQUARES

CUT FROM 2" X 2"

⅛" HARDBOARD

⅜" LIP

32⅜"

29⅝"

½" PLYWOOD

¾" PLYWOOD

⅛" HARDBOARD

3⅝"

¾" STOCK   SPACER

⅞" LIP

pieces. Center notches in all four pieces for the middle frame piece. The ends of the middle shelves are shaped as shown in the drawing. Make allowance in the length of each so they will extend into dadoes cut in the end frame pieces. Starting with the 2″ x 2″ stock, shape the two frame pieces to the sections shown in the sketch. Sand the outer edges to conform to the shelf radius. The middle frame piece also must be rounded off. Glue and screw the door parts together into a rigid framework, being careful that you get it true with all matching parts in exactly the same plane. Cut the parts and assemble the base frame in the same way.

Cut the hardboard into three sheets approximately the size required. Hardboard of this thickness can be bent without difficulty to the radius of the door and cabinet. For the 8″ radius required for the base, however, it will be necessary to moisten the panel thoroughly by leaving it in water for several hours. With the smooth side out, fasten each panel at one end and then gradually bend it into position, driving finishing nails about 1⅛″ long every 4″ or less as you go. The nailheads can be countersunk slightly and filled with putty before the finish is applied.

CURVED-DOOR QUARTER-CIRCLE CABINET

A curved-door cabinet of quarter-circle section may be desirable in some kitchen layouts in place of the half-circle one just described. To match base cabinets with a 25″ counter and a 1″ overhang, this should have two flat outer surfaces—the back and side—at right angles to each other, joined by a door (or perhaps two) bent to a 24″ radius.

A cabinet like this could be used at the end of a peninsula backed against a low divider wall—in the same manner as the square end cabinet that is illustrated immediately following. It could also be located at various other spots in the kitchen—at the end of a bank of base cabinets along a wall, in a corner by itself, adjoining a refrigerator or range, anywhere in fact where you need the clearance and added appearance that the curved surface gives. When a line of cabinets ends at a door, it would increase walking clearance and eliminate the hazard of sharp corners. Four quarter units, of course, will form a circular island. Three placed together, with the open segment as the work area, would give an island unit that could be a big work saver.

Construction of a quarter-circle unit would roughly parallel the half-circle type. Two doors could be used across the arc—or a single wide one. Here, as well as in the semicircular cabinet, the builder might like to install a curved hardboard door without a supporting framework. For the 24″ radius of the quarter-circle, $\frac{1}{4}$″ material, or perhaps $\frac{5}{16}$″, would be the best bet. Soak the panel for several hours and then leave it between wet cloths or newspapers for 48 hours. To form the panel to a permanent curvature, it must be fastened to a curved form until it has dried thoroughly. The temporary form must have a radius slightly less than the desired curvature to allow for a slight springback.

END CABINET

Uses

This cabinet was designed for a particular spot—the end of a peninsula unit dividing the kitchen and dining areas. Handy to both areas, it stores equipment needed in each. Recipes on standard 3″ x 5″ index cards can be filed in the top drawer, which also has space for several cookbooks within easy reach of the range. Lower drawers hold silver, linen, and place mats used in the dining area just around the corner. Located beside the range, the top of the cabinet serves as a convenient serving counter.

The same cabinet might also be used to advantage in some cases at the end of a line of base cabinets backed against a full wall. Your own kitchen floor plan will suggest whether you should use this one or a cabinet with normal front openings. The drawing for the cabinet was adapted from a design of the makers of Malarkey plywoods.

Materials

1″ x 2″ (nom.) stock (64 linear feet) — framing.

1″ x 4″ (nom.) stock (8 linear feet) — base.

¾″ plywood (4′ x 6′ panel) to make—

    1 pc. 17¼″ x 31⅝″ — side.

    1 pc. 24″ x 35¼″ — back.

    1 pc. 19″ x 25″ — top.

    1 pc. 16½″ x 21¼″ — bottom.

    4 pc. 4″ x 20¾″ — drawer fronts.

    1 pc. 9⅜″ x 20¾″ — drawer front.

⅝″ plywood (3′ x 4′ panel) to make—

    8 pc. 4″ x 17″ — drawer sides.

    4 pc. 4″ x 20¾″ — drawer backs.

    2 pc. 9⅜″ x 17″ — drawer sides.

    1 pc. 9⅜″ x 20¾″ — drawer back.

¼″ plywood (4′ x 6′ panel) to make—

    5 pc. 17″ x 20¾″ — drawer bottoms.

    1 pc. 4″ x 17″ — recipe file partition.

Drawer partitions as desired.

Pointers for Building

Cut and assemble the base first, using the 1″ x 4″ stock. Dimension it to allow a 3″ toe recess on two sides. Then put down the 16½″ x 21¼″ cabinet floor, allowing it to project 2¼″ on the two sides where the toe recess is to be. Cut and fit the ¾″ plywood back (the side next to the range in the drawing) and then position the assembly thus far completed and attach it to the wall. Attach the front piece of ¾″ plywood and finish the main framing at the top and front as shown in the sketches. Pieces of 1″ x 2″ stock, placed flat, serve as runners for the drawers. Others mounted on edge are guides.

A partition placed 5⅛″ from the edge of the top drawer will provide a space for 3″ x 5″ index cards. Partitions of ¼″ plywood can be added to the silver drawer as indicated—or ready-made trays can be used if you prefer.

END CABINET

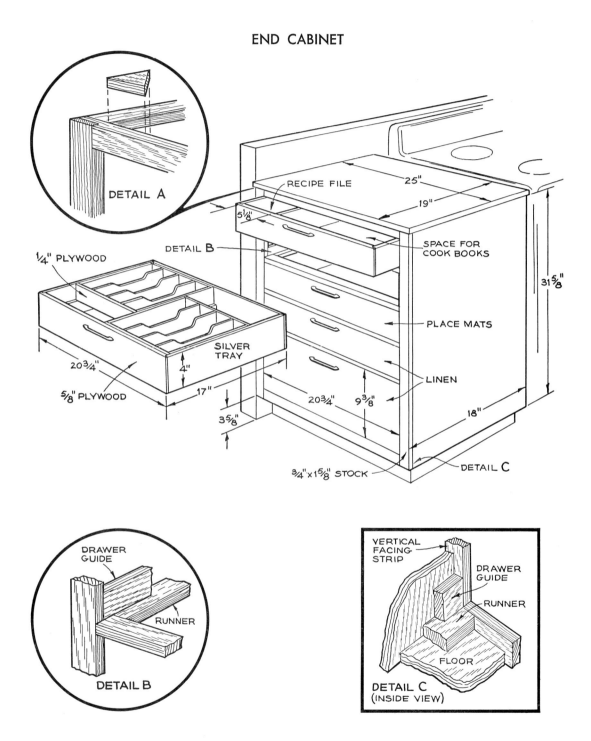

DETAIL A

1/4" PLYWOOD

DETAIL B

RECIPE FILE

5 1/8"

25"

19"

SPACE FOR COOK BOOKS

SILVER TRAY

4"

20 3/4"

17"

5/8" PLYWOOD

3 5/8"

PLACE MATS

LINEN

31 5/8"

20 3/4"

9 3/8"

18"

3/4"x1 5/8" STOCK

DETAIL C

DRAWER GUIDE

RUNNER

DETAIL B

VERTICAL FACING STRIP

DRAWER GUIDE

RUNNER

FLOOR

DETAIL C
(INSIDE VIEW)

PASS-THROUGH SERVING CENTER

Uses

This unit is a part of the Step-Saving U-Kitchen designed by the U.S. Bureau of Human Nutrition and Home Economics. It comprises most of the wall between kitchen and dining room in the original installation. But its main features—passway, sliding doors, and two-faced storage cupboards—could just as well go in a peninsula unit.

The three sliding doors back of the serving counter speed dining-room service and save many steps. They open up the passway through which food is served from the kitchen counter to a dining room side-board. In effect, this makes it possible to serve a meal in the dining room without leaving the kitchen. Double-fold doors on the kitchen side of the wall cabinet are hinged to fold back flat for convenience and safety.

Everyday and Sunday dishes stored in the wall cabinet and the corner Lazy Susan are accessible from either room. Space is provided too for large serving platters. Four small drawers under the right end of the wall cabinet also open from either room. Silver, table hot pads, and paper napkins go here. Two movable supplementary shelves between the cabinet shelves make better use of available shelf space, for flat or low objects can be placed on them. Heavy dishes and those most often used are kept on the bottom shelves of the Lazy Susan. Storage near counter level is always an excellent rule for reducing fatigue. An asbestos-covered hot pad is at hand for use under hot dishes that might mar the counter or table finish. A bullet catch holds it snugly in place while not in use.

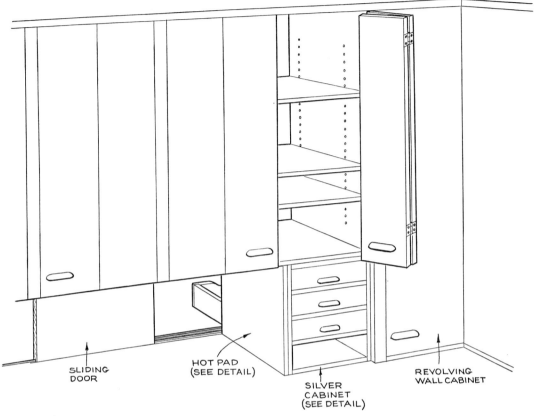

SLIDING
DOOR

HOT PAD
(SEE DETAIL)

SILVER
CABINET
(SEE DETAIL)

REVOLVING
WALL CABINET

PASS-THROUGH SERVING CENTER (A)

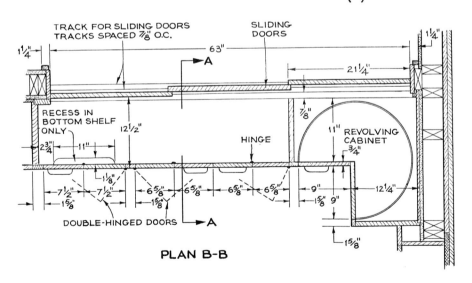

TRACK FOR SLIDING DOORS
TRACKS SPACED ⅞" O.C.

SLIDING
DOORS

RECESS IN
BOTTOM SHELF
ONLY

HINGE

REVOLVING
CABINET

DOUBLE-HINGED DOORS

PLAN B-B

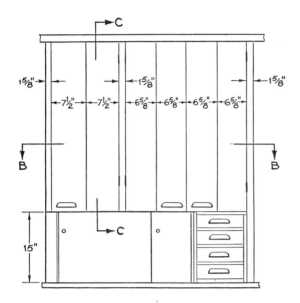

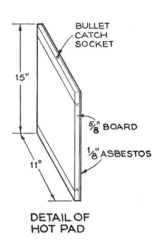

DETAIL OF
HOT PAD

PASS-THROUGH SERVING CENTER (B)

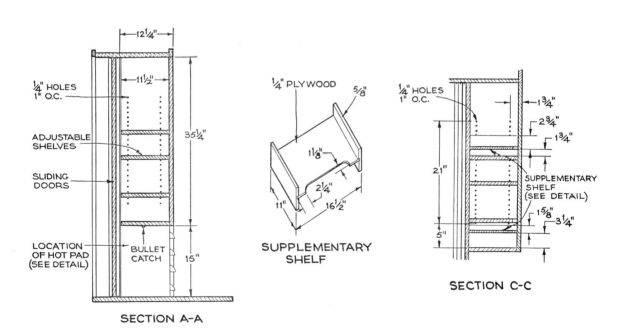

SECTION A-A

SUPPLEMENTARY
SHELF

SECTION C-C

PASS-THROUGH
SERVING CENTER
— SILVER CABINET DETAILS
(C)

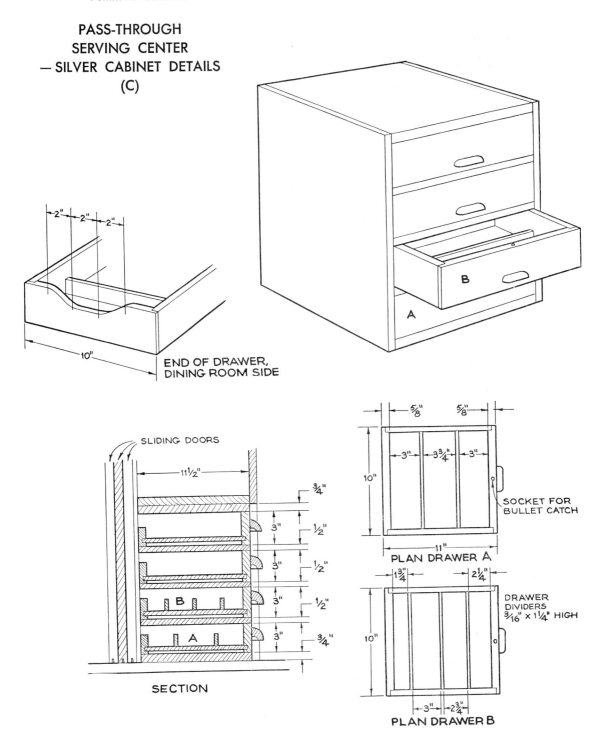

END OF DRAWER,
DINING ROOM SIDE

SLIDING DOORS

SECTION

PLAN DRAWER A

SOCKET FOR
BULLET CATCH

DRAWER
DIVIDERS
3/16" × 1 1/4" HIGH

PLAN DRAWER B

Materials (wall cupboard and silver cabinet)

1″ x 12″ (nom.) stock (30 linear feet) to make—

    1 pc. 51″ long — wall cupboard - Lazy Susan partition.

    1 pc. 36″ long — left end wall cabinet.

    1 pc. 44¾″ long — wall cupboard bottom.

    3 pc. 44″ long — adjustable shelves.

    1 pc. 15″ long — hot pad.

    2 pc. 15″ long — silver cabinet sides.

    2 pc. 10⅛″ long — top, bottom silver cabinet.

1″ x 2″ (nom.) stock (18 linear feet) to make—

    3 pc. 35¼″ long — vertical face strips.

    1 pc. 51″ long — vertical face strip.

    1 pc. 44¾″ long — horizontal face strip.

¾″ plywood (3′ x 4′ panel) to make—

    2 pc. 7½″ x 35¼″ (or 1″ x 8″ (nom.) stock) — doors.

    4 pc. 6⅝″ x 35¼″ (or 1″ x 7″ (nom.) stock) — doors.

½″ plywood — silver cabinet drawer supports.

⅝″ plywood — drawer fronts, sides, supplementary shelf ends.

¼″ plywood — drawer bottoms, supplementary shelves.

Pointers for Building

For information about the revolving cabinet, see the separate project in the chapter devoted to corner cabinets. Sliding doors can be built from scratch on the principles outlined for one of the wall cabinets in the wall cabinet chapter. However, for an installation of this size, the builder may prefer to buy a sliding-door unit complete with necessary hardware. These are available in various sizes from building supply dealers.

    The wall cabinet and silver cabinet are built on principles previously described for similar units.

10

Built-in Ovens and Cooking Tops

Streamlining of modern kitchens extends even to the range. Divided into two major units (oven and cooking top), each part can be installed for maximum efficiency and good looks. Raised to chest height, the oven typically is built into a floor-to-ceiling structure and there's no more stooping to see what's baking. Placed on or slipped into the top of a base cabinet, the cooking top becomes an integral part of its row of cabinets. Variations include built-in warming drawers (for keeping cooked foods hot), separate griddles, and complete ranges designed especially for blending into a line of base cabinets. Built-in units are available for both electricity and gas.

Anyone who can build other cabinets in this book can also build cabinets to house range built-ins. A cabinet for a sink would also suit a drop-in cooking top. The cabinets described in the sink chapter, therefore, are all possibilities for cooking tops that slip into work-counter openings. In contrast to drop-ins, some range tops are designed to rest on a cabinet just high enough to bring the cooking surface level with the kitchen work counter. Range tops are available

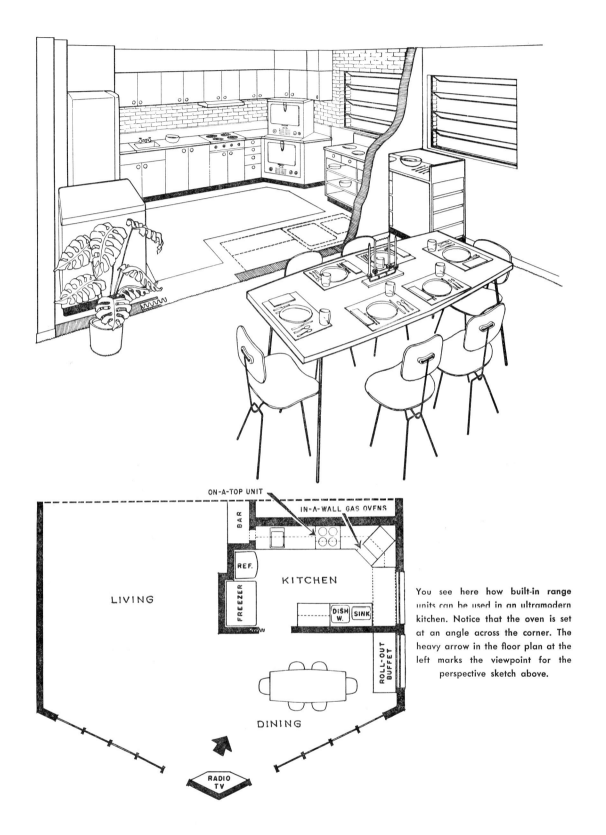

ON-A-TOP UNIT

IN-A-WALL GAS OVENS

BAR

LIVING

REF.

FREEZER

KITCHEN

DISH W.

SINK

ROLL-OUT BUFFET

DINING

RADIO TV

You see here how **built-in range** units can be used in an ultramodern kitchen. Notice that the oven is set at an angle across the corner. The heavy arrow in the floor plan at the left marks the viewpoint for the perspective sketch above.

In these sketches, and those on the facing page, the Chambers Corporation of Shelbyville, Indiana, suggests some of the ways its gas range built-ins can be applied in modern homes. Above, built-in ovens are housed in a floor-to-ceiling structure and a pair of the company's "on-a-top" cooking units rest on suitable base cabinets. Below, notice how the oven is raised to easy working height although the cabinet is not carried to the ceiling. A corner sink is another noteworthy feature of this layout.

BUILT-IN OVEN

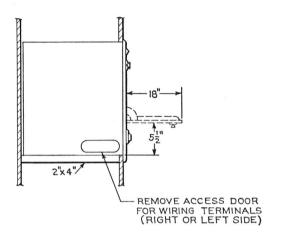

18"

5½"

2"x4"

REMOVE ACCESS DOOR
FOR WIRING TERMINALS
(RIGHT OR LEFT SIDE)

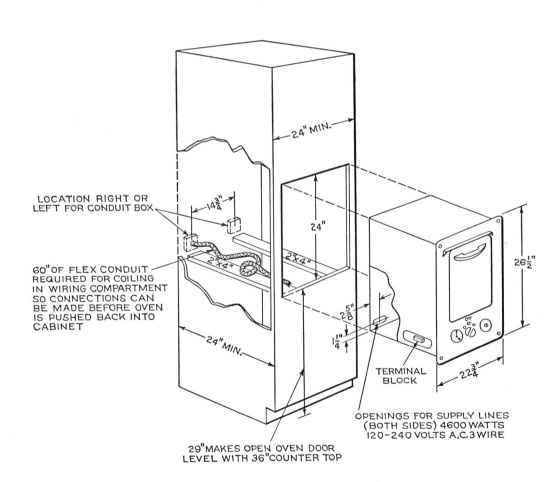

24" MIN.

LOCATION RIGHT OR
LEFT FOR CONDUIT BOX

14¾"

24"

60" OF FLEX CONDUIT
REQUIRED FOR COILING
IN WIRING COMPARTMENT
SO CONNECTIONS CAN
BE MADE BEFORE OVEN
IS PUSHED BACK INTO
CABINET

2"x4"   2"x4"

26½"

2⅝"

1¼"

24" MIN.

22¾"

TERMINAL
BLOCK

OPENINGS FOR SUPPLY LINES
(BOTH SIDES) 4600 WATTS
120-240 VOLTS A.C.3 WIRE

29" MAKES OPEN OVEN DOOR
LEVEL WITH 36" COUNTER TOP

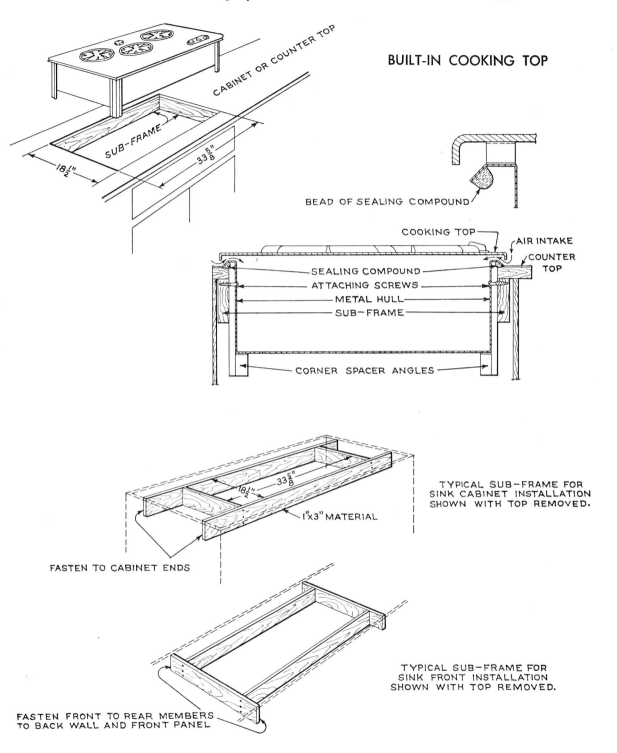

BUILT-IN COOKING TOP

CABINET OR COUNTER TOP

SUB-FRAME

18½"

33⅝"

BEAD OF SEALING COMPOUND

COOKING TOP

AIR INTAKE

COUNTER TOP

SEALING COMPOUND
ATTACHING SCREWS
METAL HULL
SUB-FRAME

CORNER SPACER ANGLES

33⅝"

18½"

1"x3" MATERIAL

TYPICAL SUB-FRAME FOR
SINK CABINET INSTALLATION
SHOWN WITH TOP REMOVED.

FASTEN TO CABINET ENDS

TYPICAL SUB-FRAME FOR
SINK FRONT INSTALLATION
SHOWN WITH TOP REMOVED.

FASTEN FRONT TO REAR MEMBERS
TO BACK WALL AND FRONT PANEL

with varying numbers of cooking units. Some include griddles.

Built-in ovens are sometimes bricked into a chimney-like structure. But this usually is for appearance only. Ovens designed for wall installation are so well insulated that no special fireproofing treatment is needed in a supporting structure. An oven can go into a simple wood cabinet fitted with a pair of horizontal 2 x 4's to provide support and serve as slides for shoving it into place.

A floor-to-ceiling cabinet as deep as the base cabinets is often used to house an oven. But the part above the oven could be omitted. A cabinet this deep (from front to back) presents awkward storage space at or above head height when utilized in conventional cupboard fashion. If oven venting is required, a vent pipe might occupy the rear of this upper part of the cabinet and a wall cabinet of standard depth the front. In certain situations, it might also be possible to use the rear space for a duct leading to a kitchen exhaust fan.

Some builders have found it convenient to stop the oven enclosure immediately above the raised oven, topping it off with a surface that can be used for open storage or display. Others have set the base low enough in the row of base cabinets so that the oven top slips under the bottom of the wall cabinets above. Some ovens need no side or top enclosure.

The accompanying drawings show cabinet construction suggested by two major manufacturers of range built-ins. In each case, the dimensions suit a specific product—a three-burner gas drop-in made by the Chambers Corporation of Shelbyville, Indiana, and a wall oven made by Thermador Electrical Manufacturing Company of Los Angeles, California. The drawings, however, are not presented here as construction plans. They are given merely to show you that range built-ins will offer no building difficulties if you wish to include them in your new kitchen. If you buy a built-in, you will receive full installation instructions to suit your particular unit.

11

Floor-to-Ceiling Cabinets

Although the modern trend is toward exclusive use of wall and base storage units with a streamlined counter arrangement, many kitchens still need cabinets or cupboards that start at the floor and rise most or all of the way to the ceiling. If closets are lacking, tall cabinets are useful for storage of brooms, mops, vacuum cleaners, ironing boards, and the like—if nothing else. In some cases, too, full-height cabinets offer a place to store reserve supplies.

Strangely enough, considering the current emphasis on separate lines of wall and base cabinets, tall storage units have gotten serious attention at some of the research centers from which kitchen cabinet styles of the future may eventually come.

On the pages that immediately follow, you will find plans for a swing-shelf storage unit. Its shelves open like the pages of a book. It departs sharply from modern kitchen-cabinet design. The home owner whose heart is set on a new or remodeled streamlined kitchen may not like its looks. It has little in common with conventional wall or base cabinets. Yet for efficiency of storage few cabinets could equal it.

The cabinet is one of several developed at the College of Home Economics of Cornell University during a study of functional kitchen storage. Mary Koll Heiner and Helen E. McCullough, who made the study, have this to say about it:

"The swing cabinet is the most compact example of functional storage here developed. It holds 150 to 175 packaged foods as well as 35 items of major equipment used first at the mix center. Through this device needless kitchen travel and the rehandling of supplies are reduced markedly. Shelving that would necessitate 57 linear feet and would require 9 feet of walking distance (pilot study) was reduced to 5 compact 24-inch units that occupy a quadrant area of less than 4 feet. First-use, ease of visibility, and ease of grasp are readily achieved on shelves ranging from 2 inches to 4½ inches for packaged food supplies. All storage is one row deep, one stack high. Order becomes automatic."

The swing feature and the narrow shelves—just wide enough for the cans or other items to be stored—are ideas that can be utilized in many ways by a home cabinet builder.

SWING STORAGE CABINET

Uses

This cabinet provides space between range and sink for storage of mixing and baking supplies and utensils. It was developed at Cornell University. Their bulletin points out:

"The upper shelves in the right-hand section hold the mixing supplies and those items used first at the sink. The wider cut-back shelves below hold the mixing and baking utensils. Bake pans, muffin tins, and other baking dishes are stored on edge on the bottom shelf and separated by plywood dividers. This eliminates stacking and the unnecessary handling which always accompanies stacking.

"The center panel in the upper part swings between the two outside sections. The small mixing and cutting tools may be hung on the right-hand surface of it and the supplies used first with boiling water are on the left-hand side. All shelves are narrow so that items are stored on them one row deep. They also are adjustable so that they may be moved up or down to fit the items placed on them."

Standing 6′ 10½″ high, the cabinet occupies only 15¼″ x 25½″ of floor space. The right-hand section should be fastened to the wall. About 29″ of free wall space is needed at the left if the left-hand section is to open fully. If desired, this section can be divided into parts. Divided slightly above the 36″ level, the upper part would clear an adjoining base-cabinet work counter. A rolling table could be used in front of the cabinet to provide a work surface.

The university bulletin recommends that if the range and sink are located on the same wall, this cabinet and a work counter should be placed between them. If sink and range are on adjacent walls, the cabinet could be placed in the corner, with the hinge side 7½″ from the corner of the room. This will allow the left door to open 90 degrees—flat against the adjacent wall.

Materials

PLYWOOD

1 4′ x 9′ panel ¼″.

1 4′ x 7′ panel ¼″.

1 4′ x 8′ panel ½″.

1 4′ x 7′ panel ¾″.

HARDWOOD

1 pc. ⅞″ x 3″ x 6′.

1 pc. ¾″ x ¾″ x 10′.

1 pc. ¾″ x ¾″ x 8′.

60′ ¼″ x ½″.

1 piano hinge 3′ 10″ long.

1 piano hinge 6′ 6″ long.

2 door catches.

12 adjustable shelf standards 6′ long.

1 rubber caster 2½″ dia.

6 doz. screws for ¼″ panels   1″-#6 flat-head.

4 doz. screws for base and shelves   1¼″-#6 flat-head.

3 doz. screws for door jambs   1½″-#7 flat-head.

2 lbs. brads #16.

23 chrome retaining strips 1″ x 23½″.

SWING STORAGE CABINET

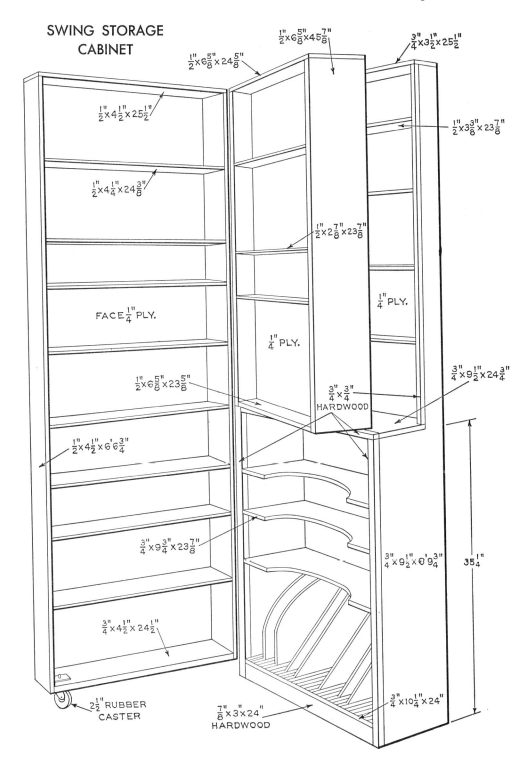

$\frac{1}{2}"\times6\frac{5}{8}"\times24\frac{5}{8}"$

$\frac{1}{2}"\times6\frac{5}{8}"\times45\frac{7}{8}"$

$\frac{3}{4}"\times3\frac{1}{2}"\times25\frac{1}{2}"$

$\frac{1}{2}"\times4\frac{1}{2}"\times25\frac{1}{2}"$

$\frac{1}{2}"\times3\frac{3}{8}"\times23\frac{7}{8}"$

$\frac{1}{2}"\times4\frac{1}{4}"\times24\frac{3}{8}"$

$\frac{1}{2}"\times2\frac{7}{8}"\times23\frac{7}{8}"$

FACE $\frac{1}{4}"$ PLY.

$\frac{1}{4}"$ PLY.

$\frac{1}{4}"$ PLY.

$\frac{1}{2}"\times6\frac{5}{8}"\times23\frac{5}{8}"$

$\frac{3}{4}"\times\frac{3}{4}"$ HARDWOOD

$\frac{3}{4}"\times9\frac{1}{2}"\times24\frac{3}{4}"$

$\frac{1}{2}"\times4\frac{1}{2}"\times6'6\frac{3}{4}"$

$\frac{3}{4}"\times9\frac{1}{2}"\times0'9\frac{3}{4}"$

$35\frac{1}{4}"$

$\frac{3}{4}"\times9\frac{3}{4}"\times23\frac{7}{8}"$

$\frac{3}{4}"\times4\frac{1}{2}"\times24\frac{1}{2}"$

$2\frac{1}{2}"$ RUBBER CASTER

$\frac{7}{8}"\times3\times24"$ HARDWOOD

$\frac{3}{4}"\times10\frac{1}{4}"\times24"$

Pointers for Building

After cutting the sides, top, and two fixed shelves of the rear unit, screw and glue the four ¾″ x ¾″ hardwood edge strips in place to serve as door jambs. For conservation of material, the three cutaway shelves in the base can be cut from the panel of ¾″ plywood. However, some builders may prefer pine stock here. Cut the indentations in these shelves 3¾″ deep, centering the cutouts 5″ from each end and rounding the inner and outer corners to a 1½″ radius.

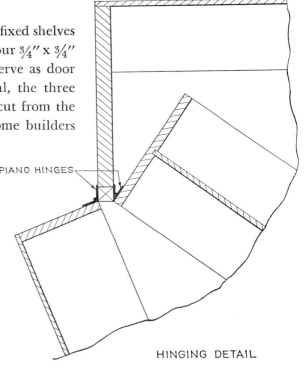

PIANO HINGES

HINGING DETAIL

The base frame consists of two 24″ lengths of ⅞″ x 3″ hardwood, installed between the sides and covered by a fixed shelf. Grooves for the shelf dividers are easily made by bradding strips of ¼″ x ½″ wood to the shelf and ¼″ plywood back. However, builders with power equipment may prefer to cut grooves in the shelf itself. Make the dividers from ¼″ plywood. Two shapes are indicated, each with a 9″ base dimension. Make the curved dividers 12″ high and curve the upper edge to a 9″ radius.

The middle swing unit is partitioned by a 24½″ x 45⅞″ panel of ¼″ plywood. Glue the edges of this panel into grooves cut in the top, bottom, and sides. Shelves 3⅜″ wide are used on the side not visible in the drawing. In the original cabinet, two rows of utensil hooks are placed across the bottom part of the unit on that side. In the rear unit, two of the shelves are cut back to a 2″ width for storage of spices. For these, you can substitute ¼″ material in place of the ½″ indicated.

Install metal shelf strips in all units to support the shelves and make them adjustable. Vertical grooves may be cut in the sides for flush-mounting of the strips, or they may be screwed directly to the sides.

Chrome strips on the shelf edges serve two functions. They cover the raw plywood grain and, projecting above the shelf surface, they keep supplies from falling off.

CANNED GOODS STORAGE CABINET

Uses

In a modern home, this spacious cabinet can take the place of the old-time pantry. Its shelves and door racks will hold most of the canned goods, bought or home-produced, that the average housewife today will want to store.

Projecting only 12½″, the cabinet will fit anywhere in the kitchen or adjoining hallway that you can find 48″ of free wall space. Cut down in width to suit, it is an ideal cabinet for a narrow wall space between two doors that pass through the same wall.

The plans are based on those for a storage cabinet shown in a U.S. Department of Agriculture Bulletin. "Easy-to-Build Kitchen Cabinets for the Remodeled Farmhouse." The plans here, in fact, differ only in that the overall depth is reduced. This reduction was made as a move toward storage shelves just wide enough for the articles to be stored; that is, if you are going to store canned goods you would make each shelf just wide enough (plus an inch or so perhaps) to take the uniform size can to be stored there. The door racks offer storage for cans of two or more sizes.

As shown, the inner shelves are in fixed positions. However, it would be simple enough to make part or all of them adjustable. You could accomplish this with movable pegs and drilled holes as shown in plans for several of the wall cabinets. In this cabinet, however, as well as in some of the wall cabinets, you may find it more convenient to use the metal shelf strips available at hardware and building supply stores.

A box step for reaching the upper shelves fits sideways under the bottom shelf. Omit this if the kitchen has a step stool stored near the cabinet.

Materials

1″ x 12″ (nom.) stock (32 linear feet) to make—

   2 pc. 88″ long — sides.

   1 pc. 46½″ long — top.

   12 pc. 11¾″ long — ends of shelves.

1″ x 6″ (nom.) stock (14 linear feet) to make—

   6 pc. 24½″ long — middle shelves.

1″ x 9″ (nom.) stock to make—

   2 pc. 88″ long — front face boards.

1″ x 3″ (nom.) stock (14 linear feet) to make—

   1 pc. 31½″ long — top facing board.

   1 pc. 31½″ long — overhead jamb.

   2 pc. 84″ long — side jambs.

1 pc. 2″ x 3″ stock 45″ long — header.

2 pc. 2″ x 3″ stock 84¾″ long — studs.

2 pc. ½″ x ⅞″ x 84″ stock ⎫
                              ⎬ door stops.
1 pc. ½″ x ⅞″ x 29″ stock ⎭

1″ half-round (18 linear feet) — door molding.

¾″ quarter-round (16 linear feet) — molding at rear corners.

1″ x 2″ (nom.) stock (48 linear feet) to make—

   7 pc. 46½″ long — back cleats.

   14 pc. 11¼″ long — side cleats.

   12 pc.   4⅛″ long — front cleats.

1 pc. ¼″ x 48″ x 88″ plywood — back.

30″ x 84″ flush panel door.

10′ ½″ x 6″ stock — door racks.

Pointers for Building

Nominal stock needs only to be cut to length to give you most of the parts for this cabinet. A good place to begin is at the front. Cut the two vertical facing boards from 1″ x 9″ stock and the top one from 1″ x 4″; cut the jamb and door stop pieces. Make a trial assembly of

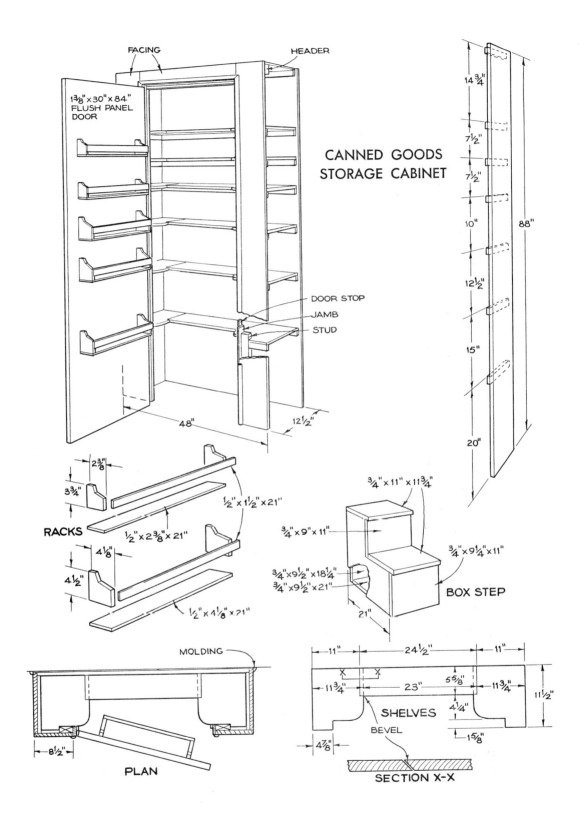

FACING

HEADER

1³⁄₈"x30"x84" FLUSH PANEL DOOR

CANNED GOODS STORAGE CABINET

14³⁄₄"

7¹⁄₂"

7¹⁄₂"

10"

12¹⁄₂"

88"

15"

DOOR STOP

JAMB

STUD

20"

48"

12¹⁄₂"

2³⁄₈"

3³⁄₄"

¹⁄₂"x1¹⁄₂"x21"

RACKS

¹⁄₂"x2³⁄₈"x21"

4¹⁄₈"

4¹⁄₂"

¹⁄₂"x4¹⁄₈"x21"

³⁄₄"x11"x11³⁄₄"

³⁄₄"x9"x11"

³⁄₄"x9¹⁄₄"x11"

³⁄₄"x9¹⁄₂"x18¹⁄₄"
³⁄₄"x9¹⁄₂"x21"

21"

BOX STEP

MOLDING

8¹⁄₂"

PLAN

11"

24¹⁄₂"

11"

11³⁄₄"

23"

5⁵⁄₈"

11³⁄₄"

4¹⁄₄"

11¹⁄₂"

X   X

SHELVES

BEVEL

4⁷⁄₈"

15⁵⁄₈"

SECTION X-X

these pieces around the flush door placed flat on the floor. Then measure the overall width of the assembly. This will enable you to take into account any local variations in the stock and show whether you should adjust other dimensions of the cabinet, especially the length of the shelves.

Screw all cleats to the back, sides, and front members. Begin assembly of the unit by screwing or nailing the ¼″ back to the wall. The sides, facing, studs, header, and top can then all go into place. Make all shelves to the shape shown and glue and nail the beveled edges together.

UTILITY CABINET

Uses

As shown, this tall cabinet provides space for broom, mop, cleaning supplies, and perhaps a vacuum cleaner. Shoe cleaning and polishing materials, or a child's toys, might go in the bottom drawer. Additional hooks would extend the usefulness of the cabinet to storage of aprons and other small items of clothing. Alternately, an ironing board might stand in the cabinet. If filled with additional shelves, it could be devoted to storage of canned goods and other food supplies.

Materials

1″ x 12″ (nom.) stock (40 linear feet).
1″ x 8″ (nom.) stock (4 linear feet).
1″ x 4″ (nom.) stock (8 linear feet).
1″ x 2″ (nom.) stock (42 linear feet).
1 pc. ¾″ plywood 36″ x 48″.
1 pc. ¼″ plywood 36″ x 88″.

Pointers for Building

Two 88″ lengths of the 1″ x 12″ stock, glued together or simply held by the shelf cleats, will be suitable for each of the cabinet sides. The door might be made of a strip of 1″ x 12″ stock and another of the

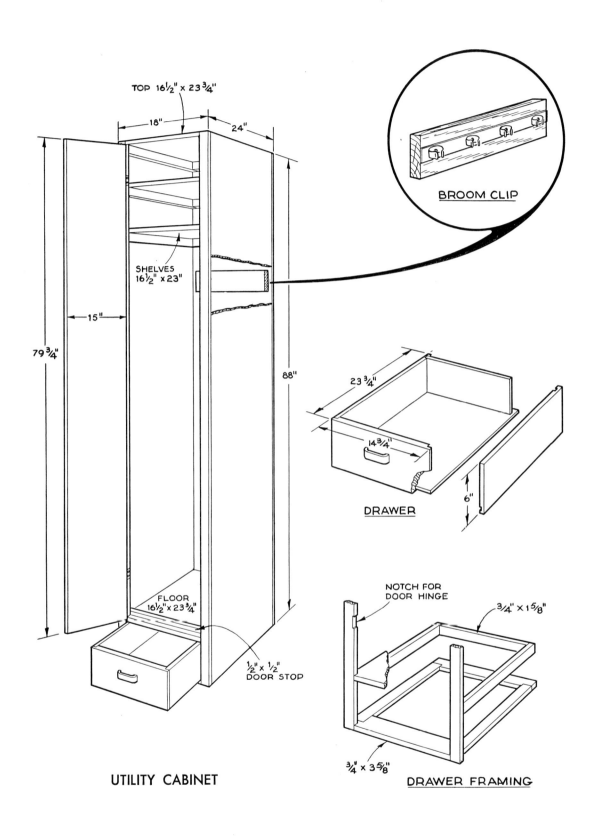

TOP 16½" x 23¾"

18"

24"

BROOM CLIP

SHELVES
16½" x 23"

15"

79¾"

88"

23¾"

14¾"

6"

DRAWER

FLOOR
16½" x 23¾"

½" x ½"
DOOR STOP

NOTCH FOR
DOOR HINGE

¾" x 1⅝"

¾" x 3⅝"

UTILITY CABINET

DRAWER FRAMING

1″ x 4″ material. Or you could use ¾″ plywood. Use ¾″ plywood for the cabinet top, the floor, and the two shelves, supporting them on cleats cut from the 1″ x 2″ stock. Two 88″ pieces of 1″ x 2″ stock also are needed for the vertical face strips. Cut ¾″ x 1⅝″ notches in the front corners of the top, floor, and the bottom drawer framing so the verticals can be inset. The drawer is standard construction. Additional pieces of 1″ x 2″ stock should be attached (not shown) to the sides just above the bottom drawer-supporting frame to act as drawer guides.

HEAVY EQUIPMENT CABINET

Uses

All kitchens need a convenient place for heavy equipment—roasters, Dutch ovens, and canning equipment. This cabinet keeps these things at a level where they are easiest to lift. The bottom compartment is for bottle storage. It might also serve for canned goods.

Materials

¾″ plywood or 1″ (nom.) stock to make—
   2 pc. 15¾″ x 6′ 8⅜″ — sides.
   1 pc. 16″ x 21¼″ — top.
   2 pc. 15¾″ x 19¾″ — shelf and bottom.
   1 pc. 15¾″ x 24″ — partition.
   1 pc. 10½″ x 15¾″ — shelf.
   1 pc. 18″ x 55″ — door.
   1 pc. 18″ x 25″ — door.
¼″ plywood (4′ x 8′ panel) to make—
   1 pc. 21¼″ x 6′ 8⅜″ — back.
   5 pc. 8½″ x 15″ — bottle shelves.
1″ x 4″ (nom.) stock (8 linear feet) — base.
1″ x 2″ (nom.) stock (20 linear feet) — door framing, shelf support.

Pointers for Building

Cut all pieces to size and assemble the base. Rip the 1″ x 2″ pine to make 11 pieces ¾″ x ¾″ x 8½″. Attach five of these to the cabinet back as cleats to support the back ends of the reclining bottle shelves, spacing them at 4″ intervals in the lower left corner. Cut a pair of notches in each of the other six pieces to hold the necks of the bottles and then nail the ¼″ plywood shelves to the bottom edges of five of them. The sixth goes at the front of the cabinet bottom. Mount the shelves at the front ends by driving screws through the partition and left cabinet side into the ends of the cleats.

Since the original was located at the end of a line of base cabinets, the drawing shows a toe recess at both the front and right sides. This of course can be varied as desired.

IDEAS

Storage Wall

One of the devices designed and tested in a Cornell functional kitchen storage study was a swing-shelf storage wall. In this case, the swinging shelves were placed on doors opening in conventional fashion, one to the right and one to the left. This made it possible to store packaged items both inside the cabinet and on the door in a row just one deep, with none behind the others. Such storage makes it easier for the kitchen worker to see and reach any desired item.

A wall storage unit like this might find a place in many homes as a divider between kitchen and dining room. Some drawers might

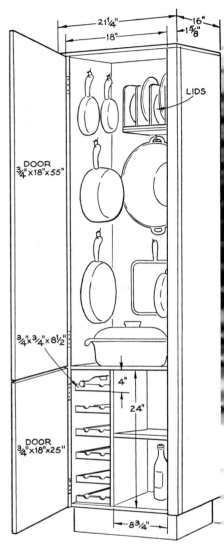

HEAVY EQUIPMENT CABINE

open both into the kitchen and the dining room. A shelf section devoted to dish storage likewise could have a door opening into each room. A counter-height shelf could serve as a pass window between the rooms.

The Cornell unit was built 16″ deep, 6′ wide, and 6′ 6″ high, all inside dimensions. It is a combination of three units, each 24″ wide, divided at a distance of 30″ from the floor. Shelves are placed above, and bins, drawers and files below.

Door Shelves

Useful storage space can often be found on inside doors, particularly the inner face of those opening into closets, stairways, and the like. Narrow shelves, with retaining strips along their edge, can be used for storage of various packaged and canned goods. The shelves can be placed between two vertical frame members, perhaps one-by-fours, mounted a short distance from each edge of the door. A shelf plus a retaining strip about 6″ above (nailed across the outer edges of the verticals) makes a handy place to store pan lids, trays, etc. A similar arrangement might also take an item as bulky as an ironing board.

Roll-out Cleaner Cabinet

A tall, narrow cabinet could have a roll-out unit in its base to store and transport a tank-type vacuum cleaner, standing on its end. Equip the unit with three or four rubber-tired casters and it can be used to move the cleaner and all accessories into other rooms of the house. Let the back of the unit serve as the cabinet door like some of the units shown and described in the chapter on vertical pull-out racks. A roll-out unit like this might also fit into a niche in a storage wall.

12

Space-Saving Dining Areas

If a modern home has dining space in the living room, or even if there is a separate dining room, the housewife usually finds it most convenient to serve at least breakfast and luncheon in the kitchen. If economy has dictated a compact kitchen, and all space must be carefully utilized, a dual-purpose unit will furnish eating facilities.

For instance, a counter that increases the kitchen work surface can do double duty as a dining table. If the kitchen floor plan includes a base-cabinet peninsula, extending the work counter about 30″ beyond the cabinets and supporting it on one or two wood or pipe posts will furnish eating space for two, and possibly three, persons. Stools can be pushed under the counter while not in use. Or, perhaps folding camp-style stools can be used and hung on hooks under the counter or on a wall. (Ordinary chairs are unsuitable at a work counter 36″ high. They can be used, however, if this section of the counter is lowered to conventional table height.) A similar arrangement might be worked out at the end of a line of base cabinets along a wall, although two persons would not be able to sit opposite each other as they would at a peninsula extension.

190

A kitchen desk often offers eating facilities for the youngsters. So does a pull-out work board under the counter, especially if it is wide enough to accommodate a place-setting on each side. Or a line of pull-out boards in wall-backed base cabinets will give leg room underneath for all hungry members of the family as they face the wall—as well as offer the chief cook additional work space wherever she happens to need it. Each of these boards can be installed as described in the chapter on base cabinets. Chairs can be used rather than stools if the boards are placed at lapboard height.

Kept narrow, an eating bar supported by brackets can sometimes be installed on a wall where the need for a passageway makes base cabinets impractical. Hinging the brackets and table surface will make it possible to drop the table against the wall while not in use.

A counter where food is placed temporarily on its way to the dining room or area can double as a breakfast table. If the kitchen has a pass-through, a narrow bar on the dining-room side will enable the housewife to serve breakfast or luncheon without leaving the kitchen. The counter on the dining-room side might be hinged to swing up, closing the pass-through. Or it could be mounted to drop down against the wall.

WINDOW-BOX TABLE

Uses

This unit adds both utility and a decorative note to the kitchen without detracting from the light-giving function of the windows. The shelves offer additional kitchen storage. The fold-down table can be used for the children's lunch or breakfast or as extra counter space. It also serves as an extension if a regular kitchen table is pushed against it. Pots of flowers spaced on the ledge behind bring colorful cheerfulness to the kitchen.

Materials

1″ x 8″ (nom.) stock (24 linear feet) to make—

   3 pc. 69½″ long (or width of your window) — shelves.

   2 pc. 26″ long — ends.

   1 pc. 69½″ long (width of this member will depend on height of
     lower edge of windows from floor and width of baseboard) —
     flower recess side.

1″ x 4″ (nom.) stock (12 linear feet) to make—

   3 pc. 25¼″ long — hinging strips.

   2 pc. 17⁹⁄₁₆″ long — folding support for table.

1″ x 2″ (nom.) stock to make—

   1 pc. 19″ long — door stop.

¾″ plywood (4′ x 8′ panel) to make—

   2 pc. 15″ x 25¼″ — doors.

   1 pc. 25¼″ x 30″ — table.

Pointers for Building

The plans for this unit appeared originally in *The Business of Farming Magazine* (published by United States Gypsum Company). As shown there, it had been designed for a specific kitchen. Except for the 30″ table height (which should be retained) the indicated dimensions therefore may not be suitable for the available spot in your kitchen. But you will be able to adapt the principles shown.

Since lumber is used in its actual width, sawing to length is mostly all that is required. However, it will be best to have the bottom of the flower recess level with the window sill. This may require ripping or planing away some of the width of the piece of 1″ x 8″ (nom.) stock indicated for the front of the recess, if the 30″ height of the table is to be retained. When you determine the width needed, by trial, it may be possible to use nominal stock of a lesser width and avoid ripping. Chisel out notches in the middle shelf for the folding leg and door stop after sawing to depth. Adjust the length of the two parts of the folding table leg by trial to be sure it brings the table

END DETAIL

- ¾"
- 7½"
- VARIABLE
- WALL
- 25¼"
- BASEBOARD

WINDOW-BOX TABLE

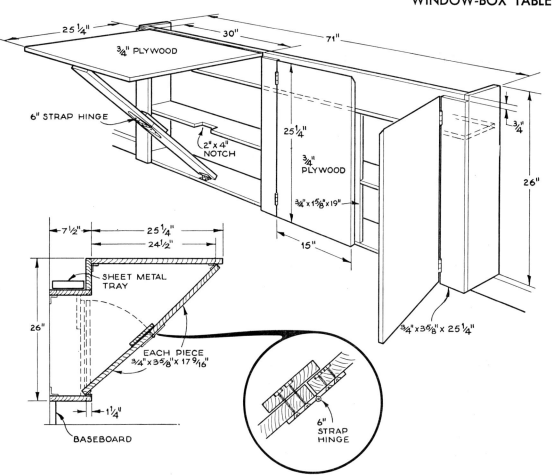

- 25¼"
- 30"
- 71"
- ¾" PLYWOOD
- 6" STRAP HINGE
- 2" x 4" NOTCH
- 25¼"
- ¾" PLYWOOD
- ¾" x 1⅝" x 19"
- 15"
- ¾
- 26"
- ¾" x 3⅝" x 25¼"
- 7½"
- 25¼"
- 24½"
- SHEET METAL TRAY
- 26"
- EACH PIECE ¾" x 3⅝" x 17 9/16"
- 1¼"
- BASEBOARD
- 6" STRAP HINGE

level. As the circled detail shows, a block bolted to the rear of the lower shelf keeps the leg from collapsing.

Shallow trays for the flower pots can be soldered together from galvanized sheet metal. However, if you do not want to attempt this job, hardware stores, dime stores and florist shops sell plastic watering coasters that will serve just as well.

FOLDING WALL TABLE

Uses

A unit like this can go where the space must be used for other purposes during most of the time, as in a hallway, for instance. However, it also makes an attractive and useful table as the major kitchen dining installation for a small family. The linoleum-covered table top is large enough for three place-settings. Necessary dishes can be stored on the shelves so as to be quickly available for use. A screen-door hook is positioned under one shelf to hold up the bending leg when the unit is closed. Decorative knickknacks might be kept on the open shelves at the bottom. A unit like this might also find uses in other rooms of the home. *The Business of Farming Magazine,* in which the original plans appeared, suggested it as a rainy-day play table for the children in the laundry or work room. For the use of children, a table height of 23¼″ from the floor was suggested instead of the 30″ in the present drawing.

Materials

1″ x 6″ (nom.) stock (20 linear feet) to make—

    2 pc. 67″ long — sides.

    3 pc. 24⅛″ long — bottom and middle shelves, top.

1″ x 5″ (nom.) stock (8 linear feet) to make—

    3 pc. 24⅛″ long — shelves. (More materials on page 196)

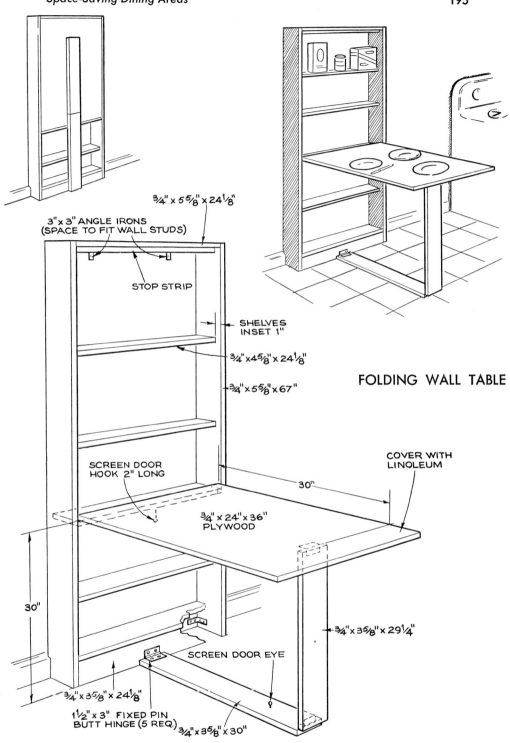

¾" x 5⅝" x 24⅛"

3" x 3" ANGLE IRONS
(SPACE TO FIT WALL STUDS)

STOP STRIP

SHELVES
INSET 1"

¾" x 4⅝" x 24⅛"

¾" x 5⅝" x 67"

FOLDING WALL TABLE

SCREEN DOOR
HOOK 2" LONG

COVER WITH
LINOLEUM

30"

¾" x 24" x 36"
PLYWOOD

30"

¾" x 3⅝" x 29¼"

SCREEN DOOR EYE

¾" x 3⅝" x 24⅛"

1½" x 3" FIXED PIN
BUTT HINGE (5 REQ.)   ¾" x 3⅝" x 30"

1″ x 4″ (nom.) stock (8 linear feet) to make—

   1 pc. 24⅛″ long — baseboard.

   1 pc. 29⅛″ long — leg unit.

   1 pc. 30″ long — leg unit.

1 pc. ¾″ plywood 24″ x 36″ — table top.

1 pc. ¾″ x ¾″ x 24⅛″ — stop strip.

5 fixed-pin butt hinges.

4 3″ x 3″ angle irons.

1 screen-door hook and eye.

Pointers for Building

If you have a power saw and if you are content to rest the shelves on cleats instead of cutting more professional dadoes, this project could be ready for painting an hour after you set to work.

Shelves set back about an inch above the table top allow the closed top to go in flush with the edges of the sides. Locate the upper stop carefully so that the top comes to rest evenly. If desired, a piece of quarter-round could be used for this strip. Position the folding leg parts by trial to be sure they hold the table level and function smoothly. Cut out the rear edges of the two side pieces as required to fit over the kitchen baseboard. Don't worry too much if you have a bad cut. Putty will fill in, and paint will hide the defect. Find the position for the screen-door hook under the hinge shelf while holding the table top up—that is, closed.

DISAPPEARING BREAKFAST NOOK

The familiar kitchen breakfast nook now has a convenient and space-saving offshoot—the disappearing breakfast nook that swings up against a wall or into a shallow cabinet. In general, it works like the folding wall table just described. But it also has fold-up benches on either side of the table.

Many variations are possible in such a unit. Table and seats can be hinged directly to the wall without a backing cabinet, the table 30″ from the floor, the benches 16″ or 18″. Mount horizontal strips on the wall, screwing them to adjoining studs. Hinge the table and benches to these. To seat four, two on each side, the table and benches should be at least 44″ long, the benches being made of 2″ stock about 12″ wide for adequate strength. For a shorter unit to seat only one on a side, 3/4″ or 1″ plywood would give the necessary rigidity to the benches and table.

Instead of two-piece folding brackets as suggested for the wall table, the table and benches might be supported by rectangular pieces of 3/4″ plywood about 12″ wide or 1″ x 12″ nominal stock and long enough to hold the three units level. Hinge these rectangular legs to the table and benches near the outward ends of the latter. The hinges will allow the legs to fold down against the table and benches when the units are raised to the wall, and drop to the floor when the units are opened out. Wood turn-buttons could be mounted on the wall to hold up the units.

Mounting the table and benches in a cabinet, rather than against the wall, will increase kitchen storage and yield a unit that many may prefer from the viewpoint of appearance. For this, the cabinet can be run from the floor to ceiling, or drop ceiling, if desired. Shelves above the upper limit needed for the benches and table may be left open or be fitted with doors. Doors also can go on the cabinet under the table. (If the table is short, two doors hinged under its center might be opened back to back to support it. Or, instead of being folded up, the table itself might be mounted to hinge down and serve as the door for the shelves below—with a hinged leg to support it when up.)

The builder should not overlook that a cabinet mounting offers a better opportunity to cushion the benches, perhaps with foam rubber. If the padding is attached permanently to the benches, allowance for its thickness must be made by reducing the front-to-back dimension of the shelves. If the pads are left free, their ends may be dropped into the cabinet niche below and behind the hinged ends of the benches.

UNDER-THE-COUNTER TABLE

Uses

While not in use, this kitchen eating center packs away snugly under the counter surface. The chairs fit on either side of the centered leg that supports the sliding table in its outward position. Their backs form a line with the fronts of the adjoining base cabinets.

The second page of drawings shows variations in the general plans —how a shallow drawer may be located above the table and space below the chair seats put to use for a drawer or bottle storage. A table unit like this would find a practical place in a very small kitchen or in one where base cabinets fill all available wall space. It is dimensioned to fit under a counter surface 36″ high.

Materials

$5/8$″ plywood (4′ x 8′ panel) to make—

    1 pc. 22$1/4$″ x 29″ — table.

    2 pc. 12″ x 13″ — chair seats.

    4 pc. 12$1/2$″ x 16$1/4$″ — chair sides.

    2 pc. 14$1/2$″ x 31$7/8$″ — chair backs (if preferred).

1″ x 4″ (nom.) stock (30 linear feet) to make—

    8 pc. 31$7/8$″ long — chair backs.

    5 pc. 14$1/2$″ long — toe recess, battens, chair brace.

1″ x 2″ (nom.) stock (4 linear feet) to make—

    1 pc. 26$3/4$″ long — table leg.

    1 pc. 13″ long — chair brace.

5 pc. 1″ x 1″ x 21$1/2$″ hardwood.

UNDER-THE-COUNTER TABLE (A)

TABLE STOP DETAIL

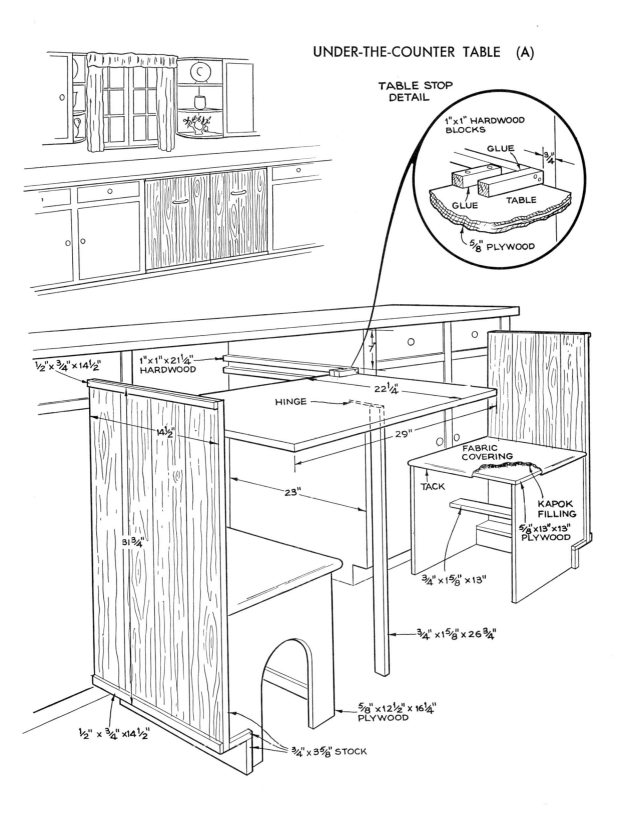

1"x1" HARDWOOD BLOCKS

GLUE

GLUE

TABLE

3/4"

5/8" PLYWOOD

1/2" x 3/4" x14 1/2"

1"x1"x21 1/4" HARDWOOD

HINGE

22 1/4"

14 1/2"

29"

23"

31 3/4"

FABRIC COVERING

TACK

KAPOK FILLING

5/8"x13"x13" PLYWOOD

3/4"x15/8"x13"

3/4" x15/8" x26 3/4"

5/8" x12 1/2" x 16 1/4" PLYWOOD

1/2" x 3/4" x14 1/2"

3/4" x35/8" STOCK

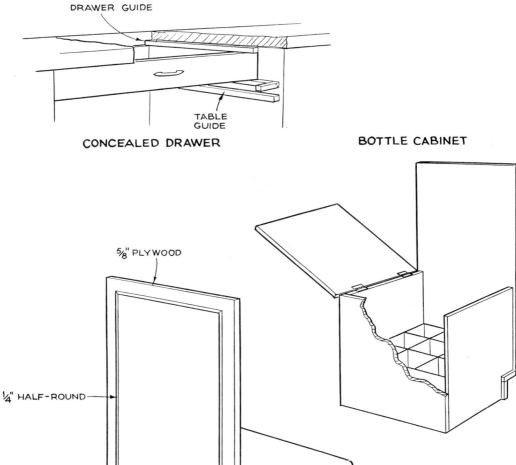

DRAWER GUIDE

TABLE
GUIDE

CONCEALED DRAWER

BOTTLE CABINET

$\frac{5}{8}$" PLYWOOD

$\frac{1}{4}$" HALF-ROUND

**UNDER-THE-COUNTER
TABLE
— ALTERNATE IDEAS
(B)**

SEAT DRAWER

Pointers for Building

Prepare the counter recess as part of the construction of the adjoining base cabinets, applying finished ends to each one and spanning them with the counter. Make the opening 29⅛″ wide, the extra ⅛″ to allow clearance for the chairs when you slide them into place. Chairs of the height shown fit under a counter 36″ high, with the counter made of ¾″ material.

Cut four table-stop blocks from the fifth piece of 1″ x 1″ hardwood in the materials list. Sand each of the other four 21¼″ pieces to a polished smoothness and wax them. Then screw one of them to the side of one base cabinet in the recess, carefully leveling it with the upper edge 8¹¹⁄₁₆″ below the counter. Mount a second one at exactly the same level on the opposite cabinet. Sink the screw heads below the surface of the strips. Then rest the table board on these strips. To assure sliding clearance, rest thin strips of cardboard on the table and push them up against the cabinets on either side. Install the upper 1″ x 1″ strips on top of the cardboard. Remove the cardboard after the strips are secure.

Mark a middle position near the outer edge of the 29″ dimension of the table and attach the 26¾″ leg there, using a small hinge. To avoid marks on the kitchen floor, you might cement a piece of rubber on the bottom end of the leg. Screw the stops to the rear edge of the table a shade over ¾″ from the edges, slide the table between the parallel strips and screw the second pair of stops to the end of the upper strips.

The width of the chairs permits use of four pieces of 1″ x 4″ (nom.) stock to make the back of each one. After sawing the two 14½″ pieces of 1″ x 4″ needed for the toe recess, rip a strip ½″ wide from the edge of one. Use this strip as the bottom batten to hold the back pieces together, the remainder for the top part of the toe recess. Rip two other ½″ strips from the fifth 14½″ piece of 1″ x 2″ and use them as the top battens on the two chairs, and shorten the remainder to make a crosswise brace if desired, under one of the chairs.

Two styles are shown for the chair sides. The open style reduces the overall weight and makes a better appearance, but you may prefer the solid type for its simplicity of construction.

CURVED-SEAT BREAKFAST NOOK

Uses

Built-in booths for serving breakfast and other light meals are favored by many persons. Here is a nook with seats curved for more comfort. You could install it in front of a window or in a corner.

This drawing was adapted from a design made by John Macsai for the Masonite Corporation. The nook utilizes the easy bending properties of this firm's tempered hardboard. A sheet of this material in black covers the table. The size of the seat and the placing of the table are based on average body measurements. The nook will seat four without crowding.

Materials

2″ x 4″ (nom.) stock (90 linear feet) to make—
  20 pc. 48″ long.
  4 pc. 18″ long.
  4 pc. 9″ long.
2″ x 6″ (nom.) stock (8 linear feet) to make—
  4 pc. 40″ long.
2″ x 8″ (nom.) stock (8 linear feet) to make—
  4 pc. 22″ long.
1 pc. ¾″ x 30″ x 50″ plywood.
1 pc. ⅛″ x 30″ x 50″ black tempered hardboard.
¼″ tempered hardboard (two 4′ x 7′ panels, one 4′ x 5′ panel) to make—
  2 pc. 40″ x 48¼″ — seat backs.
  2 pc. 18″ x 48¼″ — seat fronts.
  2 pc. 25″ x 40″ — seat ends.
³⁄₁₆″ tempered hardboard (two 4′ x 5′ panels) to make—
  2 pc. 30″ x 48¼″ — back rests.
  2 pc. 18″ x 48¼″ — seats.
1 pc. 1″ pipe 29″ long.   2 floor flanges.   2 angle brackets.

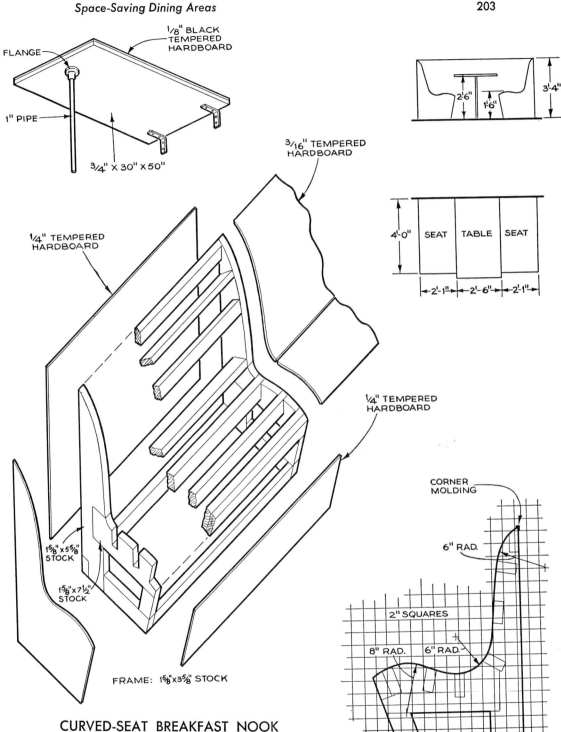

FLANGE

1/8" BLACK
TEMPERED
HARDBOARD

1" PIPE

3/4" X 30" X 50"

3/16" TEMPERED
HARDBOARD

1/4" TEMPERED
HARDBOARD

1/4" TEMPERED
HARDBOARD

3'-4"

2'-6"

1'-6"

4'-0"   SEAT TABLE SEAT

2'-1"   2'-6"   2'-1"

CORNER
MOLDING

6" RAD.

2" SQUARES

8" RAD.   6" RAD.

1 5/8" x 5 5/8"
STOCK

1 5/8" x 7 1/2"
STOCK

FRAME: 1 5/8" x 3 5/8" STOCK

CURVED-SEAT BREAKFAST NOOK

Pointers for Building

Glue together several sheets of wrapping or other paper to make a single sheet at least 26″ x 41″ in size. Carefully rule this into 2″ squares and transfer to it the squared end pattern shown. Project the bottom of the pattern to include the full height of the seat.

To make each of the four end frames required for the two seats, cut a piece 40″ long from the 2″ x 6″ lumber. Exactly 18″ from a squared end of this piece lay off a line for the upper edge of a notch $1\frac{3}{4}$″ deep into which one end of a 22″ length of 2″ x 8″ stock will fit snugly. Notching must be accurate to planed-down dimensions of lumber. Then, following the angles and dimensions indicated on your full-size pattern, cut the two $1\frac{5}{8}$″ x $3\frac{5}{8}$″ members (at the bottom and front) needed to complete the end framing. With the 2″ x 8″ horizontal member temporarily in place in its notch in the vertical 2″ x 6″ piece, transfer the contour of the seat and back rest to the two pieces, following the pattern closely. Be sure that the radii of the bends are not less than those shown. After sawing the pieces to the contour lines, cut out the indicated notches to take the 2″ x 4″ cross members of the seat—three notches on the upper edge of the 2″ x 8″ member and one in the rear bottom corner of the upright. The four members of the end frame can be joined with mortise and tenon or doweled joints glued and clamped. However, the pieces could also be butted and fastened together with long wood screws, set deep in counterbored holes where necessary. Coat the mating surfaces of the wood with glue before turning in the screws. Complete four end frames this way.

For each seat, then saw to length the ten 2″ x 4″ cross members required. Saw five to the full 48″ length of the seat. These go into the notches. Reduce the length of the other five to fit between the end frames. Then assemble the frame with screws, countersinking the heads. Plane off the edges of the cross frame members, as indicated by the plan, to the seat and back contour.

After cutting the $\frac{3}{16}$″ tempered hardboard panels to approximate size, it is necessary to increase the moisture content before bending. Do this by scrubbing warm water with a broom into the screen, or back, side until the board turns a dark chocolate brown. Then stack the four panels in pairs, smooth sides together, with wet rags or several thicknesses of wet newspaper separating the two pairs and under and on top of the stack. Allow to stand about 24 hours.

In the meantime, you can cut and apply ¼″ tempered hardboard to the back, front and ends of the seats. Cut the end piece to the exact shape of the end pattern. Fit the front and back panels to cover the edges of the end piece. When you are ready to curve the seat panels in place, let them also extend over the edges of the flat panels already in place. This will avoid down cracks.

It is a simple matter to apply the seat panels. Do it while they are still moist. Start nailing each panel at a corner to one end of the frame and wrap the panel snugly against the frame as you drive the nails. In the plans, notice that the seat and back-rest panels are butted together over the 2 x 4 frame member at the rear of the seat. Bring these edges into moderate contact.

Cement the sheet of black tempered hardboard to the table top and apply aluminum molding around the edges. Attach the end of the table to the wall with angle brackets. The 1″ pipe, with floor flanges on each end, supports the other end of the table. The seats can be fastened to the wall and floor with lag screws driven in before the panels are applied.

STANDARD BREAKFAST NOOK

Some of the construction principles shown in the preceding curved-seat eating center can be used in building a standard flat-seat nook. In this case, however, the frame can be built entirely of 1 x 4's and 1 x 2's since ¾″ plywood or 1″ stock screwed to the flat seat will help give the necessary strength and rigidity. Hardboard makes a good covering for the backs, the back rests, the ends and the heel boards of the two seats.

For the vertical members of the back frame of each seat use three or four pieces of ¾″ x 3⅝″ stock 34″ long. From the point about 16″ from the floor, where the flat seat will butt against their forward edges, taper these members upward so that the top ends just equal the milled width of a piece of ¾″ x 1⅝″ stock used to cap the verticals. This taper permits the back rest to slant away from the person seated and give more comfort. If hardboard or thin plywood is to be used on the back rest, place a horizontal frame member midway between the seat and the back cap. Mount this piece flat with its edges flush with the rear and forward edges of the verticals. Half lap joints can be used to join it to the middle vertical member (or members if four verticals are used). A ¾″ x 3⅝″ horizontal can be mounted the same way at the level of the seat frame. At the bottom, notch another ¾″ x 3⅝″ piece on edge into the rear edges of the verticals.

Let the seat frame, made of on-edge ¾″ x 3⅝″ stock, overhang the heel-board framing by about 2″. Vertical members of the heelboard framing can either stand perpendicular to the floor or be slanted slightly toward the rear to give more heel space. Let the seat board slightly overhang the free end and front of each bench. Round off these edges. Locate the two seats so that the edges of the table overhang the forward edge of each about 2″.

One way to make the table is to sandwich a flat frame of 2 x 4's between two sheets of hardboard. A handsome ladder-like support can be assembled from 2 x 2's. Place aluminum molding around the table edge and cover it to match the kitchen work counters. In building a table, consider the advisability of making it a two-level affair, that is with a shelf about 6″ under the top equal in size to the latter. This is easily accomplished by building a table in the usual way—but about 6″ lower. Then, using spacer blocks, place a second (and actual) top above the first. Such an open shelf can be used to keep table settings right at hand.

SNACK BAR

Uses

A hinged snack bar like this might be located along any free wall. Here, it backs up a peninsula dividing the kitchen and dining area. Hinging the bar so it can be dropped while not in use makes it a possibility for even a hall or narrow walkway.

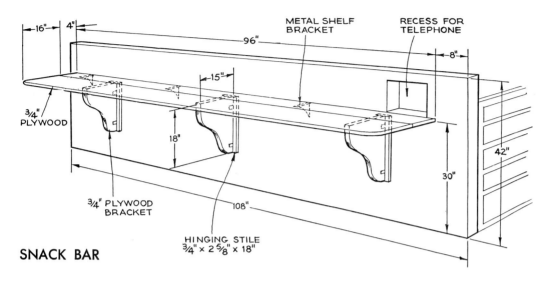

SNACK BAR

Materials

¾″ plywood (4′ x 8′ panel) to make—

    1 pc. 16″ x 8′ — bar.

    1 pc. 4″ x 8′ — ledge.

    3 pc. 15″ x 18″ — brackets.

    3 pc. 1″ x 3″ nominal stock 18″ long — stiles.

    4 3″ shelf brackets.

    6 1½″ x 1½″ hinges (for brackets).

    4 3″ x 3″ hinges (for bar).

Pointers for Building

The peninsula should follow standard wall construction, studs and any standard surfacing—lath and plaster, plaster board, etc. On the bar side, the peninsula might be faced with plywood. Frame the telephone recess as part of the peninsula construction.

Position the stiles opposite wall studs and screw them in place. Hinge the plywood brackets so they all swing in one direction. Space the bar hinges so they won't interfere with the swing of the brackets. Include some means of locking the plywood brackets to the under side of the bar when it is up. A hook and eye for each bracket will do, although a catch that latches automatically will be more convenient.

6

TABLE IDEAS

Door-mounted Breadboard

A large breadboard almost equal in size to a wide base-cabinet door can serve as both extra work surface and breakfast table. Hinge it to the inside face of the door near the top. When the door is open at right angles to the face of the cabinet and the breadboard swung up level from its normally flat position against the door, a hinged wooden bracket swung out from the other side of the door opening will support the breadboard. Make the bracket by joining two equal-length pieces of 1⅝″ x 2⅝″ stock at right angles and bracing them with a diagonal member. Hinge the bracket far enough inside the cabinet so that, when it is pivoted back parallel to the edge of the shelves, clearance will be provided for the breadboard—allowing the door to close. A snap fastener or hook and eye will lock the breadboard to the bracket in the open position.

Cantilevered Table

Starting with a modern flush-type door, you can install a table that needs no legs, yet is easily moved to the kitchen for breakfast and back to the dining room (or living room) for lunch and dinner. In addition, it makes a convenient sit-down work table in either room.

You can accomplish this by installing the door to slide back and forth in a close-fitting horizontal slot through a base cabinet and wall. Even though about 2½′ of one end of the door always remains inside the base cabinet and wall, the protruding part still gives you a table about 4′ long, enough space to serve four persons and possibly a fifth (at the end).

To make up for the lack of leg support, a strong framework of 1⅝″ x 3⅝″ stock must be installed in the base cabinet. Since down pressure on the free end of the fully opened table will multiply itself into considerable upward stress at the other end, the cabinet framework must be strong above the table as well as below. Assemble the frame with glue and screws, apply diagonal braces on either side (from front to back of the cabinet), and bolt it to the floor. If the slot passes through an existing wall, as well as the cabinet, it will be necessary to cut sections out of at least two wall studs. Nail $1\frac{5}{8}''$ x $3\frac{5}{8}''$ pieces across the cut ends of the studs, both above and below the slot, and fasten their ends securely to the adjoining studs. Screw $1\frac{5}{8}''$ x $1\frac{5}{8}''$ parallel hardwood guides inside the framework to carry the sliding door. Sand the guides smooth and wax them well. Screw a small block under the edge of the door at each end to serve as a stop. Place molding around the slot at either end.

Instead of using a door, you might build a sliding two-room table in three sections hinged together. If the middle one is made just equal to the combined depth of the base cabinet and wall, the sections on each end can be folded down flat while not in use. The length of the end sections must not, of course, exceed the height of the table from the floor, about 30''. A swing-out wooden bracket, hinged like a door, will support the end sections when the table is centered. Folding legs mounted under the end sections will enable you to pull out two sections into either room.

For either of these two-room tables, a pass-through in the wall above will make meal serving easier.

13

Handy and Decorative Accessories

Well-chosen accessories, whether they are functional or merely for looks, give the finishing touch to a kitchen. You can buy some, build others.

A small breadboard screwed to the inside of a breadbox lid puts a cutting surface conveniently at hand. A cutting board resting on narrow cleats near the upper edges of a drawer can be used in place when the drawer is pulled out—or be picked up and carried to another part of the kitchen.

Mounted on a center pivot under a utility-cabinet or closet shelf, a wood disk will support mops, brooms, and cleaning brushes on hooks around its edges. Revolve it, and you can easily reach the one you want. In a dish cupboard, a similar revolving disk will store cups out of the way.

Metal pull-out racks available at hardware stores can be mounted inside a cabinet to hold towels or pots and pans. Ready-made metal shelves screwed to the inside of cabinet doors take a wide range of articles. A narrow shelf suspended from a fixed shelf will store low

210

cans and make use of space that otherwise would be wasted. A narrow shelf resting on cleats between two fixed shelves will do the same. Metal file racks bought and placed on a shelf or door will store pot lids upright, keeping them in order in less space. Dishes, too, can be stored this way. Metal racks also are made to hold bottles on their sides, again in less space.

Units with narrow stepped shelves, bought or made at home, will bring order out of chaos in the spice and glassware departments if simply rested on a suitable cabinet shelf. Triangular shelves mounted in the corners of a cabinet that has fixed shelves spaced too far apart will help increase the storage space.

If you have no other place for the rolling pin, install hooks on the wall above the mixing counter and keep it there.

A unit with ends curving down and back to the wall, fitted under the wall cabinets, can have shelves decreasing in width from top to bottom.

Place bins about 4″ deep and the same dimension front to back against the wall at the rear of a work counter. Handy for storage of many small items—and the space won't be missed from a 24″ counter. Hinge a forward-slanting lid on the bins.

If the refrigerator stands alone, perhaps in a narrow space between two doors, see if there isn't room beside it for a counter-high shelf a few inches wide. The cook will bless you forever after. Put it on the refrigerator door-opening side, of course. A simple wood rack screwed inside a base-cabinet door, the sink cabinet perhaps, will take the paper bags that every housewife likes to collect.

A platter of awkward size will be safe and easily accessible if given its own special place under a shelf. To a narrow, fairly thick strip of wood, nail another wider strip to make an L-section assembly. Make two of these and screw them to the under side of a shelf with the protruding boards facing in—and just far enough apart so the edges of the platter can rest on them and slide in and out.

It is easy to put paper into a waste basket mounted on a shelf on the inside of a sink-cabinet door if you cut a horizontal piece about 5″ wide out of the door above the basket and hinge the cut-out piece back in place at its top edge. Push the paper through, and the hinged flap drops back in place.

These are only a few of many accessories that can be made or bought for installation in a kitchen. By bringing ingenuity into play, you will be able to dream up many more.

CHOPPING BLOCK AND KNIFE DRAWER

Uses

The original of this installation was designed to fit into a base corner cabinet with revolving shelves. But both the chopping block and drawer could be worked into a straight base cabinet 20″ wide and 24″ deep without any changes. The housewife will find many uses for a hardwood chopping block in food preparation. The cutting surface is raised $1/4$″ above the counter to prevent damage to the latter. The reason for locating a drawer for storage of sharp knives near the chopping block is obvious. Storing the knives with the cutting edges up lessens the chances of dulling them.

Materials

9 pc. 2″ x 2″ hardwood 18″ long (actual measurements).

1″ x 2″ (nom.) stock — cabinet framing.

1 pc. $3/4$″ x 4″ x $163/8$″ plywood — drawer front.

1 pc. $3/4$″ x 6″ x $151/8$″ — handle rest.

$5/8$″ plywood to make—

    2 pc. 4″ x 22″ — drawer sides.

    1 pc. 4″ x $163/8$″ — drawer back.

1 pc. $1/4$″ x $163/8$″ x 22″ plywood — drawer bottom.

1 pc. $11/2$″ x 3″ x $151/8$″ hardwood — blade holder.

1 pc. 2″ x 3″ x $151/8$″ channeled wood — paring-knife holder.

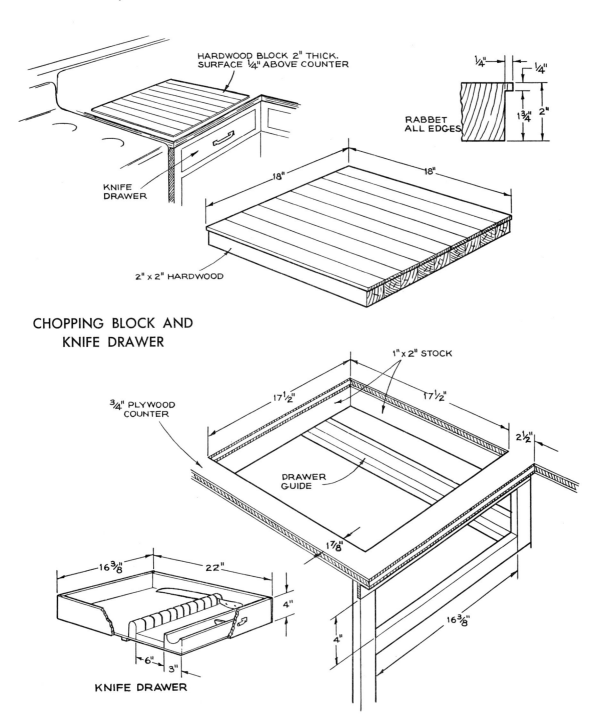

HARDWOOD BLOCK 2" THICK.
SURFACE 1/4" ABOVE COUNTER

1/4"
1/4"
RABBET
ALL EDGES
1 3/4"
2"

KNIFE
DRAWER

18"
18"

2" x 2" HARDWOOD

CHOPPING BLOCK AND KNIFE DRAWER

1" x 2" STOCK

3/4" PLYWOOD
COUNTER

17 1/2"
17 1/2"

2 1/2"

DRAWER
GUIDE

1 7/8"

16 3/8"
22"

4"

16 3/8"

4"

6"
3"

KNIFE DRAWER

Pointers for Building

The block and drawer can be fitted into any base cabinet built as suggested in this book. Construction of the drawer is conventional, as is its framing. If your lumber dealer cannot provide the channeled paring-knife block, a shop devoted to millwork undoubtedly can. Round off one edge of the 1½″ x 3″ x 15⅛″ hardwood strip with a plane and/or a sander. Saw slots 2″ deep into the 3″ dimension to take the knives. With the drawer in place in the cabinet, screw a cleat under it to keep it from opening far enough to expose the sharp knife blades.

Glue the hardwood blocks together and trim the ends and smooth the surface as required. Cut a rabbet around all edges and set the block into a hole cut in the counter, adjusting it to a snug and solid fit. Leave the block without permanent fastening so it can be removed occasionally for cleaning by reaching into the opened drawer and pressing the block upward.

UTILITY CART

Uses

This wheeled cart is a kitchen convenience with many uses. It is designed for storage in a base-cabinet recess about 23⅛″ wide, its back flush with the fronts of the adjoining cabinets. Rolled out, it provides extra work surface anywhere in the kitchen. It hauls supplies wherever you want them. Its tray and shelves are spacious enough to carry an entire meal to the dining room—or the backyard—in a single trip. It makes clearing the table easier too. The tray is removable for use alone. When the cart is in place in its base-cabinet niche, the shelves offer storage almost equal to those in a base cabinet of the same size. Just roll it out to reach the shelves. Located near the range, the cart alone might fill most of the functions of a kitchen serving center.

Materials

⅜″ exterior plywood or tempered hardboard (4′ x 4′ panel) to make—
- 1 pc. 20¼″ x 26½″ — back.
- 1 pc. 19″ x 22″ — tray.
- 2 pc. 16¼″ x 19¼″ — shelves.
- 2 pc. 4″ x 5½″ — tray handles.
- 2 pc. 1½″ x 5″ — axle supports.
- 2 pc. 3″ x 19¾″ — cleats.

1″ x 2″ (nom.) stock (40 linear feet) — framing.

1″ x 4″ (nom.) stock (4 linear feet) — base, handle brackets.

1″ quarter-round (8 linear feet).

1 broom handle or dowel — handle.

½″ dia. x 22″ steel rod — wheel shaft.

2 6″ dia. rubber-tired wheels.

2 axle clamps.

4 furniture glides.

Corner irons, flat corners, screws, etc.

Pointers for Building

Cut the framing pieces to length and cut ¼″ x ⅜″ rabbets in all except those intended for the tray support and the two end verticals. Join the frames with end laps or other joints as desired. Cut the plywood or hardboard panels and fit them into the frames. If desired, the vertical back panel can be set into a deeper rabbet and edged with quarter-round molding. For an easier and quicker job, some builders may prefer to make one-piece panels of plywood, without the framing. The tray frame and middle shelf are mounted with the ⅜″ x 3″ x 19¾″ cleats sandwiched between them and the back panel.

As shown, the tray is simply a plywood sheet with the quarter round mitered for the corners and mounted around the edges. Nail and glue the handles into notches cut in the end. The brackets for the cart handle can be shaped from 6″ lengths of ¾″ x 3⅝″ stock.

UTILITY CART

$3\frac{5}{8}$"

6"

1"

$3\frac{3}{8}$" PLYWOOD

4"

4"

1"

$1\frac{1}{2}$"

$5\frac{1}{2}$"

BROOM HANDLE

1" QUARTER ROUND

22"

19"

$\frac{3}{8}$" PLYWOOD (OUTDOOR TYPE)

$\frac{3}{8}$" X 2" X 2" FLAT CORNER

FRAME: $\frac{3}{4}$" x $1\frac{5}{8}$" STOCK

$\frac{1}{4}$" X $\frac{3}{8}$" RABBET

10"

$\frac{3}{8}$" X 3" X $19\frac{3}{4}$" PLYWOOD

$\frac{5}{8}$" X 2" X 2" CORNER IRON

$12\frac{3}{4}$"

3"

$\frac{3}{8}$" PLYWOOD

3"

WASHER

$\frac{3}{8}$" PLYWOOD

29$\frac{1}{4}$"

5"

19"

$\frac{5}{8}$" X $1\frac{1}{2}$" X 5" PLYWOOD

CLAMP

6" DIA. WHEEL

$\frac{1}{2}$" X 22" SHAFT

$\frac{1}{4}$" X $\frac{3}{8}$" RABBET

23"

FURNITURE GLIDE (4 REQ.)

$\frac{3}{4}$" x $3\frac{5}{8}$" STOCK

The handle is set in suitable holes drilled into or through the brackets. Attach the brackets by screws driven through the rear face of the panel frame. The one-by-four base is strengthened by two right-angle blocks cut from 3/4" x 35/8" material. Set this baseboard in far enough to give a toe recess equal to that in the base cabinets. Four glides spaced along the lower edge of this will make the cart easier to move in and out of the niche. Use spacer blocks under the bearing or clamp that supports the wheel shaft so as to bring the bottom of the wheel on a line with the furniture glides. Drill the ends of the rod for cotter pins to retain the wheels or thread it for axle nuts.

KITCHEN DESK

Operating a home smoothly and efficiently requires planning. A kitchen desk centralizes this paperwork.

Ideally, a planning center should include space for a telephone, housekeeping bills, cookbooks, recipe files, and writing materials. Modern kitchens tend to provide these facilities in a unit designed as part of the base cabinets. Such a unit can be installed in a variety of ways.

One of the simplest consists of a projection of the work counter at the end of a line of cabinets. This can be supported by one or more legs of metal tubing or hardwood dowel rod (clothes-pole size) or perhaps by a tier of drawers or an open-shelf whatnot. When the desk surface is supported by tubing or dowel legs, the necessary desk drawer space probably can be provided in the adjoining base cabinet. Depending on the location of the desk, it may be possible to build a telephone niche into the wall. (Amateur builders might like to note that mail-order houses sell these niches as assembled units.) It usually will be possible to locate a shelf on or near the desk for cookbooks and such.

The builder should give thought to the height of the desk surface. If placed at average counter height, a stool will be needed to raise the user to an easy working level. If a chair is to be used (a more desirable objective) the desk surface should be dropped to correspond. Give thought, too, to secondary use of the desk as a breakfast bar. A kneehole space in a peninsula arrangement of cabinets offers seating facilities for two.

A base cabinet drawer can be adapted to desk use too by hinging the drawer front to swing down. Support it by a metal elbow bracket or length of furnace chain. A pressure catch will keep the front secure while the drawer desk is closed. Use $3/8''$ or $1/2''$ stock for the drawer bottom and mount it with the under side flush with the bottom edges of the drawer sides so as to produce a full closure at the front when the hinged front is closed. A top drawer about $6''$ deep devoted to such a desk will give a writing surface at a height convenient for a person seated in an ordinary chair.

KNIFE RACK

Transparent plastic on one side allows a view of the knives for a quick selection from a knife rack that is used in the step-saving U-kitchen developed by the Department of Agriculture. The opposite side is $5/8''$ plywood. A rack like this can be mounted with the plywood side flat against the kitchen wall, or against the side of a wall cabinet or base cabinet.

Both the plastic and plywood are cut to the shape of a right-angle pie segment, that is a quarter circle with a radius of about 11 5/16''. The knives are stored blade down in suitable slots cut crosswise in a curved piece that separates the curved edges of the plastic and plywood sides by about $1\frac{1}{2}''$. A piece curved to fit can be bandsawed from a wood block and the plastic and plywood sides can then be bradded to it. Wood separators of equal width would of course go between the straight sides of the quarter-circle rack. You could also use hardboard 3/16'' thick for the curved cover. Cut the knife slots first and then moisten the hardboard before bending it.

A hardwood block about ¾″ thick, 4″ wide, and 20″ long mounted at the rear of a counter over an opening into a base cabinet will keep knives handy and protect their cutting edges. Drill and saw narrow slots crosswise on the 4″ face. Mount the block on a cabinet that has a drawer shortened enough so it won't interfere with the blades sticking down into the rear of the cabinet.

If you buy or own a knife-holder board, consider bolting the blade end flat under a wall cabinet so the board will pivot in and out.

BUILT-IN IRONING BOARD

An ironing board often presents a storage problem unless special provision is made for it. One of the simplest solutions, allowing free use of the board anywhere required, consists of a sturdy lipped shelf near the bottom of the inside surface of a closet door, plus a chain or strap with a snap fastener to hold the top of the board when the bottom is placed on the shelf.

Built-ins are of many varieties. The type that permits the narrow end to swing up and back is most frequently used. However, it also is possible to install the board flat in a long, narrow recess under the work counter of base cabinets. A door about 8″ x 60″, hinged at the bottom edge to open downward, can be used to close the horizontal recess. If the board is fitted with a bracing leg that hinges up under it, the wide end can be simply pivoted to allow the board to swing out of the recess for use. For this, it would be desirable to use a board longer than average since some of the length will be lost at the pivot end. But rather than pivot such a horizontally installed board, the builder might mount it on sturdy slides so it can be pulled out sideways. Hardwood slides salvaged from an old expanding table could be used for this. No supporting leg should be needed. Whatever method of mounting is adopted, the board should be rigid, and at the correct height to allow comfortable exertion of pressure from the ironer's shoulder. A height of 31″ or 32″ from the floor usually is about right. The builder's guide here should be the most comfortable working height for the person who will use the board most.

A special cabinet might be built to house an ironing board that folds up vertically, or it could be attached to a pantry or a tall cabinet door. A prop to support the board can consist of a pair of narrow strips assembled in ladder-like construction, the assembly being hinged under the ironing board to swing down against the floor when the board is opened for use.

A variation of this mounting consists of hinging the prop to the door or cabinet back as well as to the board. The wide end of the board is attached only while the board is in use. A loose-pin butt hinge could be used as a temporary fastener. A cleat on the door to support the end of the board and hooks to keep it from moving outward comprise another possibility. By this method, the butt end of the board swings down behind the prop. The board therefore requires less overall storage height than it does when the full length is hinged upward.

Careful fitting could install an ironing board between the studs inside a cabinet flush with the wall—or projecting only an inch or so. However, the padding normally used around a board might make it necessary to use a narrower board if it is to fit well into the recess. To make the most of the available space, let the lower part of the cabinet door serve also as the board prop. Hinge it at both ends as explained in the previous paragraph. A standard swing door will close the upper part of the wall niche. Frame the opening with suitable molding.

DRAFT COOLER

A draft cooler is a modern substitute for the old-time root cellar. It operates on the same principle as a chimney. An opening in the front near the bottom and another in the back near the top allow a current of air to pass up through the cabinet. But in this case the draft is designed to ventilate and preserve vegetables stored in drawers rather than to fan a fire. Mesh bottoms in the drawers and openings around the shelves above permit air to pass. For greater efficiency, the vent in the back should open to the outside of the house. This requirement will determine to a large extent the cooler's location in the kitchen.

A cabinet that rises from floor to ceiling will give the best draft. In depth (front to back), it might be made equal to adjoining base cabinets. If it occupies a middle location in a line of cabinets, the builder might prefer an offset on a level with the work counter to reduce the depth of the upper part to match the wall cabinets. The upper part also might be narrowed to a dimension as small as half the width of the lower. Just make sure the air current has free passage. When the kitchen layout permits, a corner location might be desirable. If the cooler stands alone, it probably would be best to use a depth of 18″ or less.

Three deep drawers in the base part of the cabinet should satisfy the vegetable and fruit storage requirements of most families. For ease of access to the stored food, swinging bins might be substituted for drawers. Wire baskets installed drawer fashion would be another good choice. The use of the shelves above would depend largely on the location of the unit.

The framing, sides, top, door, and drawer fronts of such a cabinet might be made of 1″ (nom.) stock, but it probably will be easiest to use ¾″ plywood for the shelves. To permit air passage up through the cooler, be sure to provide space around the shelves. This space can be either between the front edge of the shelves and the cabinet door or at the back.

If possible, locate the cooler so the outside vents can be placed between two studs. This will reduce the framing needed for the vents. Cover the vents with window screening. In very cold areas, hinged or sliding doors to close them on occasion would be advisable.

ROLL-FRONT CABINET

Like the old roll-top desks, roll-front kitchen cabinets belong to another age. Yet they still find favor in some modern kitchens, and the builder who wants to try his hand at making one should have no difficulty. The roll front consists of narrow strips of wood joined in a flexible mat with tape (on the back) or light wire or strong cord through drilled holes. For easier operation, the edges of the strips should be rounded off. The ends of the strips slide in grooves in the ends of the cabinets, the grooves curving gently at the top of the cabinet to carry the flexible mat to the rear. The grooves can be created by screwing properly shaped pieces of wood (strips and curved forms) to the inside faces of the cabinet ends.

A roll-front spice shelf for installation under a wall cabinet above the work counter is a useful kitchen addition. For this, the roll front should slant toward the wall from a fairly wide top shelf to a narrow one at the bottom.

WOOD BOX

Uses

Although designed as a companion piece for the wood range in the old-time farm kitchen, this wood box would find a useful place in an ultramodern kitchen that has an open fireplace. In recent kitchen planning, a fireplace has sometimes been used to bring indoors the atmosphere and advantages of open-fire cooking, especially with charcoal. This cabinet offers a convenient place for storing several bags of charcoal as well as kindling and equipment used at the fireplace. The cabinet can be used also as a hearthside serving counter.

Fitted with double-acting hinges, one lid folds down against the side of the box. A narrow, bevel-edged hook strip keeps the opposite lid (the one adjoining the wood range) in an almost upright position when open. This feature was included to prevent dust and dirt from flying on the range when wood was tossed into the box. The strip that supports the open lid provides a place for hooks or nails to hold utensils.

A baffle board keeps wood from falling out when the front doors are open. This lifts out to make it easy to remove wood bark and dirt that accumulates in the box. The kindling box rests on cleats and may be tilted or taken out for cleaning.

WOOD BOX

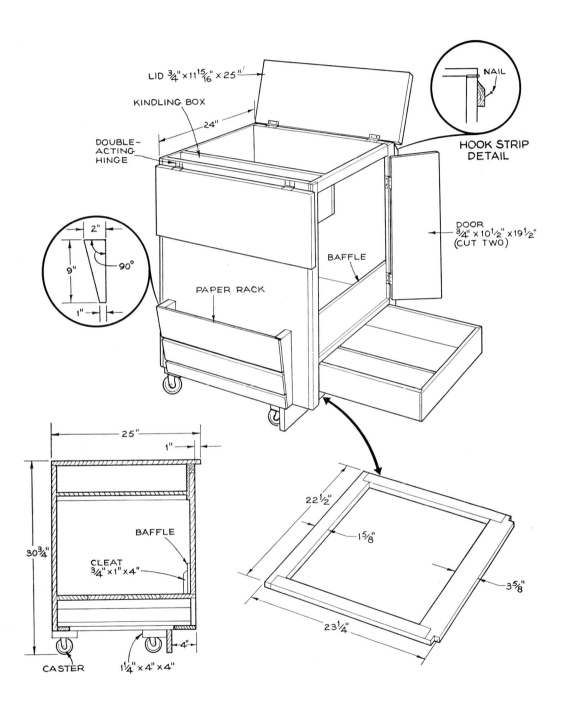

LID ¾" × 11⁷⁄₁₆" × 25"

KINDLING BOX

24"

DOUBLE-
ACTING
HINGE

HOOK STRIP
DETAIL

NAIL

DOOR
¾" × 10½" × 19½"
(CUT TWO)

2"

9"

90°

1"

BAFFLE

PAPER RACK

25"

1"

BAFFLE

CLEAT
¾" × 1" × 4"

30¾"

CASTER

1¼" × 4" × 4"

4"

22½"

1⅝"

3⅝"

23¼"

Materials

1″ x 2″ (nom.) stock (27 linear feet) — framing, drawer guides, cleats.

1″ x 4″ (nom.) stock (4 linear feet) — drawer frame, baseboard.

¾″ plywood (4′ x 8′ panel) to make—

  2 pc. 22½″ x 27″ — side panels.

  1 pc. 24″ x 27″ — back panel.

  2 pc. 10½″ x 19½ — doors.

  2 pc. 11¹⁵⁄₁₆″ x 25″ — lids.

  1 pc. 22½″ x 22½″ — bottom.

  1 pc. 2½″ x 24″ — hook strip.

  2 pc. 2″ x 9″ — paper-rack ends.

  1 pc. 4¼″ x 21″ — drawer front.

  1 pc. 5½″ x 22½″ — side kindling box.

  1 pc. 5″ x 5½″ — kindling box end.

  2 pc. 4¼″ x 22⅞″ — drawer sides.

  1 pc. 3¾″ x 20½″ — drawer back.

¼″ plywood (2′ x 4′ panel) to make—

  1 pc. 5″ x 22¼″ — baffle.

  1 pc. 5″ x 22″ — kindling box bottom.

  1 pc. 1½″ x 18″ — paper-rack slat.

  1 pc. 2½″ x 18″ — paper-rack slat.

  1 pc. 4″ x 18″ — paper-rack slat.

  1 pc. 20½″ x 22⅞″ — drawer bottom.

4 two-inch casters.

Pointers for Building

Build the front frame and the bottom drawer-supporting frame first, using the 1″ x 2″ and 1″ x 4″ stock. Attach a bottom crosspiece across the front frame 4¼″ from the bottom ends. This piece serves as the upper frame for the drawer. After the side, back, and bottom panels have been cut to size, the overall structure can then be assembled.

Use corner blocks or corner irons for strength. Screw a $\frac{3}{4}''$ x $1''$ x $4''$ cleat to the inner face of each side to hold the baffle, spacing each $\frac{1}{2}''$ plus clearance back from the front frame. This permits the baffle to be raised for removal. In mounting the casters, it may be necessary to vary the $1\frac{1}{4}''$ thickness of the mounting blocks to bring the wheel just a bit below the front baseboard.

14

Cabinet Hardware

Visit a hardware store, or glance through a catalog or the advertising columns of a home or mechanics magazine, and you will see that as a cabinet builder you have a wide choice of hinges, catches, and drawer and door pulls and knobs. Not only must you choose from general types, but you must decide on styles and materials as well: whether you'll use flat butt or concealed hinges, in plain or ornamental styles of brass, bronze, steel, chromium, wrought iron; whether you prefer a combination door latch and pull; whether you want pulls or knobs on the drawers, and in what style.

There are also new hardware items on the market that will make a handyman builder's job easier. Metal slides for drawers and Lazy Susan bearings are two examples.

HINGES

It is wise to make your hardware choice before you begin work, for it may affect design and construction. For instance, hinges must suit the type of door, that is whether it is flush, offset, or overlapping, with or without an inset.

The familiar square or rectangular butt hinge comes in two general types, swaged or flat, and with loose or fixed pins. The leaves of a swaged butt are mortised into the edges of the door and the cabinet frame. To permit the leaves to come together when the door closes, they are depressed slightly from the knuckles. As its name suggests, a flat butt is designed for mounting against the face of the door and cabinet with both leaves showing. The leaves consequently are joined to the knuckles so they form a straight line when open. Butt pins come with a variety of tips—ball, bullet, steeple, cone, button, and others.

If you want to use flat butts on a flush door, you can get them in many decorative styles. Strap, T, H, and HL hinges operate on the same principle as the ordinary butt. All of these are also available with the leaves offset for use on overlapping or lipped doors. Offset hinges usually are bent or curved to suit doors offset ⅜″ from the cabinet face.

Builders who prefer not to make hinges a display item of their cabinets can either hide them entirely or in part. Semiconcealed hinges include butts with one leaf outside and the other mortised in the edge of the other mounting member. The inside, or swinging leaf, also may be extended to wrap around the inside surface of the door, whether it is flush or lipped. For a lipped door, such hinges must suit the size of the rabbet on the rear edge. If a door overlaps without an inset, you can use semiconcealed hinges made especially for it. The swinging leaf is attached to the rear surface of the door, the fixed one to the cabinet frame outside. The swaged, or double-mortised, butt also has variations worth noting. In one, the swinging leaf is extended and bent at 90 degrees against the inside surface of the door. Another has both leaves to one side for lipped doors. This makes edge mortising unnecessary, the door rabbet being cut wide enough to provide adequate clearance for the hinge leaves when they are closed.

The pivot hinge, sometimes called a concealed hinge, is mounted in gains cut in the top and bottom edges of the door and in the frame. The edges or pivot may show. But a type with meshing leaves and lugs set into deep mortises in the vertical edges of the door and frame is truly invisible. These enable you to build cabinets without apparent hinges.

KNOBS, PULLS, AND CATCHES

The selection of door and drawer knobs or pulls is mostly a matter of personal taste and style to suit the cabinets and type of finish. But rather than buy, you may prefer to make your own. For instance, 3″ or 4″ lengths of large-diameter dowel rod screwed horizontally to drawers and vertically to doors will give you effective pulls in modern style. The dowels can be raised from the surface, if desired, by placing blocks under them. Finger grips also might be hollowed out of the sides of rectangular blocks; or blocks of suitable size can be placed on top of smaller ones. For concealed pulls in wall-cabinet doors, hollow out finger grips at the rear of the bottom edge—if the cabinet construction permits.

Door catches may be separate, or operated by a push-button on the pull. The latter may be reversible, for right- or left-hand doors, and are available for both flush and overlapping doors. Strikes can be mounted on the door frame or under a shelf. When separate door knobs or pulls are used, various types of inside spring catches are available—for installation on the door and frame, or on the door and under a shelf. These all release automatically when the door is pulled.

15

Applying the Finish

Color has come to the kitchen. Cheerful hues in paint or stains and the warm tones of natural wood are driving out laboratory white. Kitchen-appliance manufacturers are color-conscious, too, and some now offer their products in a choice of colors to match the cabinets.

Any one of three general types of finish may be selected for cabinets—paint or enamel, stain, and natural. The first two offer a wide selection of colors. A natural finish of course depends primarily on the wood itself for the desired effect.

It is axiomatic that a finish is never better than the base to which it is applied. For a finish of which you'll be proud, start with a glass-smooth surface, one on which your fingertips can detect no flaw. On wood and plywood, this calls for careful sanding. A power sander, rented if necessary, eases this job on surfaces as extensive as those of several kitchen cabinets. Leave off or remove all fasteners, pulls and knobs until the finishing operations are complete. Use progressively finer paper. When you are satisfied that the surface is glass smooth, dust it with a brush or a cloth moistened with turpentine. If you are refinishing old cabinets to match new ones, it is wise to clean down to the original surface first.

229

Paint and Enamel

Coat all knots with shellac several days before you plan to apply the first coat of paint or enamel. Painting or enameling is normally a three-coat process. The primer (the first coat) should be of a type suitable for the coats that are to follow. Directions on the can are your best guide in this. (Nail holes and cracks usually are filled after the first coat in all finishing procedures—stains and natural finishes included.) When the primer has dried thoroughly, lightly sand the surface and brush or wipe off the dust—a good rule to follow between coats with any finish. Then, apply two coats of paint or an under-coater and a coat of enamel. Flow on the enamel.

This will give you a satisfactory finish on wood or hardboards. But rotary-cut fir plywood is another matter. Its wild grain will give trouble unless a penetrating resin sealer, such as Rez or Firzite, is applied first. In most cases, this will prevent the face checking (tiny cracks) that otherwise would show up later on the finish.

The Use of Stains

Stains are used either to change or modify the color of wood without obscuring the grain. Two types are commonly used—water or oil. Oil stains are further divided into two major types—pigment and penetrating. The latter differs from the former only in having benzol in the formula to increase its penetrating qualities. Water stains come in powder form and are mixed with water, preferably hot. Although most people think only of paints or enamels as producing color, a variety of ready-mixed color stains have become available in recent years, especially for use on plywood.

Both water and oil stains may darken edge grain too much unless precautions are taken. Water itself is a good treatment in the case of a water stain. Simply soak the edge with water just before applying the stain. A light coating of shellac will usually do for an oil stain.

So that a water stain can function, the grain must first be raised. Do this by sponging the surface. When dry, smooth with fine paper or steel wool—and remove the dust particles. Brush on water stain rapidly to avoid streaks. It dries fast. Oil stain usually is wiped with a cloth a few minutes after application. This removes the surplus.

If varnish is applied directly over stain, you may notice fine pits in the surface, especially on open-grained wood. To avoid this, use a filler between the stain and first varnish coats.

Filling the Grain

There are two major types of fillers—paste and liquid. These are practically the same except that the liquid type has turpentine as a vehicle. A liquid filler is best for pine and other close-grained woods, although several coats of thin shellac are sometimes used. Brush on the filler in the direction of the grain. When dry, smooth with fine steel wool. A paste filler, designed for open-grained woods, must be thinned with turpentine just to the point where it will fill the grain pits, not too thin and not too thick. Brush it on, across the grain, and then with the grain. When it has dried enough to stay in the pores— about 15 minutes—wipe the surface with a cloth. After it has dried overnight, sand with the grain and dust the surface clean.

Simply applying a paste wax after the staining and filling operations is a short-cut to an acceptable finish. Stain waxes, available in colors, combine the staining and waxing steps. Brushing lacquer can also be used for a quick, durable one-treatment finish.

How to Use Varnish

A flat, flowing, or rubbing varnish should be selected if you want a varnish finish. The flowing type gives a high gloss. Flat and rubbing types give a satiny effect. The usual system of staining and varnishing wood may include six steps, the first being application of the stain. For open-grain woods, follow this with a filler. Then comes a sealer coat, shellac perhaps, if the stain contains aniline dye. Thin the first coat of varnish in the proportion of one-half pint turpentine to a gallon of varnish. Sand the surface lightly when dry with fine sandpaper. Apply the second varnish coat without thinning, and sand as before. If a dull rubbed finish is wanted, let the third coat dry hard— about 72 hours. Then rub it with powdered pumice and water to an even dull finish. Brush on varnish with the grain, crossbrush, and then brush again with the grain. Be sure to allow ample drying time between coats, keeping the room clean and dust-free during the drying period. Keep brushes and varnish can free of dust too.

Finishing Plywood

A blond finish, often seen on plywood surfaces in the living room these days, would also be suitable for plywood kitchen cabinets. For this, thin a flat white wall paint with turpentine, apply it with a brush or rag, and after a few minutes wipe off the excess with a cloth. This treatment has a softening effect on the plywood grain. Follow this with clear lacquer and wax.

Plywood may be given a great variety of colors and shades with a stain glaze treatment. White the panel first with a coat of white undercoat thinned with an equal amount of turpentine. If more grain is desired, wipe or dry-brush this coat. After it has dried, sand lightly. Then apply clear resin sealer or thinned white shellac. Again sand lightly when dry. Now, for the color, apply colored undercoat or enamel thinned as for the first coat, wiping or dry-brushing to the desired tone. Sand lightly when dry, apply flat varnish, and steel-wool it lightly when dry.

The main job of a natural finish is to protect the wood surface. You'll want to use this primarily on hardwood plywood and pine. Water-white lacquer or white shellac will do nicely. Two or more coats, each steel-wooled lightly, will produce a durable finish. Wind up with paste wax. Two coats of water-clear varnish, followed by wax, will give a finish that is more water-resistant, however. In pine, yellow beeswax or tinted nonshrinking crack fillers are frequently used to fill holes and cracks. For a natural finish on fir plywood, use a clear sealer instead of the white you would use under paint or enamel. When dry, smooth it with fine steel wool, and then apply two or three coats of clear brushing lacquer, smoothing with steel wool between coats. As the final step, rub on a paste wax.

Although tedious and slow, an oil-rubbed finish is worth considering for wood work surfaces in the kitchen. For this, you use linseed oil—either boiled linseed thinned with turpentine or raw linseed alone. After each rubbing, wipe off the excess. Repeat the rubbing four or five times to fill the pores of the wood. The more the finish is rubbed, the better it will be. Hot dishes placed on a rubbed finish will not turn it white.

16

Kitchen Lights and Appliances

Work-saving efficiency and a pleasant environment are major objectives in planning a modern kitchen. Good illumination and the careful selection and proper placement of modern appliances—a gas or electric range and refrigerator, and such electrical conveniences as a dishwasher, garbage grinder, towel dryer, and ventilating fan—will make a big contribution toward achievement of these twin goals.

Consideration of wiring and plumbing needs should go hand-in-hand with basic kitchen-layout planning. Even though an electrician and plumber will make all connections, the cabinet builder should know the location of lights and appliances before he begins work so as to make any necessary allowances or changes in construction.

Artificial lighting should include both general illumination and direct light where it is most needed—at the sink, range, and mix center. Incandescent and daylight-type fluorescent lamps can be combined to drive out the shadows.

Because there is no lighting superior to natural daylight, kitchen planners nowadays strive for the maximum in window area. This

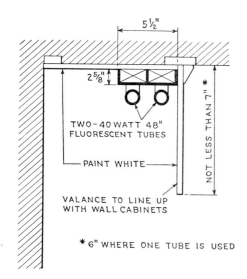

LIGHT OVER SINK

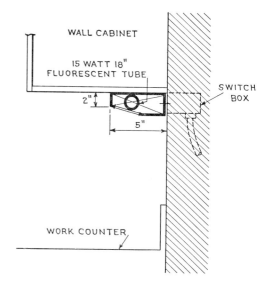

UNDER-CABINET LIGHT

SECTION DRAWINGS—COURTESY WESTINGHOUSE

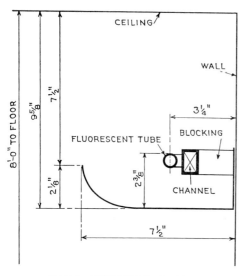

WALL-MOUNTED COVE

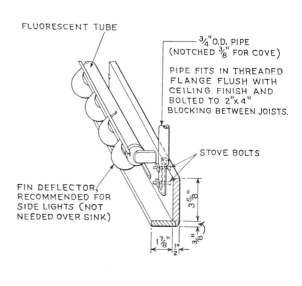

CEILING-MOUNTED COVE

should never be less than 15 to 20 percent of the floor area, and up to 25 percent if possible. But a compromise with storage needs is sometimes necessary. It may be impossible or impractical, especially in a small kitchen, to omit cabinets from a wall where otherwise a window could go. However, the kitchen should have at least one large window, preferably two. Custom suggests a long one over the sink. This is desirable, but in some very efficient layouts the sink faces a wall or is located in a peninsula. You should consider this point in the first planning stage. If yours is a remodeling job, relocating a window or putting in one or two new ones may make the difference between a cheerful kitchen and one that is not.

Installation of such electrical conveniences as a garbage unit, an automatic washing machine, or a clothes dryer normally calls for an electrician or plumber, and sometimes both, but the handyman builder can often take a hand in installing two other important units —an automatic dishwasher and a kitchen ventilating system.

Dishwashers are available in three types—as a part of a sink, as a self-contained cabinet with its own top, or as a unit for installation under a work counter of standard height. By choosing the latter, a builder can space adjoining cabinets to suit the dishwasher and bridge it with a continuous counter.

Avoid Electrical Overloads

Whether you build or remodel, be sure to plan the wiring circuits to avoid overloads. If you remodel, don't make the mistake of assuming that your present wiring is adequate. Chances are it was not installed to handle all the many electrical conveniences that help make the modern kitchen a room in which a housewife finds it a pleasure to spend her working hours.

An electric range and hot-water heater each demands its own circuit. It is also advisable to have an individual circuit for the refrigerator, the dishwasher, the freezer, and any other motor-driven appliance that may have a momentary starting load as high as 1,000 watts. Otherwise, an overload can occur if other appliances are in use when the motor starts. Appliances that have known, fixed loads— toaster, waffle iron, coffee maker, roaster, and the like—can be grouped on the same circuit so long as the total wattage, if all were in use simultaneously, does not exceed the maximum carrying capacity of the circuit. The plate on an electrical appliance will show either its amperage or wattage. If amperage is given, multiply the figure by 115 to get the wattage. Electrical codes usually require at least one 20-ampere circuit for kitchen, dining room, and laundry appliances—with independent 15-ampere circuits for the lights. This means that appliances with a total wattage exceeding 2,300 should never be used simultaneously on a 20-ampere circuit. To avoid this possibility, or at least reduce the chance of it, provide convenience receptacles for each appliance at the point of use and combine the various receptacles into a circuit that will not be overloaded even if all appliances assigned to it are in use at the same time. Special-purpose outlets that will take a plug only for a particular appliance are an additional safeguard. To avoid stooping, install kitchen plug-in wall outlets at about waist height. You will want several in the space between the work counter and the bottom of the wall cabinets.

How to Install Cove Lights

General illumination is not limited to the conventional overhead lamp suspended from the ceiling. Instead of this, you might choose from two types of concealed lighting—cove or recessed. The first provides illumination at the edges of the ceiling, utilizing hidden fluorescents. Cove lighting may be used along one or two walls—or may completely encircle the room. A recessed fixture is set flush in the ceiling, usually in the center. This also might be used over the dining area of a combination kitchen-dining area. It is frequently installed, too, in a soffit board above a sink.

The drawing of the step-saving U-kitchen in the opening chapter shows how a cove can be used for general illumination of the work areas. In this case, lengths of 3/4" outer-diameter pipe suspend the cove from the ceiling. The upper ends of the pipe were screwed into flanges set flush with the ceiling finish and bolted to 2" x 4" blocking between the joists. Each piece of pipe was cut lengthwise for about 2" at the bottom and drilled for two stove bolts run through the face of the cove, which is 1/2" stock 4" wide. Fluorescent fixtures were attached to the rear of this board and a 2" strip of 3/8" wood was rabbeted to the inside of the lower edge at right angles. This piece hides the fixture and helps reflect part of the light to the ceiling for indirect lighting. Light also spills down the front of the wall cabinets, illuminating the work areas.

Coves are sometimes used for indirect lighting alone. For this, a cove can be attached directly to the wall or the front surface of a drop ceiling (soffit) when the latter is used to fill space between the top of wall cabinets and the ceiling. The fixture can be attached to the wall or soffit face, with blocking behind it to bring the centerline of the fluorescent tube out about $3\frac{1}{4}''$. For the cove, attach a $3''$ strip of wood at right angles to one edge of a length of stock $7''$ wide and mount the latter at right angles to the wall about $2''$ below the fixture, using small shelf brackets placed above. The $3''$ front strip should point upward to hide the fixture.

A cove might be made also by soaking a $10''$ strip of $\frac{1}{8}''$ hardboard for several days, and then curving the front edge upward on an easy radius. Mount this on a permanent form until thoroughly dry. For maximum efficiency, apply white enamel to the interior of a cove. Best light distribution will be obtained if it is about $10''$ below the ceiling.

Hiding Secondary Lights

To avoid glare, secondary kitchen lights should not be in the direct line of sight. A sink light can be hidden behind a valance, or can be mounted in a soffit board; or perhaps a combination of valance and soffit can be used. A bridging soffit above the sink offers a natural place for a recessed light. Various fixtures are available to shine light downward through an opening in the soffit board. Although not required, a decorative valance may be desirable below the soffit flush with the adjoining wall cabinets. A valance may be used, too, either with or without a soffit, to conceal a long fluorescent light. The handyman builder can cut a valance in a variety of designs. If unable to find a suitable pattern, he should have no difficulty creating an original design and sawing it out. Or he can buy valance boards by the foot at a local lumber yard.

Some modern ranges have built-in lights. If yours doesn't, you should consider whether there isn't some way to place one above or near it without robbing the cook of storage space or interfering with installation of a ventilation system. In many cases a fluorescent fixture can be attached to the bottom of a shelf or cabinet directly above the range.

At the mix center and other strategic spots along the work counter, conceal fluorescents under the wall cabinets, locating them back against the wall. Each of these should have its own control switch.

The final touch in kitchen lighting, one that is not used as often as it could be, provides illumination inside the cabinets, particularly in the dark recesses of cupboard-type base units. Space usually can be found for a small incandescent light. Let the hinge side of the cabinet door operate a spring-type door switch—like the one in your refrigerator—and you will have real convenience.

Ventilating Fans

Only in comparatively recent years has the importance of an adequate kitchen ventilating system become apparent—and many builders still tend to slight it. Such a system should carry off grease-laden cooking fumes, reduce the humidity that builds up in a kitchen, and help keep the room cool and more comfortable.

No matter what type of range is used, tiny particles of fat, moisture, and smoke are given off during the process of cooking. Floating with the air currents, these particles may spread all through the house if a ventilating system is lacking. As they cool, the particles settle on the walls, ceiling, woodwork, furniture, draperies, and rugs. Besides spreading cooking odors, the airborne grease and dirt makes house cleaning a more burdensome and costly task.

In modern, well-insulated homes, harmful condensation results from moisture trapped inside. A U.S. Government publication notes: "Insulation is not complete without ventilation. When a house is tightly built, weatherproofed, and insulated, it is more necessary than ever to have good ventilation. You will need controlled ventilation throughout all parts of the house to carry off stale air and excess moisture." The report notes that adequate window area, located to provide cross ventilation, will help a ventilating fan do its job.

Your guide in buying a ventilating fan should be its ability to move air. Consult the manufacturer's literature for this—that is, how many cubic feet of air it is designed to move in a minute. Ideally, all air in a kitchen should be changed once every two or three minutes. For a small kitchen, aim for a two-minute change. To determine the fan-capacity required, compute the number of cubic feet of air in the kitchen and divide by the air-change figure selected—either two or three minutes.

A kitchen fan can be installed in various ways. The simplest is in a window. A fan also can go in a wall, in the ceiling, in a cabinet, or in a furred-down ceiling above wall cabinets. A cabinet installation, with the inlet grille in the cabinet bottom, will hide the unit from sight.

To carry off fumes quickly, the fan should be placed near the range, above it if possible. But a compromise location may be necessary, either for appearance or to improve the overall efficiency of the air-exhaust system. If placed on the same wall with a window that is frequently open, a fan will set up a semicircular current, leaving a big pocket of stale air on the opposite side of the room. The ideal location permits the fan to draw air across the entire kitchen, preferably from the other part of the house, and then over the range—and out. When the house has warm-air heat, an exhaust system like this may make damper adjustment necessary.

Frequently a duct is installed from the fan to the outside of the house. This may go in the ceiling, wall, or soffit assembly. To reduce air friction, a duct should be kept short, with curving instead of sharp bends. For the same reason, a round duct is preferable to a square one. It is important that all ducts be tight. Otherwise, grease may seep through and spoil the kitchen finish. When you buy a fan, ease of cleaning it is a major point to consider. Eventually, grease collecting behind the inlet will reduce the efficiency of the unit.

Most exhaust systems carry the air up from the range—and then out of the house. But it is sometimes possible to exhaust the air downward by a wall duct and discharge it through another leading across the basement to an outer wall. In a system like this, it is advisable to have a cleanout door at the base of the wall duct so that grease and dirt may be removed frequently. An accumulation of grease inside a duct is a fire hazard.

Some exhaust fans designed for installation above a range include a collecting hood. Since a hood can be a decorative asset to the kitchen, here is a place where a handyman builder can give any artistic bent free play—by designing a hood to suit his particular situation and shaping it from copper or other sheet metal.

In contrast to building a handsome new cabinet, selecting, buying, and installing a ventilating system may seem like work you would rather avoid. But don't. Do the job while your cabinets are still new—and the ventilating system will help keep them looking that way.

Index

Index

243

Spoon holder, 28
Staining cabinets, 230
Step board, 121
Stool, 79, 80, 81, 121, 183, 199
Stopped dado, 28
Storage wall, 188
Sugar storage, 40, 61, 63
Supplementary shelves, 166, 168, 211
Swinging bins, 93
Swinging shelves, 21, 23, 56, 139, 178, 184, 188
Swing-shelf wall cabinet, 56

Table linens, storage of, 106, 163
Tables, 190
Tall cabinets, 177
Tempered Presdwood, 17
Thermador, 176
Thye, Lenore Sater, 4, 48, 49
Toaster storage, 120, 159
Tool hanging cabinet, 55
Towel rack, 122, 125, 134
Trash disposal, 71, 75, 119, 150, 155, 211
Tray storage, 54, 96, 116, 119
Triangle work plan, 3, 4
Triangular shelves, 211
TV set in kitchen cabinet, 154
Two-faced cabinets, 1, 158, 167
Two-room table, 208
Typical cabinet dimensions, 7

U-kitchen, 2, 4, 5, 157
Under-counter table, 198
United States Gypsum Company, 192
Utensil cabinet, 106, 138
Utility cabinet, 185
Utility cart, 214

Vacuum-cleaner storage, 185, 189
Varnishing cabinets, 231
Vegetable bin, 48, 91, 120, 130, 134
Ventilating fan, 235, 238
Vertical pull-out board, 133
Vertical pull-out racks, 124

Wall Lazy Susan, 147
Wall oven, 171
Wall shelves, 58
Wall vegetable bin, 48
Warming drawers, built-in, 171
Wastebasket rack, 71
Waxed paper storage, 56
Window-box table, 191
Wire vegetable bin, 91
Wiring a built-in oven, 174
Wiring in kitchen, 233
Wood box, 222
Work centers, 4, 37, 40